Survival

GLOBAL POLITICS AND STRATEGY

Volume 65 Number 5 | October–November 2023

'The fallout from the break with France over submarine procurement was spectacular and unfortunate, but not critical and apparently reparable. The United States, however, has gone to far greater lengths than France to support Australia's ambitions, to the point of sharing some security "crown jewels" in the form of nuclear-propulsion technology. If AUKUS is seen as strengthening the strategic linkage between the US and Australia, and as an American endorsement of a close ally, unravelling it would likely have the reverse effect.'

Nick Childs, The AUKUS Anvil: Promise and Peril, pp. 17–18.

'The question the West should be asking is not whether the female population of Afghanistan is being treated badly, but whether Western disengagement is making their situation worse.'

James M. Cowan, Calibrating Engagement with the Taliban, p. 38.

'Wagnerites … could also follow the path of unemployed mercenaries throughout history, using their skills in violence to become marauders and extortionists. Some … returning home to Russia are already reported to be doing exactly that.'

Kimberly Marten, Whither Wagner? The Consequences of Prigozhin's Mutiny and Demise, p. 56.

Survival

GLOBAL POLITICS AND STRATEGY

Volume 65 Number 5 | October–November 2023

Contents

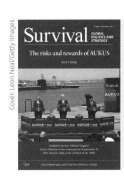

Cover: Leon Neal/Getty Images

On the cover
Australian Prime Minister Anthony Albanese, US President Joe Biden and British Prime Minister Rishi Sunak hold a press conference during the AUKUS summit on 13 March 2023 in San Diego, California.

On the web
Visit www.iiss.org/publications/survival for brief notices on new books on Economy; Cyber Security and Emerging Technologies; Middle East; and South Asia.

Survival **editors' blog**
For ideas and commentary from *Survival* editors and contributors, visit www.iiss.org/blogs/survival-blog.

Survival
GLOBAL POLITICS AND STRATEGY

The International Institute for Strategic Studies

2121 K Street, NW | Suite 600 | Washington DC 20037 | USA
Tel +1 202 659 1490   E-mail survival@iiss.org   Web www.iiss.org

Arundel House | 6 Temple Place | London | WC2R 2PG | UK
Tel +44 (0)20 7379 7676   E-mail iiss@iiss.org

14th Floor, GFH Tower | Bahrain Financial Harbour | Manama | Kingdom of Bahrain
Tel +973 1718 1155   E-mail iiss-middleeast@iiss.org

9 Raffles Place | #49-01 Republic Plaza | Singapore 048619
Tel +65 6499 0055   E-mail iiss-asia@iiss.org

Pariser Platz 6A | 10117 Berlin | Germany
Tel +49 30 311 99 300   E-mail iiss-europe@iiss.org

Survival Online www.tandfonline.com/survival and www.iiss.org/publications/survival

Aims and Scope *Survival* is one of the world's leading forums for analysis and debate of international and strategic affairs. Shaped by its editors to be both timely and forward thinking, the journal encourages writers to challenge conventional wisdom and bring fresh, often controversial, perspectives to bear on the strategic issues of the moment. With a diverse range of authors, *Survival* aims to be scholarly in depth while vivid, well written and policy-relevant in approach. Through commentary, analytical articles, case studies, forums, review essays, reviews and letters to the editor, the journal promotes lively, critical debate on issues of international politics and strategy.

Editor **Dana Allin**
Managing Editor **Jonathan Stevenson**
Associate Editor **Carolyn West**
Editorial Assistant **Conor Hodges**
Production and Cartography **Alessandra Beluffi, Ravi Gopar, Jade Panganiban, James Parker, Kelly Verity**

Contributing Editors

William Alberque	**Chester A. Crocker**	**Melissa K. Griffith**	**Irene Mia**	**Karen Smith**
Målfrid Braut-	**Bill Emmott**	**Emile Hokayem**	**Meia Nouwens**	**Angela Stent**
Hegghammer	**Franz-Stefan Gady**	**Nigel Inkster**	**Benjamin Rhode**	**Robert Ward**
Aaron Connelly	**Bastian Giegerich**	**Jeffrey Mazo**	**Ben Schreer**	**Marcus Willett**
James Crabtree	**Nigel Gould-Davies**	**Fenella McGerty**	**Maria Shagina**	**Lanxin Xiang**

Published for the IISS by
Routledge Journals, an imprint of Taylor & Francis, an Informa business.

About the IISS The IISS, a registered charity with offices in Washington, London, Manama, Singapore and Berlin, is the world's leading authority on political–military conflict. It is the primary independent source of accurate, objective information on international strategic issues. Publications include *The Military Balance*, an annual reference work on each nation's defence capabilities; *Survival*, a bimonthly journal on international affairs; *Strategic Comments*, an online analysis of topical issues in international affairs; and the *Adelphi* series of books on issues of international security.

SUBMISSIONS

To submit an article, authors are advised to follow these guidelines:

- *Survival* articles are around 4,000–10,000 words long including endnotes. A word count should be included with a draft.
- All text, including endnotes, should be double-spaced with wide margins.
- Any tables or artwork should be supplied in separate files, ideally not embedded in the document or linked to text around it.
- All *Survival* articles are expected to include endnote references. These should be complete and include first and last names of authors, titles of articles (even from newspapers), place of publication, publisher, exact publication dates, volume and issue number (if from a journal) and page numbers. Web sources should include complete URLs and DOIs if available.
- A summary of up to 150 words should be included with the article. The summary should state the main argument clearly and concisely, not simply say what the article is about.

- A short author's biography of one or two lines should also be included. This information will appear at the foot of the first page of the article.

Please note that *Survival* has a strict policy of listing multiple authors in alphabetical order.

Submissions should be made by email, in Microsoft Word format, to survival@iiss.org. Alternatively, hard copies may be sent to *Survival*, IISS–US, 2121 K Street NW, Suite 801, Washington, DC 20037, USA.

The editorial review process can take up to three months. *Survival*'s acceptance rate for unsolicited manuscripts is less than 20%. *Survival* does not normally provide referees' comments in the event of rejection. Authors are permitted to submit simultaneously elsewhere so long as this is consistent with the policy of the other publication and the Editors of *Survival* are informed of the dual submission.

Readers are encouraged to comment on articles from the previous issue. Letters should be concise, no longer than 750 words and relate directly to the argument or points made in the original article.

Survival: Global Politics and Strategy (Print ISSN 0039-6338, Online ISSN 1468-2699) is published bimonthly for a total of 6 issues per year by Taylor & Francis Group, 4 Park Square, Milton Park, Abingdon, Oxon, OX14 4RN, UK. Periodicals postage paid (Permit no. 13095) at Brooklyn, NY 11256.

Airfreight and mailing in the USA by agent named World Container Inc., c/o BBT 150-15, 183rd Street, Jamaica, NY 11413, USA.

US Postmaster: Send address changes to Survival, World Container Inc., c/o BBT 150-15, 183rd Street, Jamaica, NY 11413, USA.

Subscription records are maintained at Taylor & Francis Group, 4 Park Square, Milton Park, Abingdon, OX14 4RN, UK.

Subscription information: For more information and subscription rates, please see tandfonline.com/pricing/journal/TSUR. Taylor & Francis journals are available in a range of different packages, designed to suit every library's needs and budget. This journal is available for institutional subscriptions with online-only or print & online options. This journal may also be available as part of our libraries, subject collections or archives. For more information on our sales packages, please visit librarianresources.taylorandfrancis.com.

For support with any institutional subscription, please visit help.tandfonline.com or email our dedicated team at subscriptions@tandf.co.uk.

Subscriptions purchased at the personal rate are strictly for personal, non-commercial use only. The reselling of personal subscriptions is prohibited. Personal subscriptions must be purchased with a personal cheque, credit card or BAC/wire transfer. Proof of personal status may be requested.

Back issues: Taylor & Francis Group retains a current and one-year back-issue stock of journals. Older volumes are held by our official stockists to whom all orders and enquiries should be addressed: Periodicals Service Company, 351 Fairview Avenue, Suite 300, Hudson, NY 12534, USA. Tel: +1 518 537 4700; email psc@periodicals.com.

Ordering information: To subscribe to the journal, please contact T&F Customer Services, Informa UK Ltd, Sheepen Place, Colchester, Essex, CO3 3LP, UK. Tel: +44 (0) 20 8052 2030; email subscriptions@tandf.co.uk.

Taylor & Francis journals are priced in USD, GBP and EUR (as well as AUD and CAD for a limited number of journals). All subscriptions are charged depending on where the end customer is based. If you are unsure which rate applies to you, please contact Customer Services. All subscriptions are payable in advance and all rates include postage. Subscriptions are entered on an annual basis, i.e., January to December. Payment may be made by sterling cheque, dollar cheque, euro cheque, international money order, National Giro or credit cards (Amex, Visa and Mastercard).

Disclaimer: The International Institute for Strategic Studies (IISS) and our publisher Informa UK Limited, trading as Taylor & Francis Group ('T&F'), make every effort to ensure the accuracy of all the information (the 'Content') contained in our publications. However, IISS and our publisher T&F, our agents and our licensors make no representations or warranties whatsoever as to the accuracy, completeness or suitability for any purpose of the Content. Any opinions and views expressed in this publication are the opinions and views of the authors, and are not the views of or endorsed by IISS or our publisher T&F. The accuracy of the Content should not be relied upon and should be independently verified with primary sources of information, and any reliance on the Content is at your own risk. IISS and our publisher T&F make no representations, warranties or guarantees, whether express or implied, that the Content is accurate, complete or up to date. IISS and our publisher T&F shall not be liable for any losses, actions, claims, proceedings, demands, costs, expenses, damages and other liabilities whatsoever or howsoever caused arising directly or indirectly in connection with, in relation to or arising out of the use of the Content. Full Terms & Conditions of access and use can be found at http://www.tandfonline.com/page/terms-and-conditions.

Informa UK Limited, trading as Taylor & Francis Group, grants authorisation for individuals to photocopy copyright material for private research use, on the sole basis that requests for such use are referred directly to the requestor's local Reproduction Rights Organization (RRO). The copyright fee is exclusive of any charge or fee levied. In order to contact your local RRO, please contact International Federation of Reproduction Rights Organizations (IFRRO), rue du Prince Royal, 87, B-1050 Brussels, Belgium; email ifrro@skynet.be; Copyright Clearance Center Inc., 222 Rosewood Drive, Danvers, MA 01923, USA; email info@copyright.com; or Copyright Licensing Agency, 90 Tottenham Court Road, London, W1P 0LP, UK; email cla@cla.co.uk. This authorisation does not extend to any other kind of copying, by any means, in any form, for any purpose other than private research use.

Submission information: See https://www.tandfonline.com/journals/tsur20

Advertising: See https://taylorandfrancis.com/contact/advertising/

Permissions: See help.tandfonline.com/Librarian/s/article/Permissions

All Taylor & Francis Group journals are printed on paper from renewable sources by accredited partners.

October–November 2023

 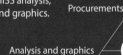

The AUKUS Anvil: Promise and Peril

Nick Childs

The 'enhanced trilateral security partnership' between Australia, the United Kingdom and the United States, known as AUKUS, emerged in September 2021.[1] Since then it has acquired almost mythical status. This is due mainly to the strategic loft and immense national ambition of the initiative: it aims to secure for the Royal Australian Navy a capability in submarines with nuclear propulsion – a technology shrouded in secrecy that only six countries now possess – and thereby to elevate and consolidate allied power.[2] AUKUS has acquired the label 'too big to fail'.[3] That remains to be seen. For all three countries there are serious questions about whether defence-industrial capacities and economic growth will be sufficient, and political commitment durable enough, to sustain the project. Given the enterprise's large scale, long span and the potential strategic rewards and risks, it will be the anvil on which a key set of relationships, capabilities and effects will either be forged or broken. For all the commitments proclaimed, work undertaken and decisions unveiled so far, the formidable challenges of fulfilling the arrangement also raise the question of what the strategic fallout will be if it is not fulfilled.

The promise

It is difficult to overestimate the potential significance of this tripartite submarine undertaking. While the initial AUKUS announcements studiously avoided references to China, that nation's growing challenge to the

Nick Childs is IISS Senior Fellow for Naval Forces and Maritime Security.

Survival | vol. 65 no. 5 | October–November 2023 | pp. 7–24   https://doi.org/10.1080/00396338.2023.2261239

West was clearly the motivating force behind it. AUKUS is perhaps the most important multilateral initiative so far that is intended to readjust a maritime balance in the Pacific that seemed to be inexorably shifting in China's favour.

If things go according to plan, Australia will join an elite fraternity of like-minded nations operating nuclear-powered submarines; the submarine-production capacity of the three partners will significantly increase; and, by the middle of the century, about a dozen extra such submarines could be added to the combined inventories of the AUKUS navies. The result will be 'a new global and interoperable nuclear-powered submarine capability'.[4] The debate will continue over whether this project reinforces deterrence or raises tensions; whether nuclear-powered submarines are the right strategic choice for Australia; whether they risk obsolescence as undersea-surveillance technologies improve; and whether they tie Canberra into far greater strategic dependence on the US. For now, though, the nuclear-powered-submarine option looks like the most potent, survivable and operationally independent means of establishing a long-range power-projection capability for Australia.

From the outset, AUKUS also contemplated cooperation on other key defence capabilities, initially identified as cyber, artificial intelligence, quantum technologies and undersea-warfare technologies. To this second pillar hypersonic and counter-hypersonic capabilities, electronic warfare, innovation and information-sharing have been added.[5] Some have argued that the second pillar could become at least as significant as the first, but that will depend on nurturing further cooperation in these areas, possibly including with other partners as well. Submarines are the main focus here.

Notwithstanding the steadily reiterated message that the project will necessarily span decades and even generations, the unveiling itself was something of a sea-change moment, particularly for Australia. Canberra, not Washington, initiated AUKUS. It was also an inflection point for the US, which agreed only for the second time to share its nuclear-submarine propulsion technology, having done so with the UK in 1958. It also symbolised the seismic evolution under way in the United States' defence and security posture in the region and globally – in particular the dawning realisation of the need to embrace allies and partners more closely and rely on their capabilities to sustain credible deterrence.[6] The UK, meanwhile, functioned as a linchpin in bringing the tripartite partnership together after the Royal Australian Navy chief of navy had secretly broached the idea with his Royal Navy counterpart.[7] Should it pan out, AUKUS could validate and reinforce the UK's revived and enhanced engagement in the Pacific theatre, and therefore its position as a medium power with a global perspective and reach. It would also shore up Britain's future in the nuclear-submarine business and offer the broader prospect of a bonanza in high-tech jobs and manufacturing.

The run-up

The Royal Australian Navy had toyed with the ambition of procuring nuclear-powered attack submarines (SSNs) in the past. Given the tyrannies of distance in patrolling the waters of potential strategic interest to Australia, SSNs' ability to remain submerged and undetected, transit underwater at high speed for practically unlimited periods, and support a powerful range of systems and weapons always offered significant operational advantages over conventionally powered attack submarines (SSKs). Until recently, however, those assets had never seemed quite enough to justify the potential costs and complexity of procurement, or the political challenge of overcoming a national aversion to crossing the political–military threshold of nuclear propulsion.[8]

The strategic horizons, however, were darkening significantly when Canberra decided in April 2016 to replace its flotilla of six ageing *Collins*-class conventional attack subs. It was clear that Australia's subsurface force needed boosting, and the Department of Defence had decided to double hull numbers to 12. But the choice was still for a conventional vessel of French design dubbed the *Attack* class. The design chosen, described as 'regionally superior', was in effect a conventionally powered version of the latest French nuclear-attack-submarine design.[9] The government's 2020 Defence Strategic Update foretold a rapidly deteriorating strategic environment.[10] A more hostile future looked set to arrive early, calling into question whether the *Attack* class would meet requirements of survivability and lethality by the time the first boats started entering service, projected by then to be in the 2030s.[11]

Warning signs also appeared that the French submarine deal was not in the best of health, with growing expressions of concern about delays, cost escalations and the level of workshare for Australia: the Australian government was losing confidence in France's ability to deliver. Alliance management was another matter. Operational considerations did not soften France's well-publicised indignation at having been 'stabbed in the back' by the AUKUS partners.[12]

Optimal pathway

Operational necessity also does not mitigate the challenges facing the AUKUS partners in delivering 'at least eight' nuclear-powered submarines for the Royal Australian Navy.[13] When the second major milestone of AUKUS was promulgated 18 months after the initial announcement, and the leaders of the three countries revealed the long-awaited conception of an 'optimal pathway' to Australia's new submarine capability, the very complexity of the proposal underscored just how much the undertaking will strain the armed forces and industrial capacities of all three countries.[14]

On 13 March 2023, at the US naval base in San Diego, California, with a US Navy nuclear-powered submarine as a backdrop, US President Joe Biden, Australian Prime Minister Anthony Albanese and UK Prime Minister Rishi Sunak set out their phased approach. It includes embedding Australian military and civilian personnel with the US Navy, Royal Navy and the American and British submarine-industrial bases from 2023, as well as increasing port visits by US Navy submarines to Australia and starting similar UK visits in 2026; forward rotations of US and UK submarines to Australia from as early as 2027; the sale of three of the US current-generation *Virginia*-class submarines to Australia in the early 2030s to create a 'sovereign capability' for Australia in the operation of such vessels, plus an option for up to two more if needed; and the joint development of a new submarine, SSN-AUKUS, based on the UK's next-generation nuclear-powered-submarine design but also incorporating Australian and cutting-edge US technology. SSN-AUKUS is slated to serve both the Royal Navy and Royal Australian Navy as an enduring future capability, with the first SSN-AUKUS to be delivered to the Royal Navy in the late 2030s and to the Royal Australian Navy in the early 2040s.

Beyond the new operational capability, and critical to the overall objective, the biggest prize for Australia will be a sustainable, indigenous building capacity for new-generation submarines, save for the nuclear-propulsion plant based on highly enriched uranium, which will allow the Australian submarines to operate for a full 35-year service life without refuelling.[15] The plant will be constructed in the UK and delivered as essentially sealed units to comply with Australia's nuclear non-proliferation commitments. Even so, the demands placed on Australia of nuclear stewardship – not just in operation but also in safe oversight – and of establishing the necessary shipbuilding and support infrastructure will be stiff.

Timing, even if it is not everything, remains a critical issue. A major criticism of AUKUS was that it would not bear fruit in time to be relevant. The 2023 Australian Defence Strategic Review emphasised that the ten-year warning the country's defence planners had previously identified was no longer valid.[16] Yet the most optimistic forecast of when Australia could take delivery of a first indigenously built nuclear-powered submarine was the late 2030s, more likely the early 2040s. Furthermore, Australia could face a submarine gap, as the current *Collins* class would be unlikely to function for that long, even with a planned service-life extension programme. To address these worries, the March 2023 announcement outlined a stepladder approach involving initially small but important incremental developments in the early years, including some capability upgrades.

The uptick in visits of US submarines to the Western Australia submarine base, HMAS Stirling, is meant to help expand the Royal Australian Navy's knowledge of SSNs. One of the most significant early steps on the AUKUS ladder, from 2027, will be the establishment at HMAS Stirling of a forward rotational presence of up to four US Navy *Virginia*-class submarines and one Royal Navy *Astute*-class SSN, the formation to be known as 'Submarine Rotational Force – West'. Included in the bargain are upgrades to HMAS Stirling. Undoubtedly a key factor in Washington's assessment of the value of AUKUS is access within a few years to an additional forward-operating base for an enhanced submarine flotilla, which would complicate the calculations of China's military planners. Australia has also undertaken to add a second submarine base on its eastern seaboard.

All three partners have committed to significantly enhancing their respective submarine-industrial bases. Canberra has additionally pledged a significant financial injection firstly into US submarine-production capacity and then proportionately into the UK's industry as well. The partners have openly acknowledged the challenges, and none have unblemished recent records in meeting similar ones. Moreover, while it may be possible to sustain broad support for the enterprise while these challenges remain notional, when they start to ramify in the form of delays, cost overruns, organisational shortfalls, or clashes of priorities, the risks to the overall project will intensify.

Hovering contingencies

The partner with the biggest stake and proportionately the most on its plate is, of course, Australia. Along with the March announcement of the optimal pathway came the shock of the first official cost estimate for the AUKUS submarine project to 2055: A$368 billion (US$236bn). Official Australian documents prefer to focus on the less gobsmacking figure of 0.15% of GDP that this amount represents.[17] Another leavening factor is that the dollar amount includes a hefty 50% contingency, some or all of which may not be required. And the defence budget is also supposed to grow from 2.0 to 2.2% of GDP. Still, the complexity of the undertaking and the risk of cost overruns exceeding the contingency provision could increase financial pressures.[18]

For the Australian government, AUKUS is also about investment in a high-technology industrial future, with an estimated 4,000 direct jobs being created in developing the new Submarine Construction Yard in Osborne, South Australia, some 4,000–5,500 to run the shipyard, and around 20,000 across Australia. Yet some analysts have suggested that Australia currently is not producing enough engineers and technicians to furnish the estimated 8,000 personnel with nuclear-related training needed to develop, build, operate and maintain the submarines, let alone the management and regulatory talent and infrastructure required to run and oversee the process effectively.[19]

A key objective is for Australia to be 'sovereign ready' to operate and support its own *Virginia*-class submarines from about 2033, just a decade away. For the Royal Australian Navy, on the personnel front alone, that task looks difficult enough. Last July, the first three Australian naval officers graduated from the US Navy's foundation nuclear-propulsion course.[20] They will still require further training to become nuclear-qualified. A decade is barely long enough for the Royal Australian Navy to develop a sufficient cadre of personnel at all the necessary levels to start operating nuclear-powered submarines. A more streamlined but equally rigorous training process may be necessary to meet the 2033 deadline. On top of that, the Royal Australian Navy will likely need at least double the number of highly trained personnel to crew the new flotilla compared to the *Collins* class. The Royal Australian Navy will also need to anticipate the heightened challenge of personnel retention since the crews on the new SSNs might be asked to go on much longer tours than those operating an SSK.

In addition, there remain questions about when and how the new submarines themselves will materialise. Some lingering uncertainty exists over whether US International Traffic in Arms Regulations will be amended so as to allow for the required technology transfer.[21] Assuming the export-control hurdle can be surmounted, as appears likely, the first procurement step calls for the proposed sale of three and possibly up to five *Virginia*-class submarines to Australia, starting in the early 2030s. Critically, this would still be conditional on the approval of the US Congress. Furthermore, as it is, the US industrial base is struggling to fulfil the pre-existing requirement of delivering the new *Columbia* class of nuclear-powered ballistic-missile submarine (SSBN) – the US Navy's top priority – as well as new *Virginia*-class boats on time and in the numbers contracted for. The navy's inventory of non-SSBN submarines hovers around the 50 mark, a long way short of the long-term goal of between 66 and 72 boats, with America's admirals looking to minimise an anticipated near-term dip in numbers at a crucial strategic moment as remaining *Los Angeles*-class boats, the *Virginias*' forerunners delivered late in the Cold War, are decommissioned.

According to the Royal Australian Navy, the details about which boats the US will transfer and when it will do so have yet to be worked out. However, the Royal Australian Navy's working assumption is that the US Navy would provide two existing submarines and order a third newly built vessel, likely the Block III or IV version of the design most recently in US Navy service, each with a minimum of 20 years of service life remaining.[22]

To offset the impact on US Navy force levels, the US Navy would need the two US submarine yards between them to deliver new boats at the rate of one *Columbia* and two *Virginia*s a year for the rest of the decade and into the 2030s. Adding the Australian requirement is estimated to raise the *Virginia* production quota to at least 2.3 per year. Hence the Australian initiative to boost investment in America's submarine-construction infrastructure. However, despite considerable US investment to bolster the two yards' capacity, some US$3–4bn pledged so far, the delivery rate on *Virginia*-class boats is currently running at about 1.4 per year, and it will be five years before it reaches two.[23]

Compounding these obstacles is a backlog of maintenance and support requirements that has significantly reduced the readiness and availability of the US Navy's current submarine fleet. While the navy is planning a US$2.2bn injection to shore up the corresponding infrastructure, given estimates that the overall submarine-industrial base has shrunk by some 70% from the end of the Cold War, US industry's ability to absorb significant cash infusions appears to have limits due to skill shortages and supply-chain bottlenecks. The US government and promised Australian funding may be enough to lift capacity in time, but industrial realities and American priorities seem likely to cast a persistent shadow over AUKUS's prospects.[24]

A maintenance backlog has reduced readiness

Potential impediments also abound on the UK side. Britain's industrial base is significantly smaller than America's and also has its work cut out to deliver a new-generation SSBN (the *Dreadnought* class), complete the *Astute* SSNs and gear up for the *Astutes'* successor. For much of the 18-month AUKUS assessment period, the UK seemed to be battling the impression that it would be the junior AUKUS partner, seeking at best consolation prizes, and the assumption that the eventual submarine solution would be an American one. The UK's recent record on submarine delivery – though to an extent attributable to political decisions to string it out to ease budget shortfalls rather than incapacity – has been poor, and the *Astute* programme has gained a reputation for being troubled. The 2015 UK Strategic Defence and Security Review tacitly acknowledged the problems by announcing a new organisational structure for the defence-nuclear enterprise.[25] And the *Astute* design seemed to be out of the running for AUKUS at an early stage, partly because key components, such as the nuclear reactor, were already out of production.

Nevertheless, the UK's next-generation design is seen as a viable basis for meeting Australia's SSN-AUKUS requirements, as the US Navy's next submarine design, the SSN(X), scheduled for procurement in the mid-2030s, looks to be too much for the Royal Australian Navy to handle. It will likely be larger and more sophisticated than the *Virginia* class, and significantly more expensive at an estimated US$5.6–7.2bn per copy compared to US$4.3bn for the latest Block V *Virginia*s.[26]

The SSN-AUKUS design project may increase the UK's chances for staying in the nuclear-powered-submarine construction and operating business. The country's current low force level (four SSBNs and seven *Astute*-class SSNs planned) leaves it at the ragged edge of viability as a nuclear-powered-submarine constructor. The Royal Navy's ambition is to regrow the force to perhaps a dozen new attack boats in addition to the SSBNs. That was always going to require significant additional funding. The AUKUS arrangement bolsters the rationale for authorising it. On top of that, the proposed addition of extra cutting-edge US technology – a vertical-launch system for cruise missiles and perhaps future remote technology, plus an enhanced reactor plant – could yield a better submarine for the Royal Navy than it would otherwise have been able to design and afford. The success of AUKUS could also yield greater short-term influence for the UK, linked to its ability to deploy forces with substantial combat capability to the region in the form of increased numbers of submarines. The more established Australia becomes in delivering that kind of capability with the UK's help, however, the less need there may be for the UK to do the same.

Overall, the SSN-AUKUS piece of the submarine package is the most fragile one because the uncertainties are the greatest. The details of the design remain essentially unknown, at least to the public. So do specifics about what the production plan will look like, how integrated it will be, and particularly how the labour will be divided between BAE Systems' UK yard at Barrow-in-Furness and Australia's Osborne facility. Furthermore, the apparent introduction of a US–Australia command system could threaten the UK's expertise and industrial stake in that technological area, as could non-British weapons systems, if selected, in another. The greater the number of potential divergences between British and Australian requirements, the greater the risks of delays and cost increases.

To meet the planned delivery dates of a first Royal Navy SSN-AUKUS submarine by the late 2030s and a first Royal Australian Navy vessel by the early 2040s, work would have to start on the new vessels before the end of this decade. UK industry – BAE Systems and Rolls-Royce in particular – are already ramping up capabilities to deliver on the new propulsion system. BAE Systems aims to grow its Barrow workforce from 10,000–11,000 people to around 17,000.[27] Rolls-Royce has announced it plans nearly to double the size of its Raynesway reactor-production facility.[28] Meeting these targets will be a challenge. Special concern has arisen about the shortage of nuclear expertise, with both the defence and the civilian sector aiming at expansion – the latter to build new nuclear-power-generation capacity. This has led the government to inaugurate a UK Nuclear Skills Task Force.[29] While tough 'no poaching' agreements will surely be part of the AUKUS framework, there will undoubtedly be a strong temptation for skilled UK workers and even submarine personnel to opt for a new life in Australia.

Australia's option to buy a fourth and fifth *Virginia*-class submarine is a hedge against delays in SSN-AUKUS procurement, or even its failure as a design. A lack of clarity as to how many SSN-AUKUS submarines might be built is another uncertainty that makes the programme especially vulnerable. The Australians could at some point 'jump ship' and opt for a US solution after all for its indigenous submarine design. Meanwhile, the UK may be pressed to deliver on another key element of the contribution contemplated by the AUKUS deal: the forward deployment of an *Astute* to the Pacific for extended periods starting in 2027. A maximum of seven SSNs will be available over the next decade and a half at least, and a report was recently published highlighting a period when none of the current submarines were at sea.[30] Given these factors and demands to support national and NATO requirements closer to home, it remains unclear whether it will be sensible or plausible to dispatch an *Astute* to the Pacific.[31]

Possible blowback

AUKUS has long been recognised as a high-reward, high-risk enterprise, particularly with respect to the submarine pillar. Heavy lifting will be required to make it all come together. The fallout that could arise from the severe faltering or abandonment of the project would depend on the precise circumstances and context, and on when the crisis occurs. China is likely to remain a peer competitor of the United States for decades to come, and the intensity of great-power competition does not appear likely to abate in the short run. But it could diminish over AUKUS's long time span – undercutting the rationale for much of the project – and perhaps be supplanted by another global challenge of a very different character. Meanwhile, economic and budgetary pressures, notably in a post-Brexit Britain beset by relatively weak economic growth, could force painful choices among military, and between military and civilian, priorities. Maintaining coherence against the ebbs and flows of politics in all three countries is a known challenge, with a resurgence of isolationist impulses in the US a particular Australian and British anxiety.

Canberra could also change its mind as the economic burden grows and the country has to confront some of the more politically sensitive AUKUS undertakings, such as managing all the radioactive waste produced. Furthermore, Australia's Defence Strategic Review has produced a key judgement that Australia can no longer afford to maintain a range of balanced forces and must concentrate on a more focused posture.[32] Increased AUKUS pressures could force an even greater narrowing of choices and cuts in other capabilities to the point at which the opportunity costs of AUKUS appeared unsustainable. Torpedoing the enterprise would pose risks to the credibility of Australia's overall defence posture, and could jeopardise its relationship with the United States, a critical ally. The fallout from the break with France over submarine procurement was spectacular and unfortunate, but not critical and apparently reparable.[33] The United States, however, has gone to far greater lengths than France to support Australia's ambitions, to the point of sharing some security 'crown jewels' in the form of nuclear-propulsion technology. If AUKUS is seen as strengthening the strategic linkage between the US and Australia, and as an American endorsement of a close ally, unravelling it would likely have the reverse effect. The alliance would survive, but Washington would regard Canberra as a diminished partner.

Washington could also get cold feet, calculating that the deal's potential impacts on America's defence capabilities were prohibitive and returns marginal. While alternative arrangements could conceivably dilute perceptions of American unreliability, regional and global powers might still assess such a turn of events as evidence of uncertainty about Washington's strategic commitment.

The UK may be even more vulnerable to the consequences of AUKUS's failure than the other partners. Its global defence standing – and more acutely its vaunted 'special relationship' with the United States – could suffer profoundly. The nuclear partnership has been one of the most tangible elements of that relationship. Were the UK to lose the industrial opportunities AUKUS offers, its own national nuclear-powered-submarine programme might begin to look increasingly tenuous and difficult to sustain, with maintaining a submarine-based nuclear deterrent the chief but increasingly burdensome justification. Getting out of the nuclear-powered-submarine business or having to rely almost wholly on the Americans for the technology and even the supply of submarines – assuming the US could even cope with that – would inevitably diminish its overall strategic standing. However, the UK Defence Equipment Plan 2022–2032 underscored that the country's nuclear capability – including nuclear weapons – accounted for the largest single cost of procurement, at £59.7bn out of total planned expenditures of £236.5bn over ten years.[34] There may come a point at which the opportunity cost of incurring that expense becomes too great to bear.

Pings from the past

Some of the cross-currents and impulses that have featured in the evolution of AUKUS echo the deliberations and exchanges that led to the 1958 agreement between the UK and the US on sharing submarine nuclear-propulsion technology.[35] In the mid-1950s, there was growing concern in the Royal Navy that its experimentation with new submarine propulsion based on hydrogen peroxide was getting nowhere, and that the service's capabilities were falling farther and farther behind those of its rivals and potential opponents. UK research on submarine nuclear propulsion took a back seat to military and civil nuclear work. This state of affairs prompted the UK to take a more proactive approach in seeking access to US nuclear-propulsion technology.

A 1957 visit to UK waters by the USS *Nautilus*, the first nuclear-powered submarine, quelled British scepticism by clearly demonstrating its massively superior performance. There were legislative hurdles to overcome, and US Navy concerns to be assuaged that any support to the UK should not impede its own efforts to develop nuclear propulsion for its fleet. But shared concerns about Soviet advances helped cement the United States' agreement to share the nuclear-propulsion technology with the UK.

The US and the UK's early Cold War relationship also produced a cautionary tale about the potential impact of one partner's scrapping a programme that was critical for the other.[36] In the early 1960s, the UK was looking to an American air-launched ballistic missile, the *Skybolt*, to prolong the effective life of its 'V bomber' nuclear-strike force. When, in late 1962, the US decided to cancel *Skybolt*, UK prime minister Harold Macmillan hurried to Nassau for talks with US president John F. Kennedy to persuade him to sell Britain the US *Polaris* submarine-launched ballistic-missile system to offset the unsustainability of the bomber force precipitated by the *Skybolt*'s cancellation. Macmillan argued that Britain would otherwise have to review its entire global defence posture, which could produce a deep and strategically damaging rift in Anglo-American relations. The UK's standing as a major power and a member of NATO seemed to do the trick, but perhaps there was also an understanding on the American side about the implications of this decision for the stability of the British government. The US reluctantly agreed, with the proviso that the UK's *Polaris* force would also be assigned to NATO.[37]

In the 1960s, of course, both the UK and the US could fall back on very extensive defence-industrial bases and much larger armed forces, including the submarine forces from which to draw resources. The regulatory environments in both countries and globally were also considerably less onerous.[38] The Royal Navy's first SSN, HMS *Dreadnought*, with a US-supplied reactor, was commissioned into service just five years after the joint agreement was concluded. Britain's first *Polaris* SSBN, HMS *Resolution*, embarked on its first patrol in June 1968, less than six years after the Nassau meeting. Sixty years ago, the two parties did not have to consider generational factors to the extent that they do today, when the aims of the AUKUS submarine project cannot be fulfilled in much less than a quarter of a century.

*   *   *

The AUKUS partners agree that the potential strategic dividends of the arrangement currently outweigh the risks. For Australia and the UK, AUKUS has the character of a national endeavour given the scale and gravity of its demands. AUKUS will likely drive a significant change in the shape, focus and character of their respective armed forces, particularly their navies. For the United States, the direct costs and benefits are part of a broader calculation of what an enhanced relationship with Australia offers, including growing options for forward basing other critical assets and a wider deterrent posture. As the project unfolds, however, and particularly as divisive issues become more urgent, maintaining political and strategic alignments among the three capitals will inevitably become more challenging. AUKUS could become a foundational relationship among the three comparable in its strategic cohesiveness to the Anglo-American nuclear relationship. But failure to deliver, or delivering at too high a price, could have equally adverse consequences.

Notes

1   White House, 'Joint Leaders Statement on AUKUS', 15 September 2021, https://www.whitehouse.gov/briefing-room/statements-releases/2021/09/15/joint-leaders-statement-on-aukus/.

2   The AUKUS programme adopts the common classification of SSN for the types of submarine to be procured and built under the project. In *The Military Balance* and *The Military Balance+* digital

database, the IISS classifies the types of submarines involved, which will include a vertical-launch system (VLS) for cruise and other guided missiles, separately from traditional torpedo launchers, as SSGNs. Both these classifications are distinct from the strategic nuclear-powered submarines equipped with nuclear-armed ballistic missiles, referred to as SSBNs.

3   Daniel Hirst, 'AUKUS Nuclear Submarine Deal Will Be "Too Big to Fail", Richard Marles Says', *Guardian*, 17 March 2023, https://www.theguardian.com/australia-news/2023/mar/17/aukus-nuclear-submarine-deal-will-be-too-big-to-fail-richard-marles-says.

4   UK Foreign, Commonwealth & Development Office, 'First Sea Lord's Sea Power Conference 2023: Minister Trevelyan's Keynote Speech', 16 May 2023, https://www.gov.uk/government/speeches/minister-for-indo-pacific-anne-marie-trevelyan-delivers-keynote-speech-at-first-sea-lords-sea-power-conference-2023.

5   See White House, 'FACT SHEET: Implementation of the Australia–United Kingdom–United States Partnership (AUKUS)', 5 April 2022, https://www.whitehouse.gov/briefing-room/statements-releases/2022/04/05/fact-sheet-implementation-of-the-australia-united-kingdom-united-states-partnership-aukus/.

6   See, for example, Charles Edel, 'The AUKUS Wager', *Foreign Affairs*, 4 August 2023, https://www.foreignaffairs.com/united-states/aukus-wager.

7   See Larisa Brown, '"Like a Scene from le Carré": How the Nuclear Submarine Pact Was No 10's Biggest Secret', *The Times*, 18 September 2021, https://www.thetimes.co.uk/article/like-a-scene-from-le-carre-how-the-nuclear-submarine-pact-was-no10s-biggest-secret-dj7z5f8bh.

8   See James Goldrick, 'Going Nuclear: Assessing Australia's Nuclear-powered Submarine Plans', *Jane's Navy International*, 1 October 2021, https://customer.janes.com/Janes/Display/BSP_6575-JNI.

9   See Mike Yeo, 'French Design Wins Australia's Next Generation Submarine Competition', *US Naval Institute News*, 26 April 2016, https://news.usni.org/2016/04/26/french-design-wins-australias-next-generation-submarine-competition.

10 See Australian Government Defence, '2020 Defence Strategic Update', 1 July 2020, https://www.defence.gov.au/about/strategic-planning/2020-defence-strategic-update.

11 See Euan Graham, 'Australia's Serious Strategic Update', International Institute for Strategic Studies, 3 July 2020, https://www.iiss.org/online-analysis/online-analysis//2020/07/apacific-australia-defence-update.

12 See Zoya Sheftalovich, 'Why Australia Wanted Out of Its French Submarine Deal', *Politico*, 16 September 2021, https://www.politico.eu/article/why-australia-wanted-out-of-its-french-sub-deal/.

13 Australian Government Defence, 'Joint Media Statement: Australia to Pursue Nuclear-powered Submarines Through New Trilateral Enhanced Security Partnership', 16 September 2021, https://www.minister.defence.gov.au/statements/2021-09-16/joint-media-

statement-australia-pursue-nuclear-powered-submarines-through-new-trilateral-enhanced-security-partnership.

14 See White House, 'Joint Leaders Statement on AUKUS', 13 March 2023, https://www.whitehouse.gov/briefing-room/statements-releases/2023/03/13/joint-leaders-statement-on-aukus-2.

15 French nuclear-powered submarines use lower-enriched uranium and need to refuel two or three times during their service lives.

16 See Australia Government Defence, 'National Defence: Defence Strategic Review 2023', 24 April 2023, p. 24, https://www.defence.gov.au/about/reviews-inquiries/defence-strategic-review.

17 Australian Submarine Agency, 'The Aukus Nuclear-powered Submarine Pathway', 13 March 2023, p. 50, https://www.asa.gov.au/aukus.

18 See Karl Dewey, 'AUKUS Submarine Funding Surfaces in Latest Australian Defence Budget', International Institute for Strategic Studies Military Balance blog, 2 June 2023, https://www.iiss.org/online-analysis/military-balance/2023/06/aukus-submarine-funding-surfaces-in-latest-australian-defence-budget/.

19 See Gregor Ferguson, 'Building a Nuclear Workforce Will Take Time', Australian Financial Review, 20 August 2023, https://www.afr.com/policy/foreign-affairs/building-a-nuclear-work force-will-take-time-20230803-p5dtp9.

20 See Sam LaGrone, 'First Australian Sailors Graduate from Navy Nuclear Power School, Set to Serve on U.S. Navy Subs in Hawaii', US Naval Institute News, 7 July 2023, https://news.usni.org/2023/07/07/first-australian-sailors-graduate-from-nuclear-power-school-set-to-serve-on-u-s-navy-subs-in-hawaii.

21 See Bryant Harris, 'AUKUS Standoff: Australia, UK Wait on Congress to Approve Pact', Defense News, 5 September 2023, https://www.defense news.com/congress/2023/09/05/aukus-standoff-australia-uk-wait-on-congress-to-approve-pact/.

22 See Australian Senate Foreign Affairs, Defence and Trade Legislation Committee, 'Estimates', Official Committee Hansard, 31 May 2023, https://parlinfo.aph.gov.au/parlInfo/download/committees/estimate/26914/toc_pdf/Foreign%20Affairs,%20Defence%20and%20Trade%20Legislation%20Committee_2023_05_31_Official.pdf;fil eType=application%2Fpdf.

23 See 'Navy Virginia-class Attack Submarine Program and AUKUS Submarine Proposal: Background and Issues for Congress', Congressional Research Service, 5 September 2023, pp. 12–33, https://sgp.fas.org/crs/weapons/RL32418.pdf.

24 See Megan Eckstein, 'Allies Target Early AUKUS Milestones to Keep 20-year Plan on Track', Defense News, 7 September 2023, https://www.defensenews.com/naval/2023/09/07/allies-target-early-aukus-milestones-to-keep-20-year-plan-on-track/.

25 See HM Government, 'National Security Strategy and Strategic Defence and Security Review 2015: A Secure and Prosperous United Kingdom', 23 November 2015, pp. 35–6, https://assets.publishing.service.gov.uk/government/uploads/system/uploads/attachment_data/

file/478936/52309_Cm_9161_NSS_SD_
Review_PRINT_only.pdf.

26 See Ronald O'Rourke, 'Navy Next
Generation Attack Submarine
(SSN(X)) Program: Background and
Issues for Congress', Congressional
Research Service, 4 August 2023,
https://crsreports.congress.gov/
product/pdf/IF/IF11826.

27 See Daniel Pye, 'Ben Wallace Confirms
that Barrow Workforce Will Grow',
NW Mail, 31 January 2023, https://
www.nwemail.co.uk/news/23287247.
ben-wallace-confirms-barrow-work
force-will-grow/.

28 See, for example, Harry McNeil,
'Rolls-Royce Submarines Expand
Raynesway Site in Derby', Naval
Technology, 13 June 2023, https://
www.naval-technology.com/news/
rolls-royce-submarines-expand-
raynesway-site-derby/?cf-view.

29 See UK Ministry of Defence and
Department for Energy Security and
Net Zero, 'New Taskforce to Build UK
Nuclear Skills', 1 August 2023, https://
www.gov.uk/government/news/new-
taskforce-to-build-uk-nuclear-skills;
and Sylia Pfeifer and Rachel Millard,
'UK Ministers Plan Task Force to Plug
Nuclear Skills Gap', *Financial Times*,
1 August 2023, https://www.ft.com/
content/2e420836-c529-484b-a119-
9f0b833acb08.

30 See 'Why Are No Royal Navy
Attack Submarines at Sea?', *Navy
Lookout*, 29 August 2023, https://
www.navylookout.com/why-are-no-
royal-navy-attack-submarines-at-sea/.

31 See Tanya Ogilvie-White and John
Gower, 'A Deeper Dive into AUKUS:
Risks and Benefits for the Asia-Pacific',
Asia-Pacific Leadership Network,
October 2021, p. 22, https://cms.apln.
network/wp-content/uploads/2021/10/
A-Deeper-Dive-into-AUKUS-1.pdf.

32 See Andrew Carr, 'Australia's
Archipelagic Deterrence', *Survival*,
vol. 65, no. 4, August–September 2023,
pp. 79–100.

33 See Eglantine Staunton, 'France–
Australia: Salving the Wounds of
AUKUS', *Interpreter*, Lowy Institute,
2 February 2023, https://www.
lowyinstitute.org/the-interpreter/
france-australia-salving-wounds-aukus.

34 UK Ministry of Defence, 'The Defence
Equipment Plan', November 2022,
p. 39, https://assets.publishing.service.
gov.uk/government/uploads/system/
uploads/attachment_data/file/1120332/
The_defence_equipment_plan_2022_
to_2032.pdf.

35 For background, see Peter Hennessy
and James Jinks, *The Silent Deep: The
Royal Navy Submarine Service Since 1945*
(London: Allen Lane, 2015), pp. 132–81.

36 See *ibid.*, pp. 205–16.

37 That said, the boats have always
been under sole UK command, with
the UK government retaining the
right to decide on their weapons' use
in circumstances of supreme national
interest, so the real force of the
NATO commitment has remained
somewhat murky.

38 See Ogilvie-White and Gower, 'A
Deeper Dive into AUKUS', p. 15.

A Fragile Convergence: The US–Japan–South Korea Camp David Summit

Robert Ward

The United States–Japan–South Korea summit that took place at Camp David, Maryland, on 18 August 2023 was historic for a number of reasons. Firstly, this first-ever 'stand-alone' summit between the three countries was an achievement in itself.[1] Although Japan and South Korea are treaty allies of the US, their bilateral relationship has long been volatile, reflecting differences over their shared history, notably what many Koreans see as Japan's failure to atone fully for its brutal colonisation of the Korean Peninsula in 1910–45. The Japanese government's coercive assimilation measures in these years included the banning of the Korean Hangul script and the requirement that Koreans adopt Japanese names. The colonial regime also administered forced-labour programmes that moved workers within Korea, as well as to Japan and elsewhere.[2]

The current warming of Japan–South Korea ties, while encouraged by the US, has been driven mainly by the intense diplomatic activity of South Korean President Yoon Suk-yeol and Japanese Prime Minister Kishida Fumio since the East Asia Summit in November 2022. Their 'Phnom Penh Statement' issued at that summit effectively marked the first step on the way to Camp David.[3] Since then, Yoon and Kishida have held two summits, one in Tokyo and one in Seoul, and they also met at the G7 Hiroshima Summit in May and the NATO Vilnius Summit in July. One symbolic highlight of this diplomacy was the paying of respects during the G7 summit by Yoon

Robert Ward is IISS Japan Chair and Director of Geo-economics and Strategy.

Survival | vol. 65 no. 5 | October–November 2023 | pp. 25–36   https://doi.org/10.1080/00396338.2023.2261241

and Kishida at the Hiroshima monument to Korean victims of the atomic bombing of the city.

The speed of improvement in Tokyo–Seoul ties is all the more remarkable given that it follows the most serious deterioration since the normalisation of relations in 1965. Recent tensions include a diplomatic row in 2018 over what Japan claimed was the directing of a fire-control radar by a South Korean naval destroyer at a Japanese Maritime Self-Defense Force patrol plane, which South Korea denied; and the approval in 2019 by a South Korean court of the seizure of some Japanese corporate assets in South Korea to fund the compensation claims of forced labourers. Japan subsequently curbed the export of some critical materials to South Korea and removed the country from its preferential 'white list' for exports. Also in 2019, South Korea threatened to cancel bilateral intelligence-sharing under the General Security of Military Information Agreement (GSOMIA), an important operational link between the two American allies.

This chill followed the collapse of a deal brokered by the US in 2015 between Park Geun-hye, then president of South Korea, and Japanese prime minister Abe Shinzo to settle 'finally and irreversibly' the issue of compensation for 'comfort women', a euphemism for Korean women who were used as sex slaves by the Imperial Japanese Army before and during the Second World War.[4] The deal was reviled in South Korea and discredited by Park's impeachment and removal from office in 2017, and by her subsequent imprisonment in 2018. The succeeding Moon Jae-in administration prioritised rapprochement with North Korea and had no interest in reviving the deal or in engaging more broadly with Japan. US president Donald Trump's lack of concern for the Japan–South Korea relationship and his idiosyncratic engagement with Pyongyang did little to encourage productive diplomacy.

Given this recent history, the fact that the Camp David meeting took place at all was remarkable. The acknowledgement in the summit's Joint Statement that the three countries need to respond to 'regional challenges, provocations, and threats that affect our collective interests and security' represented a notable upgrade of the language about 'shared prosperity and security' in the Phnom Penh Statement.[5] The US until now had only limited success in trying to cement security ties between Japan and South

Korea, both allies of critical strategic importance.[6] Japan and South Korea have traditionally been reluctant to acknowledge security links, reflecting, inter alia, fears in Japan of being ensnared in a conflict with North Korea and lingering suspicions among some Koreans of Japanese militarism.

Drivers and outcomes

The key driver of the rapprochement at Camp David, and of US President Joe Biden's clear desire to build on it, has been the deterioration of the strategic environment in the Indo-Pacific since Russia's illegal invasion of Ukraine in February 2022. Indeed, Kishida explicitly linked the European and Asian security theatres in his keynote speech to the IISS Shangri-La Dialogue in June 2022, in which he observed that 'Ukraine today may be East Asia tomorrow'.[7] South Korea's first Indo-Pacific strategy, launched by the Yoon administration in late 2022, also reflects concerns in Seoul about stability beyond the Korean Peninsula in seeking to 'expand comprehensive security cooperation'.[8] The strategy represents a significant departure from the Moon administration's New Southern Policy, which focused on India and the Association of Southeast Asian Nations (ASEAN).

The list of strategic concerns shared by Japan, South Korea and the United States is long. China's accelerating military build-up, increasingly menacing behaviour towards Taiwan and harassment of some ASEAN members over territorial disputes in the South China Sea are threats to regional maritime security, and in particular to Japan's and South Korea's sea lanes of communication. North Korea's nuclear-weapons programme threatens the security of all three countries. The deepening strategic relationship between China and Russia, which have been carrying out joint patrols near Japan and South Korea, is reinforcing the connection between European and Asian security.[9] Reports of Russian–North Korean cooperation, which includes the supplying by Pyongyang of weapons for Moscow's war against Ukraine, are also a source of strategic anxiety.[10]

The three countries agreed to hold trilateral meetings between leaders, foreign and defence ministers, and national-security advisers on 'at least' an annual basis, meetings that will complement existing trilateral foreign- and defence-ministry gatherings. There will also be annual meetings between the trio's finance, commerce and industry ministers, as well as a Trilateral Indo-Pacific Dialogue to coordinate policy towards the region.[11]

A stand-alone statement was released to emphasise the countries' 'Commitment to Consult' in response to regional threats and challenges, which contained the same 'collective interests and security' formulation from the Joint Statement. The Commitment to Consult is clear, however, that it is not 'intended to give rights or obligations under international or domestic law', and therefore is not legally binding.[12] This caveat may have been designed to head off Chinese concerns about the emergence of an Asian NATO, and to assuage domestic concerns in Japan and South Korea about entering into alliance-like commitments.

In the military arena, the Camp David participants agreed to hold 'annual, named, multi-domain trilateral exercises on a regular basis'. This was another push to institutionalise interaction between the three and will build on existing exercises. The fact that exercises will be held in more than one physical domain reflects the scale of the perceived security challenge from China and elsewhere, and a desire to include South Korea in wider regional, multilateral exercises in the East China Sea. The Joint Statement also referred to the 'real-time sharing of missile warning data' as part of the trio's efforts to deter and respond to North Korea's 'advancing nuclear and missile threats'.[13]

The importance of Japan and South Korea in US economic-security policy, particularly in advanced technology, was reflected in the summit's acknowledgement of trilateral cooperation in areas including supply-chain security, technology security and standards, critical materials, artificial intelligence, quantum computing and scientific research. There has been encouraging recent evidence of technology cooperation between Japan and South Korea, including the agreement during Kishida's visit to Seoul in May 2023 to reinforce semiconductor supply chains, and the announcement by South Korea's largest semiconductor maker, Samsung Electronics, that it plans to build a new facility for making prototype chips in Yokohama, near Tokyo.[14] Preferential access to the United States' electric-vehicle (EV) market under the Biden administration's Inflation Reduction Act is also tightening trilateral links, especially in the strategically important area of EV batteries.

In 2022, Japan held a 9% share of the global market for lithium-ion batteries and South Korea 19%, compared with 60% for China.[15]

Strategic implications

The Camp David Summit adds to the Biden administration's successful thickening of the United States' network of allies and partners in the region. A sustained US–Japan–South Korea minilateral would complement other formal and informal groupings that have appeared in recent years, such as the AUKUS security pact between Australia, the United Kingdom and the US; the Quadrilateral Security Dialogue (known as the 'Quad') involving Australia, India, Japan and the US; the 'new' Quad comprising Australia, Japan, the Philippines and the US; the 'Chip 4 Alliance' (Japan, South Korea, Taiwan and the US); and the US–Japan–Australia Trilateral Infrastructure Partnership. These smaller groupings offer the advantage of flexibility to the US and its partners in addressing specific strategic issues. The US has also been making efforts to draw countries into the Indo-Pacific Economic Framework (IPEF) it launched in 2022, which, while not offering market access to the US, is intended by Washington to become a key channel for economic rule-making in the region. Japan and South Korea are both participants in IPEF discussions.

China's reaction to the Camp David Summit was predictably acidic, with the Xinhua news agency describing Japan and South Korea as 'sacrificial lambs' in an American bid for 'hegemonic power' and asserting that the summit would escalate tensions in the region.[16] China's banning of all Japanese marine-product imports on 24 August, ostensibly a reaction to the release of waste water from Japan's disabled Fukushima nuclear plant, may have also been an attempt to drive a wedge between Japan and South Korea, where there are also concerns about the Fukushima discharge. Japan has been on the receiving end of Chinese economic coercion before, notably in 2010, when a flare-up in the territorial dispute over the Senkaku/Daioyu islands, which Japan controls but China claims, resulted in a brief halting of exports from China to Japan of rare-earth minerals critical for Japan's electronics industry. The possible resumption of the China–Japan–South Korea Summit, which reports suggest may take place this year for the first time since 2019, will be key in ascertaining China's stance. Japan and South Korea will go into the summit with a stronger relationship and greater strategic alignment than at any time since their 2015 meeting with China.

A fragile convergence

The last time Japan and South Korea enjoyed such strong ties was in the late 1990s, during the premiership of Obuchi Keizo in Japan and the presidency of Kim Dae-jung in South Korea. In 1998, Kim visited Tokyo, where he addressed the Diet (Japanese parliament) and met Japan's emperor. The visit resulted in a joint declaration calling for a 'partnership towards the twenty-first century'.[17] That same year, Kim began a staged lifting of the long-standing ban on imports of Japanese films, CDs and other cultural items, and the two countries even agreed to co-host the FIFA World Cup in 2002. While these moves were partly driven by Kim's need to boost South Korea's beleaguered economy after the 1997 Asian financial crisis, his willingness to set aside the history issue, arguing that this should not define future relations, as well as his moral authority as a critic and victim of South Korea's military dictatorships, contributed to the breakthrough.[18]

This rapprochement lost momentum, however, after Kim's departure from office in 2003. Tensions mounted as Koizumi Junichiro, who served as Japan's prime minister from 2001 to 2006, made repeated visits to Tokyo's Yasukuni Shrine, where the spirits of Japan's war dead, including those convicted of war crimes following the Second World War, are honoured. The decision by Japan's Shimane prefectural assembly in 2005 to establish a day honouring Takeshima, an island that is claimed by both Japan and South Korea and that the latter calls Dokdo, did not improve the situation, nor did the expressed ambivalence of the first Abe administration in 2006–07 towards the Japanese government's 1993 'Kono Statement', in which Japan acknowledged the coercive way in which 'comfort women' had been recruited.[19] The placing of a 'comfort woman' statue in front of the Japanese Embassy in Seoul in 2011; the visit by Lee Myung-bak to Takeshima/Dokdo in 2012 (the first such visit by a South Korean president); and the succeeding Park administration's desire to cleave more closely to China kept relations frosty until the brief thaw in 2015.

Another potential pitfall in the relationship arises from the questioning in South Korea of the legitimacy of the 1965 normalisation treaty.[20] Japan's view is that the treaty settled all financial claims between the two governments 'completely and finally'.[21] South Korea's first fully civilian president, Kim Young-sam, came to office in 1992. Since then, the country's democracy has matured and flourished, and its citizens have become more willing to challenge the decisions made by leaders from its authoritarian past. This includes Park Chung-hee, who was South Korea's president at the time of the 1965 treaty. Park's decision not to secure compensation payments for individuals has been particularly controversial. This may remain a lingering source of friction between Tokyo and Seoul, despite Yoon's efforts to resolve the forced-labour issue by setting up a fund to which South Korean companies will contribute to pay compensation to individuals.

Each of the three leaders also faces political headwinds at home. Biden faces a highly unpredictable US presidential election in November 2024. A win by Trump would cast a long shadow over the United States' diplomatic engagements with all its allies and partners. Yoon's rapprochement with Japan, meanwhile, is controversial at home. South Korean presidents are only allowed, under the country's constitution, to serve for one term, though during that term they wield considerable executive power. This has allowed Yoon to innovate in foreign policy despite his People Power Party not having a majority in the National Assembly. Yoon's popularity ratings are low at just over 30%, partly reflecting the unpopularity of his policy towards Japan.[22] National Assembly elections are due in April 2024 and will inevitably be seen as a referendum on Yoon's forward-leaning foreign policy.

Kishida is also likely to call a general election in either late 2023 or early 2024. While continued opposition weakness suggests that Kishida's ruling Liberal Democratic Party (LDP) is likely to do well, the prime minister's support ratings have been volatile, largely for domestic reasons. Kishida also faces an LDP leadership election in September 2024, which he will have to win if he is to retain the premiership. There is also some scepticism in the Japanese government about the sustainability of Seoul's warmth towards Tokyo. Memories of the failure of the 2015 'comfort women' agreement, in aid of which Abe sought support among reluctant conservatives in his own party and elsewhere in making a landmark apology for 'the incurable physical and psychological wounds' inflicted on the women, remain vivid in Tokyo.[23] Press reports also suggest some alarm in Tokyo at the speed with which the trilateral summit was arranged.[24]

Even assuming that closer trilateral cooperation can be maintained, it is unclear how such cooperation could close several strategic gaps between Japan and South Korea. One such gap relates to nuclear weapons. Kishida's government has emphasised the need to bring about a world without nuclear weapons – indeed, this was reflected in the Camp David Joint Statement. By contrast, Yoon has said that South Korea could consider developing a nuclear-weapons capability or asking the US to deploy nuclear weapons on the Korean Peninsula, with polls suggesting that a majority of the public supports this.[25] The Joint Statement made no mention of trilateral coordination on extended deterrence. (Japan and South Korea each have bilateral Extended Deterrence Dialogues with the US.) Given the stark differences in each country's nuclear stance, the setting up of a trilateral coordination channel might simply serve to highlight these differences.

Another gap exists between each country's policies on China. Although Japan and South Korea have converged under Yoon, South Korea's special strategic concern with North Korea, and China's position as a key interlocutor with Pyongyang, mean that Tokyo's and Seoul's China strategies are unlikely to be fully aligned. Fears in Seoul of being trapped in a US–Japan conflict with China over Taiwan will therefore persist, especially given the speed with which Tokyo is seeking to boost its defence and response capabilities in the event of a crisis involving the island.[26]

Attempts over the past 25 years to deepen Japan–South Korean strategic ties have foundered under the weight of historical baggage and differing conceptions of national interest. Such differences retain the potential to reverse any progress made at Camp David. The Camp David Summit is unlikely to initiate a structural change in the Japan–South Korea relationship. Past failures, however, occurred in starkly different geopolitical circumstances and during a time of enduring expectations that China's influence would be relatively benign. The Camp David Summit in one sense reflected a revision of these expectations. It contained, to be sure, an element of diplomatic housekeeping in the consolidation of cooperation already under way. Yet it also embodied the hope that solidarity in facing common threats will prove strong enough to ensure that the relationship between Japan and South Korea remains broadly constructive and sufficiently healthy to reinforce the United States' growing latticework of allies and partners in the region.

Notes

1   US Embassy and Consulates in Japan, 'Trilateral Leaders' Summit of the United States, Japan, and the Republic of Korea', 19 August 2023, https://jp.usembassy.gov/trilateral-leaders-summit-us-japan-south-korea/#:~:text=President%20Biden%20welcomed%20Japanese%20Prime,David%20during%20the%20Biden%2DHarris.

2   Victor D. Cha, 'Bridging the Gap: The Strategic Context of the 1965 Korea–Japan Normalization Treaty', *Korean Studies*, vol. 20, 1996, p. 125.

3   White House, 'Phnom Penh Statement on US–Japan–Republic of Korea Trilateral Partnership for the Indo-Pacific', 13 November 2022, https://www.whitehouse.gov/briefing-room/statements-releases/2022/11/13/phnom-penh-statement-on-trilateral-partnership-for-the-indo-pacific/.

4   Ministry of Foreign Affairs of Japan, 'Japan–ROK Summit Telephone Call', 28 December 2015, https://www.mofa.go.jp/a_o/na/kr/page4e_000366.html.

5   White House, 'The Spirit of Camp David: Joint Statement of Japan, the Republic of Korea, and the United States', 18 August 2023, https://www.whitehouse.gov/briefing-room/statements-releases/2023/08/18/the-spirit-of-camp-david-joint-statement-of-japan-the-republic-of-korea-and-the-united-states/.

6   One early example of this was the 'Korea clause' in the November 1969 communiqué between US president Richard Nixon and Japan's prime minister Sato Eisaku. This was the first public recognition by Japan that South Korea's security 'was essential to Japan's own security', although support for the clause ebbed and flowed with the Japanese governments that followed. The communiqué came at a time of increased security tensions in Asia against the background of the Vietnam War and the threat of a newly nuclear China. See 'The Nixon–Sato Communique', *New York Times*, 22 November 1969, p. 14, https://timesmachine.nytimes.com/timesmachine/1969/11/22/issue.html; and Victor D. Cha, *Alignment Despite Antagonism: The US–Korea–Japan Security Triangle* (Stanford, CA: Stanford University Press, 1999), chapter 1.

7   Prime Minister's Office of Japan, 'Keynote Address by Prime Minister Kishida Fumio at the IISS Shangri-La Dialogue', 10 June 2022, https://japan.kantei.go.jp/101_kishida/statement/202206/_00002.html.

8   Republic of Korea, Ministry of Foreign Affairs, 'Introducing the Indo-Pacific Strategy', https://www.mofa.go.kr/eng/wpge/m_26382/contents.do.

9   For a map of Chinese and Russian joint patrols and exercises, see Yuka Koshino and Robert Ward, 'Japan Steps Up: Security and Defence Policy Under Kishida', *Asia-Pacific Regional Security Assessment 2023: Key Developments and Trends* (Abingdon: Routledge for the IISS, 2023), p. 119.

10   See, for example, James Politi, 'North Korea's Kim Plans to Visit Putin to Discuss Arms Sales, US Says', *Financial Times*, 4 September 2023, https://www.ft.com/content/11cc1d36-6783-4ab0-96d1-edd27d06b54d.

11   White House, 'The Spirit of Camp David'.

12   White House, 'Commitment to Consult', 18 August 2023, https://www.whitehouse.gov/briefing-room/statements-releases/2023/08/18/commitment-to-consult/#:~:text=We%2C%20the%20leaders%20of%20Japan,our%20collective%20interests%20and%20security.

13   White House, 'The Spirit of Camp David'.

14   Samsung already has a research and development facility in the city. See Kotaro Hosokawa, 'Samsung to Build Chip Development Facility in Japan', Nikkei Asia, 13 May 2023, https://asia.nikkei.com/Business/Tech/Semiconductors/Samsung-to-build-chip-development-facility-in-Japan.

15   'Chugoku Sei, Sentan Hin de Sekai Shea Kakudai, 22 Nen Chosa' 中国勢、先端品で世界シェア拡大22年調査 [China expands global share of advanced products, 2022 survey], *Nihon Keizai Shimbun*, 5 September 2023, https://www.nikkei.com/article/DGKKZO74169420V00C23A9MM8000/.

16   Huaxia, 'Xinhua Commentary: Trilateral Meeting at Camp David Stokes Embers of Cold War', Xinhua, 20 August 2023, https://english.news.cn/20230820/55275e1196b14b6db7d7a099c91e842c/c.html.

17   Ministry of Foreign Affairs of Japan, 'Japan–Republic of Korea Joint Declaration: A New Japan–Republic of Korea Partnership Towards the Twenty-first Century', 8 October 1998, https://www.mofa.go.jp/region/asia-paci/korea/joint9810.html.

18   In 1973, for example, Kim Dae-jung was kidnapped from a hotel in Tokyo by agents from the Korean Central Intelligence Agency on account of his criticism of Park Chung-hee's regime. In 1980, he was sentenced to death after the uprising in Gwangju triggered by the coup that brought Chung Doo-hwan to power, although this sentence was later commuted to a prison sentence.

19   Ministry of Foreign Affairs of Japan, 'Issues Regarding History, Statement by the Chief Cabinet Secretary', 4 August 1993, https://www.mofa.go.jp/a_o/rp/page25e_000343.html. For an account of the deterioration in bilateral ties in this period, see Kimiya Tadashi, *Nikkan Kankei Shi* 日韓関係史 [A history of Japan–South Korea relations] (Tokyo: Iwanami Shinsho, 2021), pp. 169–71.

20   Lee Jong Won et al., *Sengo Nikkan Kankei Shi* 戦後日韓関係史 [A contemporary history of Japan–South Korea relations since the Second World War] (Tokyo: Yuhikaku, 2017), p. 252.

21 See United Nations, 'No. 8473 Agreement on the Settlement of Problems Concerning Property and Claims and on Economic Cooperation Between Japan and the Republic of Korea. Signed at Tokyo, on 22 June 1965', Treaty Series, 1966, p. 260, https://treaties.un.org/doc/Publication/UNTS/Volume%20583/volume-583-I-8473-English.pdf.

22 Kim Han-joo, 'Yoon's Approval Rating Inches Up to 33 pct', Yonhap News Agency, 21 July 2023, https://en.yna.co.kr/view/AEN20230721003000315.

23 Ministry of Foreign Affairs of Japan, 'Japan–Republic of Korea Relations, Announcement by Foreign Ministers of Japan and the Republic of Korea at the Joint Press Occasion', 28 December 2015, https://www.mofa.go.jp/a_o/na/kr/page4e_000364.html.

24 Kiyomiya Ryo, Nishimura Keishi and Inada Kiyohide, 'Nichibeikan, "Zenrei Nai Reberu" de Anpo Kyoryoku e, Mae Nomeri no Beikoku, Nikkan wa?' 日米韓、「前例ないレベル」で安保協力へ前のめりの米国、日韓は？ [Towards unprecedented Japan–US–South Korea security cooperation: forward-leaning US, but what about Japan and South Korea?], Asahi Shimbun, 19 August 2023, https://www.asahi.com/articles/ASR8M62SRR8MUTFK00B.html.

25 Choe Sang-hun, 'In a First, South Korea Declares Nuclear Weapons a Policy Option', New York Times, 12 January 2023, https://www.nytimes.com/2023/01/12/world/asia/south-korea-nuclear-weapons.html.

26 Koshino and Ward, 'Japan Steps Up', pp. 121–6.

Calibrating Engagement with the Taliban

James M. Cowan

Since the United States withdrew from Afghanistan two years ago and the Taliban quickly took over the country, Western governments, including the United Kingdom, have been understandably reluctant to engage with an Islamist regime that has hosted al-Qaeda and trampled on human rights – particularly those of women. At the same time, completely isolating the regime could have perverse security, geopolitical and humanitarian consequences.[1]

A controversy related to the vexing effort to get the balance right erupted following a July visit by UK Member of Parliament Tobias Ellwood to Afghanistan as the guest of the HALO Trust, the British mine-clearing non-governmental organisation with extensive operations in the country. (I am the organisation's CEO.) After an otherwise informative week, Ellwood circulated a video on social media in which he suggested unconditional support for the Taliban. He soon deleted the video after drawing criticism both from former soldiers and from the humanitarian sector.[2] The incident created much heat, but perhaps less light.

A cooler analysis

While Ellwood, by his own admission, overstated his case, there was nevertheless a case to be made. The real question is not whether there is a problem with human rights in Afghanistan – there clearly is – but

Major General (Retd) James M. Cowan is CEO of the HALO Trust and the former commander of the International Security Assistance Force in Helmand province. An earlier version of this essay appeared on the *Survival* Editors' Blog on 14 August 2023 at https://www.iiss.org/online-analysis/survival-online/2023/08/should-the-uk-engage-with-the-taliban-government/.

Survival | vol. 65 no. 5 | October–November 2023 | pp. 37–41   https://doi.org/10.1080/00396338.2023.2261243

whether, by standing back, the United Kingdom is making matters worse. For the first time in 44 years, Afghanistan is largely at peace, and even in traditional strongholds there is no effective armed opposition. While the Islamic State – Khorasan Province remains a threat, the Taliban has established a reasonable level of security and cracked down on corruption. It has destroyed a large part of this year's poppy crop with a resolve that eluded the West. This does not mean these problems have been eradicated or that they could not re-emerge, but the reality is that most Afghans, notably those who live outside Kabul, value new-found peace and security.

For anyone who knew rural Afghanistan during the recent war, it is a bittersweet experience to return. It is now possible to travel to Lashkar Gah and from there to Marjah, Nad-e Ali, Nahr-e Saraj and Nawa-i Barakzai without body armour or weapons. The visitor may reflect on the reasons why, instead of making peace with the Taliban in the aftermath of 9/11, the West waged a long and half-hearted war before making its precipitous exit.[3] The consequences of that failure are everywhere to be seen: the elders of one village in Marjah who had fled the fighting have returned 13 years later to a barren land contaminated by improvised explosive devices. Some 132 people have died in mine accidents in Marjah alone since October 2018. While Westerners could visit Helmand until 2014, very few, if any, visited after 2018, when fighting peaked.

Violence, corruption and narcotics may have all been dramatically reduced, but on the other side of the ledger there are real concerns: the ban on work for women, loss of education for girls, violence towards members of the old regime and absolutist rule. The Taliban's treatment of women and girls has rightly drawn the most condemnation. But the question the West should be asking is not whether the female population of Afghanistan is being treated badly, but whether Western disengagement is making their situation worse.

The HALO model

HALO Afghanistan has 2,200 staff operating across 23 provinces. The last two years have seen a surge of activity into the south, with nearly 1,000 deminers working in southern provinces. HALO creates local employment, with 20 Afghans currently dependent upon each HALO breadwinner. Both the Taliban and the international community regard HALO's work as a good thing. It is therefore an apolitical means of bridging the chasm of mutual distrust. Because HALO believes in making its case patiently and privately, the charity employs more women now than it did when the Western-supported government was in power. Its female employees work in mixed-gender survey teams and are respectful of traditional Afghan social norms.

Much of HALO's work involves clearing rural irrigation systems of explosive devices to enable agriculture. In a country where famine is real, the basic need to feed people transcends all others. HALO's work in other areas has also benefited Afghanistan. The UN secretary-general's Special Representative believes that a significant part of the education problem in Afghanistan is that in rural areas, far too few children (boys or girls) go to school. Many schools are surrounded by improvised landmines and many teachers are unwilling to work in such dangerous circumstances. Because it has the confidence of the de facto authorities, HALO has been able to react to natural disasters such as last year's earthquake and recent heavy flooding, bringing heavy equipment and logistical expertise to bear in support of the relief operation.

Notwithstanding these other humanitarian responsibilities, HALO supports the country's women and girls, and does not shy away from raising the matter of their rights with even the most hardline members of the Taliban. Some moderate Taliban are uncomfortable with the group's harsh current policy and are amenable to discussion. The European Union and United Nations operations in Afghanistan are both headed by women and want the UK to return.

*   *   *

The West has a duty to help Afghanistan's entire population, which is living in highly precarious economic conditions. Other national and international interests are salient. The UK and its allies have legitimate security, narcotics and migration concerns. Afghanistan has huge mineral resources that could help the green transition, but that will be exploited by others – notably

Russia and China – if Western countries stand aside. Russia and China are far less likely to be respectful of human rights.[4]

Through its long history, Afghanistan has experienced three essential political conditions: a secular government backed by an external power (the British Empire, the Soviet Union, the NATO coalition) that has sought to modernise a traditional society; a conservative indigenous government that has imposed peace upon a country prone to war; and civil war.

The present Taliban government is vulnerable to the usual tensions of any coalition, but it has proved to be more enduring than some may have wished. Short of another invasion and occupation, there is no prospect of a secular, Western-style government re-emerging. The Taliban's detractors must know that Afghanistan's strongest hope lies in nudging the current regime away from its unworldly posture towards a more pragmatic one. This will require patience that may have to be measured in decades. The alternative is to subject Afghanistan once more to the horrors of its third and perhaps more normal condition – civil war. In that case, nobody's human rights would be served.

Notes

[1] See Arne Strand and Astrid Suhrke, 'Quiet Engagement with the Taliban', *Survival*, vol. 63, no. 5, October–November 2021, pp. 35–46.

[2] The *Daily Mail* has preserved the video for posterity. See 'Tory MP Ellwood Hails "Transformation" of Afghanistan by the Taliban', *Daily Mail*, 17 July 2023, https://www.dailymail.co.uk/video/news/video-2981441/Video-Tory-MP-Ellwood-hails-transformation-Afghanistan-Taliban.html.

[3] See, for example, Toby Dodge, 'Afghanistan and the Failure of Liberal Peacebuilding', *Survival*, vol. 63, no. 5, October–November 2021, pp. 47–58; and Laurel Miller, 'Biden's Afghanistan Withdrawal: A Verdict on the Limits of American Power', *Survival*, vol. 63, no. 3, June–July 2021, pp. 37–44.

[4] See Laurel Miller, 'Protecting US Interests in Afghanistan', *Survival*, vol. 64, no. 2, April–May 2022, pp. 25–34; and Graeme Smith and Ibraheem Bahiss, 'The World Has No Choice But to Work with the Taliban', *Foreign Affairs*, 11 August 2023, https://www.foreignaffairs.com/afghanistan/world-has-no-choice-work-taliban.

Noteworthy

Indicted, again

'1.   The Defendant, DONALD J. TRUMP, was the forty-fifth President of the United States and a candidate for re-election in 2020. The Defendant lost the 2020 presidential election.

2.   Despite having lost, the Defendant was determined to remain in power. So for more than two months following election day on November 3, 2020, the Defendant spread lies that there had been outcome-determinative fraud in the election and that he had actually won. These claims were false, and the Defendant knew that they were false. But the Defendant repeated and widely disseminated them anyway – to make his knowingly false claims appear legitimate, create an intense national atmosphere of mistrust and anger, and erode public faith in the administration of the election.

3.   The Defendant had a right, like every American, to speak publicly about the election and even to claim, falsely, that there had been outcome-determinative fraud during the election and that he had won. He was also entitled to formally challenge the results of the election through lawful and appropriate means, such as by seeking recounts or audits of the popular vote in states or filing lawsuits challenging ballots and procedures. Indeed, in many cases, the Defendant did pursue these methods of contesting the election results. His efforts to change the outcome in any state through recounts, audits, or legal challenges were uniformly unsuccessful.

4.   Shortly after election day, the Defendant also pursued unlawful means of discounting legitimate votes and subverting the election results. In so doing, the Defendant perpetrated three criminal conspiracies:

   a.   A conspiracy to defraud the United States by using dishonesty, fraud, and deceit to impair, obstruct, and defeat the lawful federal government function by which the results of the presidential election are collected, counted, and certified by the federal government, in violation of 18 U.S.C. § 371;

   b.   A conspiracy to corruptly obstruct and impede the January 6 congressional proceeding at which the collected results of the presidential election are counted and certified ("the certification proceeding"), in violation of 18 U.S.C. § 1512(k); and

   c.   A conspiracy against the right to vote and to have one's vote counted, in violation of 18 U.S.C. § 241.

Each of these conspiracies – which built on the widespread mistrust the Defendant was creating through pervasive and destabilizing lies about election fraud – targeted a bedrock function of the United States federal government: the nation's process of collecting, counting, and certifying the results of the presidential election ("the federal government function").'

Excerpt from the federal indictment against former US president Donald Trump filed on 1 August 2023.[1]

Survival | vol. 65 no. 5 | October–November 2023 | pp. 42–44   https://doi.org/10.1080/00396338.2023.2261244

'Defendant Donald John Trump lost the United States presidential election held on November 3, 2020. One of the states he lost was Georgia. Trump and the other Defendants charged in this Indictment refused to accept that Trump lost, and they knowingly and wilfully joined a conspiracy to unlawfully change the outcome of the election in favor of Trump. That conspiracy contained a common plan and purpose to commit two or more acts of racketeering activity in Fulton County, Georgia, elsewhere in the State of Georgia, and in other states.

[…]

At all times relevant to this Count of the Indictment, the Defendants … constituted a criminal organisation whose members and associates engaged in various related criminal activities including, but not limited to, false statements and writings, impersonating a public officer, forgery, filing false documents, influencing witnesses, computer theft, computer trespass, computer invasion of privacy, conspiracy to defraud the state, acts involving theft, and perjury.

[…]

The manner and methods used by the Defendants and other members and associates of the enterprise to further the goals of the enterprise and to achieve its purposes included, but were not limited to, the following:

1. **False Statements to and Solicitation of State Legislatures**
    Members of the enterprise … appeared at hearings in Fulton County, Georgia, before members of the Georgia General Assembly on December 3, 2020, December 10, 2020, and December 30, 2020. At these hearings, members of the enterprise made false statements concerning fraud in the November 3, 2020, presidential election.

2. **False Statements to and Solicitation of High-Ranking State Officials**
    Members of the enterprise … made false statements … to Georgia officials, including the Governor, the Secretary of State, and the Speaker of the House of Representatives. Members of the enterprise also corruptly solicited Georgia officials … to violate their oaths to the Georgia Constitution and to the United States Constitution by unlawfully changing the outcome of the November 3, 2020, presidential election in Georgia in favor of Donald Trump.

3. **Creation and Distribution of False Electoral College Documents**
    Members of the enterprise … created false Electoral College documents and recruited individuals to convene and cast false Electoral College votes at the Georgia State Capitol, in Fulton County, on December 14, 2020. After the false Electoral College votes were cast, members of the enterprise transmitted the votes to the President of the United States Senate, the Archivist of the United States, the Georgia Secretary of State, and the Chief Judge of the United States District Court for the Northern District of Georgia. The false documents were intended to disrupt and delay the joint session of Congress on January 6, 2021, in order to unlawfully change the outcome of the November 3, 2020, presidential election in favor of Donald Trump.

4. **Harassment and Intimidation of Fulton County Election Worker Ruby Freeman**
    Members of the enterprise … falsely accused Fulton County election worker Ruby Freeman of committing election crimes in Fulton County, Georgia. These false accusations were repeated to Georgia legislators and other Georgia officials in an effort to persuade them to unlawfully change the outcome of the November 3, 2020, presidential election in favor of Donald Trump.

5. **Solicitation of High-Ranking United States Department of Justice Officials**
   Members of the enterprise … corruptly solicited high-ranking United States Department of Justice officials to make false statements to government officials in Fulton County, Georgia, including the Governor, the Speaker of the House of Representatives, and the President Pro Tempore of the Senate. In one instance, Donald Trump stated to the Acting United States Attorney General, "Just say that the election was corrupt, and leave the rest to me and the Republican congressmen."

6. **Solicitation of the Vice President of the United States**
   Members of the enterprise … corruptly solicited the Vice President of the United States to violate the United States Constitution and federal law by unlawfully rejecting Electoral College votes cast in Fulton County, Georgia, by the duly elected and qualified presidential electors from Georgia.

7. **Unlawful Breach of Election Equipment in Georgia and Elsewhere**
   Members of the enterprise … corruptly conspired in Fulton County, Georgia, and elsewhere to unlawfully access secure voting equipment and voter data. In Georgia, members of the enterprise stole data, including ballot images, voting equipment software, and personal voter information. The stolen data was then distributed to other members of the enterprise, including members in other states.

8. **Obstructive Acts in Furtherance of the Conspiracy and the Cover Up**
   Members of the enterprise … filed false documents, made false statements to government investigators, and committed perjury in judicial proceedings in Fulton County, Georgia, and elsewhere in furtherance of and to cover up the conspiracy.'

Excerpt from an indictment against Trump and his associates filed in Fulton County, Georgia, on 14 August.[2]

Alliance happy

'If I sound optimistic, it's because I am. Today, our Alliance remains a bulwark of global security and stability as it's been for more than seven decades. NATO is stronger, more energized, and, yes, more united than ever in its history. Indeed, more vital to our shared future.'

US President Joe Biden speaks at the NATO summit in Vilnius, Lithuania, on 12 July 2023.[3]

'If I seem like I'm happy, it's because I am. This has been a great, great meeting.'

Biden speaks at a press conference with Yoon Suk-yeol, president of South Korea, and Kishida Fumio, prime minister of Japan, following a meeting at Camp David on 18 August.[4]

Sources

1 United States District Court for the District of Columbia, 'United States of America v. Donald J. Trump', Case 1:23-cr-00257-TSC, 1 August 2023, https://www.justice.gov/storage/US_v_Trump_23_cr_257.pdf.
2 Fulton County Superior Court, 'The State of Georgia v. Donald John Trump', Case 23SC188947, 14 August 2023, https://www.politico.com/f/?id=00000189-f730-dc32-ab89-f7fc1f760000.
3 White House, 'Remarks by President Biden on Supporting Ukraine, Defending Democratic Values, and Taking Action to Address Global Challenges', Vilnius Summit, 12 July 2023, https://www.whitehouse.gov/briefing-room/speeches-remarks/2023/07/12/remarks-by-president-biden-on-supporting-ukraine-defending-democratic-values-and-taking-action-to-address-global-challenges-vilnius-lithuania/.
4 White House, 'Remarks by President Biden, President Yoon Suk Yeol of the Republic of Korea, and Prime Minister Kishida Fumio of Japan in Joint Press Conference', Camp David, MD, 18 August 2023, https://www.whitehouse.gov/briefing-room/speeches-remarks/2023/08/18/remarks-by-president-biden-president-yoon-suk-yeol-of-the-republic-of-korea-and-prime-minister-kishida-fumio-of-japan-in-joint-press-conference-camp-david-md/.

Whither Wagner? The Consequences of Prigozhin's Mutiny and Demise

Kimberly Marten

Yevgeny Prigozhin, leader of the Russian paramilitary outfit known as the Wagner Group, and other senior members of the group were confirmed dead by Russian authorities on 27 August 2023, days after a suspicious crash of Prigozhin's private jet on Russian territory. Early indications suggested sabotage by way of a planted bomb.[1] Until Prigozhin turned against the Russian military leadership and attempted a mutiny last June, the organisation had been a crucial element of Russia's recent projection of power and influence in the Central African Republic, Libya, Mali, Sudan, Syria and Ukraine, and therefore a major factor in Russian President Vladimir Putin's revanchism. The demise of its key figures brings into question whether and how the Wagner Group and other similar Russian paramilitaries will operate in the future. Indeed, Moscow may now become even more dependent on similar security contractors as its financial and military resources become increasingly depleted from its invasion of Ukraine and international sanctions.[2]

The Wagner Group and the Russian state

Many source materials on the Wagner Group are impossible to verify with any degree of certainty. The Russian military-intelligence agency, known as the GRU, is closely connected to Wagner's operations and conducts many foreign-influence campaigns. Prigozhin himself was crucial to Putin's covert efforts to project Russian influence for years. For example, Prigozhin admitted that he controlled the Internet Research Agency, which attempted

Kimberly Marten is professor of political science at Barnard College and Columbia University.

Survival | vol. 65 no. 5 | October–November 2023 | pp. 45–64   https://doi.org/10.1080/00396338.2023.2261245

to manipulate public opinion in the 2016 US presidential election.[3] Various other companies linked to Prigozhin have spread disinformation throughout Africa, as well as in India and the United Kingdom.[4] He directed media and social-media companies notable for their disinformation campaigns in Russia and abroad. While some foreign intelligence agencies from adversaries of Russia may have incentives to spread false information, it is fairly clear that both the Wagner Group and Prigozhin himself were fully dependent on Kremlin support for their operations, and in turn served as instruments of the Russian state.[5] Though often portrayed as a private military company or mercenary outfit, the Wagner Group was probably a GRU creation.[6] Satellite images confirm that, from 2015 until the 2023 mutiny, it trained close to the GRU special-operations (*spetsnaz*) 10th Special Mission Brigade base in Molkino, Russia.[7] In virtually every place it deployed abroad except Ukraine, and now perhaps Belarus, investigative journalists have discovered that it executed contracts with foreign actors with Russian state assistance. After the mutiny, Putin revealed that the Wagner Group's funding came from the Russian state, but the proportions of its funding from Russian-assisted foreign contracts and direct state payments remain murky.[8]

Prigozhin was fully dependent on Kremlin support

Prigozhin had no combat experience and owed his rise entirely to Putin. During the Soviet era, he spent nine years in prison for organised theft and burglary.[9] He then began his career as a grocer and restaurateur in St Petersburg, when Putin worked for the mayor's office and apparently determined what businesses could legally operate in the city.[10] After Prigozhin's death, Putin confirmed he had known him since the early 1990s.[11] When Putin became president of Russia, Prigozhin was awarded state contracts for the Kremlin's catering, the Moscow regional school district's food supplies, and the Russian Ministry of Defence's catering and cleaning.

Infighting between Prigozhin and the Defence Ministry began in 2017, amid accusations of Prigozhin's embezzlement and the ministry's refusal to pay amounts due on his contracts.[12] This episode may help explain the Defence Ministry's apparent unwillingness to stop the Wagner Group from attacking US special-operations forces in Deir ez-Zor, Syria, in February 2018. The ministry's denial to US forces that Wagner forces were Russian assets assured a no-holds-barred American response, with Russian commanders assenting to US airstrikes.[13] Since the Wagner Group lacked air-defence systems, it suffered hundreds of casualties. The Russian Ministry of Defence refused even to send helicopters to the battlefield to evacuate the wounded, although they were later flown back to Russian military hospitals on military aeroplanes.[14] Prigozhin claimed in June 2023 that the Defence Ministry designed the attack and intended to set the Wagner Group up for failure.[15] Tensions became more pronounced as Prigozhin lambasted the ministry and its leadership for poor decision-making in Russia's war in Ukraine, and especially its failures to provide his forces with adequate ammunition.

The Prigozhin-led mutiny on 23–24 June, involving thousands of Wagner Group forces stationed in eastern Ukraine, appeared to be a reaction to Russian Defence Minister Sergei Shoigu's order that the fighters sign direct contracts with the ministry, which would have cut Prigozhin out of the financial loop.[16] While several of Wagner's senior commanders in Ukraine were battle-hardened veterans of the group's previous deployments in Syria and Africa, most of the mutineers were probably former Russian prisoners, recruited by Prigozhin in summer 2022 in exchange for the promise of amnesty after six months' combat service, and survivors of Russia's brutal and underequipped spring offensive in Bakhmut, in which the Wagner Group played a prominent role.[17]

During the mutiny, Wagner Group forces shot down six Russian military helicopters and an aeroplane, reportedly killing 13 airmen. They rolled into Rostov-on-Don in southwestern Russia, occupying the Southern Command military headquarters and other security-service buildings. A convoy of their military trucks (including some armoured vehicles) advanced to within 200 kilometres of Moscow. Prigozhin demanded Shoigu's removal and that of Chief of the General Staff Valery Gerasimov. Although the Russian state often punishes criticism of Russia's war in Ukraine with imprisonment, Prigozhin also said that Putin's main justifications for the war were based on lies because Putin had been misled by his advisers: Ukraine and NATO had not been about to attack Russia, Ukraine did not need de-Nazification, and Ukrainian President Volodymyr Zelenskyy would have been willing to negotiate. In a ranting video posted on his Telegram social-media channel, Prigozhin fumed: 'What was the war for? The war was needed for Shoigu to receive a hero star ... The oligarchic clan that rules Russia needed the war.'[18] Prigozhin was careful not to express any personal disloyalty to Putin, in spite of the violence and mayhem his mutiny caused.

In any case, several thousand Wagner forces with a few armoured vehicles spread out along Russia's long M-4 highway probably could not have staged a successful coup on their own. Putin and the Kremlin are defended by the elite Kremlin Regiment of the Federal Protective Service. More than 300,000 members of Russia's National Guard, including brutal special forces in every city who specialise in riot control, also report directly to Putin. Prigozhin might have believed, however, that significant numbers of Russian uniformed troops would mutiny alongside him. That did not occur. US officials believe that General Sergei Surovikin, whom Prigozhin identified as his go-between in negotiations with the Defence Ministry, had foreknowledge of the mutiny.[19] Surovikin was not seen for more than two months following the mutiny. US officials believe he was detained, then released in early September.[20] The day before the August plane crash, he was relieved of his command of Russia's air and space forces. Thirteen other senior military officers were detained following the mutiny, and 15 were either suspended from duty or fired by mid-July.[21]

Putin's response to the mutiny was muddled, which made him look weak. He called its leaders traitors, criminals and terrorists, and vowed they would be brought to account.[22] Russian state television showed embarrassing police raids on Prigozhin's St Petersburg office and home, displaying ridiculous disguises and wigs, multiple fake passports, and piles of cash and gold. The announcers called him a traitor and a criminal, this time by name.[23] Yet a local online newspaper, *Fontanka*, reported that authorities had returned $111 million to Prigozhin.[24] While the authorities shut down his business centre and media outlets, social-media sites associated with him continued to operate.[25] His catering firms continued to secure Kremlin contracts.[26] While Russian authorities confiscated the heavy weapons of the mutineers and closed the Wagner Group's training base in Molkino, they allowed the force to move to neighbouring Belarus under a deal nego-tiated with Belarusian President Alyaksandr Lukashenka. Within a few weeks, Prigozhin was shown on social media encouraging Wagner Group forces there to train for future deployments to Africa. He was then shown back in St Petersburg, meeting with African representatives to Putin's Russia–Africa Summit and offering to send Wagner to help coup leaders in Niger. Meanwhile, Russian independent-media reports indicated that the Wagner Group was still recruiting inside Russia.[27] Advertisements for new enlistees were reported in Poland and Latvia, and in six languages on Facebook and Instagram.[28]

Then, on 23 August, a private plane registered to Prigozhin, having flown back to Russia from an apparent visit to the Central African Republic and Mali, crashed halfway to St Petersburg on a flight originating in Moscow. Prigozhin and several of the Wagner Group's senior staff died. One was Dmitry Utkin, a former GRU *spetsnaz* officer known by the *nom de guerre* 'Wagner' because of his fondness for Nazi culture, who gave the group its name, first commanded it in eastern Ukraine in 2014 and was considered a hero by many Wagner fighters. Another was Valery Chekalov, known to have responsibility for Wagner Group logistics, as well as Prigozhin's Evro Polis oil- and gas-security firm in Syria.[29]

Even if Wagner Group members are outraged by these events, they are unlikely to be able to destabilise the Russian state. After the post-mutiny closure of the Molkino base, all organised Wagner formations were relo-cated outside of Russian territory. The Wagnerites in Belarus are mostly poorly trained former Russian prisoners who lack heavy weapons. Those in Syria and Africa depend on the Russian military air base in Khmeimim, Syria, for transit, and would have a tough time returning to Russia without the support of the Defence Ministry.

The Wagner Group in Belarus

Under the deal with Lukashenka, the Wagner Group mutineers relocated from eastern Ukraine to neighbouring Belarus without their heavy weapons. Independent satellite images indicated that several thousand were housed in a reconstructed military base in the centre of the country, near the rural village of Tsel'.[30] They conducted joint training exercises with Belarusian forces along the Polish border at Brest, and Lukashenka joked in a meeting with Putin that Wagner forces 'want to go west' into Poland.[31] Given that the troops involved were poorly trained and lightly armed, however, they could not have invaded any country successfully. The Belarusian state did release a video of what appeared to be a few Wagner Group troops training its conscripts.[32] But the force is unlikely to add much sophistication or depth to Belarusian defence preparedness, and it remained unclear who was paying them.[33] Their only realistic use was as an infantry element of a future Russian military force staging from Belarus.[34] What neighbouring NATO members Poland, Lithuania and Latvia most feared was that Wagner could exacerbate illegal migrant flows into their countries or engage in other forms of hybrid warfare.

This particular group may constitute the Wagner Group forces most loyal to Prigozhin, since he was responsible for most of them having been released from Russian prisons in return for their service. Given reports of violent criminal acts by similar Wagner fighters who have returned home, keeping a large group of battle-hardened Russian ex-convicts busy outside of Russian territory, but near enough for Russian intelligence to monitor and Russian military forces to reach if necessary, may provide passive domestic security benefits for Russia.[35]

The Wagner Group in Syria

Wagner Group infantry supported the Russian military in Syria for several years starting in 2015, and in 2020 Wagner recruited former Syrian rebels to fight with them in Libya on behalf of warlord Khalifa Haftar. The Wagner Group's last combat role in Syria appears to have been in late 2021, and more recently they have been deployed there in smaller numbers, estimated in the hundreds, primarily to guard oil and gas facilities pursuant to contracts reached between the Syrian government and Prigozhin's Evro Polis firm.[36] These facilities are relatively low-value resources, and may primarily constitute a means for Russia to ensure that it retains an economic position in Syria over the long term.[37] Wagner's presence there may also have been designed to block competitive efforts by the Iran-backed Lebanese militia

Hizbullah to gain control over Syrian pipeline and shipping links across the border into Lebanon.[38]

During the mutiny, several thousand regular Russian military forces deployed in Syria worked with local authorities to cut off Wagner's communications, detain local Wagner commanders for questioning, and force Wagner fighters either to sign new individual contracts with the Russian Defence Ministry or leave on Russian military aeroplanes.[39] Reportedly only a few dozen Wagner forces left, out of the hundreds on the ground. This may indicate that Wagner forces far from home – volunteers who have risked their lives and watched their comrades die – had little real attachment or loyalty to Prigozhin, whose whole justification for the mutiny was to avoid having his forces sign contracts with the Defence Ministry. He was, after all, a man who never engaged in combat himself, but got wealthy off the labour and sacrifices of those who did.

It remains unclear exactly what it means that these Wagner fighters signed contracts with the Defence Ministry. Consumed by its war in Ukraine, the ministry likely has limited administrative bandwidth and few extra funds to devote to guarding oil and gas enterprises in Syria. It might therefore make sense to transfer those Wagner forces to a different Russian paramilitary group, one more known for its loyalty to the Defence Ministry. One such group is Redut, which means 'Redoubt', and was formerly known as Shchit, meaning 'Shield'.[40] It has been guarding natural-gas and phosphate facilities in Syria since 2018 for businesses associated with Russian oligarch Gennady Timchenko's Stroytransgaz firm.[41] Timchenko's ties with Putin also began in St Petersburg in the early 1990s, including through reputed organised-crime dealings involving an oil terminal and shipping port.[42] He is probably much closer to Putin at a personal level than Prigozhin ever was, and is certainly far wealthier than Prigozhin was.[43] Redut has an additional long-term association with Russia's huge Gazprom natural-gas conglomerate, the prior owner of Stroytransgaz.[44] Units from Redut fought in the early days of Russia's Ukraine war, although they reportedly did not perform well.[45] The Russian Defence Ministry seems to have firmer control of Redut than Wagner. It is possible that Redut has absorbed the Wagner fighters in Syria, given the similarities of their recent guard-duty profiles there. In any case, the presence of several thousand regular Russian forces in the country, which outnumber Wagner forces by a factor of ten, has likely eased the subjugation of the Wagner Group in Syria to Defence Ministry oversight.

The Wagner Group in Africa

Since Russia was slow to return to Africa after the Soviet collapse in 1991, its commercial presence there is small compared with that of other foreign states.[46] The Wagner Group became an alternative mechanism for Putin to establish influence on a continent that Putin considers ripe for great-power competition. Wagner forces began to deploy to Sudan and the Central African Republic in late 2017 to help Moscow regain a foothold by dominating the security landscape in certain countries. At the time of the June mutiny, the Wagner Group is believed to have had 1,000–1,500 troops on the ground in both the Central African Republic and Mali, several hundred in Libya and dozens in Sudan.

The Wagner Group has secured contracts to train local forces in all of the African countries into which it has ventured, including its failed counter-insurgency effort in Mozambique in 2019. In so doing, it has made Moscow a necessary player for ensuring the security of several of the continent's authoritarian regimes, propping them up in the Central African Republic, Mali and eastern Libya while fighting off opposition forces and at times targeting civilians.[47] Furthermore, Prigozhin's media and social-media networks in Africa have glorified Russia and tarred the French presence on the continent, magnifying entrenched anti-colonial historical narratives. In Mali, Wagner effectively forced France to withdraw its counter-terrorism forces in 2022, and Prigozhin employees worked directly with the Malian junta in spring 2023 to expel the United Nations peacekeeping operation.[48] Wagner has also provided weapons and advice to the rebel Rapid Support Forces faction in Sudan's civil war.[49] In both the Central African Republic and Sudan, Russia has used the Wagner Group to seize and guard gold mines and smuggle gold to the United Arab Emirates.[50] This has likely helped Putin fund his war in Ukraine despite sanctions against Russia and Russian-produced gold.

The Wagner Group or a successor could conceivably take advantage of recent coups in Burkina Faso and Niger and use its existing support for rebels in Chad to establish major footholds in each of those countries, too.[51] But even the fully intact, pre-mutiny incarnation of the group had a mixed track record in Africa. It suffered a massive rout in Mozambique in 2019, failed to help Haftar take Tripoli in 2020 and faces a surge in terrorist attacks in Mali.[52] In this light, other African countries may think twice before retaining a presumptively weaker Wagner – and less stable Russia – to help them.

As of early September, no evidence of significant change in any Wagner Group African deployments had emerged since the mutiny. While there were reports of Wagner forces leaving their bases in the Central African Republic, officials explained it as a normal annual rotation of forces.[53] New Wagner forces came pouring into the country in July to help President Faustin-Archange Touadéra successfully manage a referendum that enabled him to extend his term.[54] There was also no evidence that any of Russia's African partners would hesitate to accept change in Wagner's leadership provided the force itself were effective. Fidèle Gouandjika, a senior adviser to Touadéra, famously said: 'If it's not Wagner anymore and they send Beethoven or Mozart, it doesn't matter, we'll take them.'[55] Indeed, some African officials may have expected a changing of the guard. A few days before Prigozhin's plane crash, Russian Deputy Defence Minister Yunus-bek Yevkurov visited Haftar in Benghazi to propose setting up a new security support group under GRU oversight.[56] Haftar has long expressed displeasure about Wagner's work and expenses, dating back to its failed 2020 effort to help him take Tripoli using Syrian ex-rebels.[57] The GRU might be a better overseer of the Wagner Group than the Defence Ministry as a whole, since its long-standing responsibilities for foreign-military training, arms sales and foreign-influence campaigns better match Wagner's strengths.[58]

The utility of expeditionary Wagner Group forces

While Wagner once offered Russia plausible deniability for its actions abroad, that vanished after the 2018 Deir ez-Zor battle. By summer 2018, members of the Russian legislature were referring to the Wagner Group by name.[59] The following December, Putin mentioned it in his annual scripted press conference.[60] The Wagner Group began recruiting online, and investigative journalists began reporting on Wagner activities around the globe.[61] The only arena in which deniability, albeit now implausible, still seems to matter to Russia is the United Nations, where Moscow has used its Security Council veto to interfere with the work of sanctions experts seeking to report on Wagner Group activities in Libya and the Central African Republic.[62]

The Wagner Group has allowed Russia to extend its martial reach far beyond its borders at relatively low cost, without putting regular Russian military forces in harm's way. Many other governments have also used private military companies to avoid official military casualties.[63] What distinguishes Russia's instrumentalisation of the Wagner Group, though, from at least the recent experiences of most other countries is its use as a main combat element in both Syria and Ukraine, where it has suffered heavy personnel losses.[64]

Alternatives going forward

With Prigozhin gone, there are reports that various actors, ranging from Russia's civilian foreign-intelligence agency (the SVR) to Prigozhin's young son Pavel, are vying to seize parts of his complex business empire.[65] It is too early to know whether this posturing is realistic, or just wishful thinking by the competitors. The Russian Defence Ministry or the GRU, which is subordinate to the General Staff, could assume direct control of all Wagner Group operations.[66] Prigozhin's final trip to Africa may have reflected his own concerns that the GRU was attempting a takeover of his assets.[67] But without some other paramilitary group to take on Wagner's former role, such a dispensation would entail serious costs for Russia. Wagner and Prigozhin's global reach did not just involve armed activities. It was multifaceted, substantially clandestine and hydra-headed, with many businesses hidden behind shell companies.[68] Many of these, as noted above, centred on commercial security provision in Syria and Africa, as well as media and social-media outlets, but they range from a movie studio and catering companies in Russia to timber and gold-mining concessions in the Central African Republic. Military officers might not be well suited to managing these companies. Furthermore, placing the forces themselves under direct military control would presumably increase the costs of managing them to the Russian state while undercutting the operational flexibility and ingenuity which the group once enjoyed. Finally, given Russia's status as a permanent member of the UN Security Council, it would be politically fraught for it to send regular forces anywhere in the face of UN sanctions. On balance, bureaucratising and regularising the Wagner Group would largely erase its benefits to Russia.

A second possibility is that the Wagner Group could be kept much as it is, with a new set of Kremlin-approved senior managers taking over Prigozhin's roles. Putin may have waited two months before eliminating Prigozhin – assuming, credibly, that this is what in fact happened – to allow his intelligence services to gather information about the vast range of Prigozhin's and Chekalov's activities and holdings with an eye to clearing the path for others to replace them. Putin said he met with 35 Wagner commanders and Prigozhin in the Kremlin in July, and proposed as a new leader Andrey Troshev, a founding member of Wagner and one of its senior commanders in Syria, with previous combat experience in Afghanistan and Chechnya.[69] Putin claimed that many of the Wagnerites nodded, while Prigozhin said that they had not agreed.[70] Prigozhin fired Troshev in late June, following reports that Troshev had informed the Kremlin about the mutiny in advance.[71]

If not Troshev, Timchenko, in spite or because of his Redut connections, could be a contender. Another might be Konstantin Pikalov, who reportedly served as the link between the Defence Ministry and Wagner Group operations in Africa, and who recently opened a branch of his services in Crimea.[72] Pikalov is now expanding his African ambitions.[73] Yet another could be Konstantin Malofeev, a shady Russian monarchist billionaire who helped foment uprisings in eastern Ukraine in 2014 and finance armed groups in the Russian-occupied Donbas region.[74] All four candidates are subject to Western sanctions. Putin could also choose a relatively unknown Putin crony, as Prigozhin was when he first became a military contractor. A newcomer would lack the acumen and experience that Prigozhin had developed via Wagner's African activities, but Prigozhin and his team did not generally act alone, usually enjoying the overt or implied cover of Russian diplomats and officials. In the Central African Republic, Valery Zakharov, a former GRU officer not directly affiliated with Wagner, initially served as Touadéra's security adviser, and was eventually replaced by Vitali Perfilev, a Wagnerite.[75]

A third option for Putin would be to fragment the Wagner empire, with local commanders pledging direct loyalty to Putin or the Defence Ministry. As of 2010, over a dozen Russian security firms were known to exist.[76] A variety of new ones have appeared in Russia's Ukraine war, and the Russian state is encouraging big businesses such as Gazprom, state ministries such as the Russian space agency, and regional leaders in Russia including Chechnya's Ramzan Kadyrov to create their own militias to fight in Ukraine.[77] It is plausible that new groups could merge with existing Wagner formations – or that Wagner units could be refashioned into new companies. While this would do nothing to expand Wagner operations, it could keep the existing deployments functioning to advance Russia's interests. It could also make it harder for Western countries to track their activities, restoring some of the discreetness that Prigozhin lost by way of his penchant for self-promotion.

*   *   *

The viability of any of these scenarios would of course depend on cooperation from local Wagner commanders still in place, or at least from replacements who could command the loyalty of Wagner's enlistees. While Wagnerites might not wish to pledge fealty to a new management team, the apparent willingness of most of those in Syria to accept new orders after the mutiny suggests that the transition could be easier than it might seem. Wagnerites have always known they were ultimately working for the Russian state. Given the recent proliferation of small mercenary groups formed by authoritarian Middle Eastern and African countries, Wagnerites could offer their services elsewhere, although the pay is usually low.[78] They could also follow the path of unemployed mercenaries throughout history, using their skills in violence to become marauders and extortionists.[79] Some Wagnerites returning home to Russia are already reported to be doing exactly that.

Notes

1   See, for example, Julian E. Barnes et al., 'Blast Likely Downed Jet and Killed Prigozhin, U.S. Officials Say', *New York Times*, 24 August 2023, https://www.nytimes.com/2023/08/24/us/politics/plane-crash-prigozhin-explosion.html.

2   See Kimberly Marten et al., 'Potential Russian Uses of Paramilitary Groups in Eurasia', Center for a New American Security, September 2023.

3   See, respectively, 'Russia's Prigozhin Admits Links to What U.S. Says Was Election-meddling Troll Farm', Reuters, 14 February 2023, https://www.reuters.com/world/europe/russias-prigozhin-admits-links-what-us-says-was-election-meddling-troll-farm-2023-02-14; and Special Counsel Robert S. Mueller III, 'Report on the Investigation into Russian Interference in the 2016 Presidential Election', vol. 1, US Department of Justice, March 2019, https://www.justice.gov/archives/sco/file/1373816/download.

4   See Elena Cryst, 'Stoking Conflict by Keystroke', Stanford Internet Observatory, 15 December 2020, https://cyber.fsi.stanford.edu/io/news/africa-takedown-december-2020; and UK Foreign, Commonwealth & Development Office, 'UK Exposes Sick Russian Troll Factory Plaguing Social Media with Kremlin Propaganda', 1 May 2022, https://www.gov.uk/government/news/uk-exposes-sick-russian-troll-factory-plaguing-social-media-with-kremlin-propaganda.

5   For background analysis, see Kimberly Marten, 'The GRU, Yevgeny Prigozhin, and Russia's Wagner Group: Malign Russian Actors and Possible US Responses', written testimony before the US House of Representatives Foreign Affairs Subcommittee on Eurasia, Energy, and the Environment, 7 July 2020, https://www.congress.gov/116/meeting/house/110854/witnesses/HHRG-116-FA14-Wstate-MartenK-20200707.pdf; Kimberly Marten, 'Russia's Use of Semi-state Security Forces: The Case of the Wagner Group', *Post-Soviet Affairs*, vol. 35, no. 3, May 2019, pp. 181–204; and Kimberly Marten, 'Russia's Use of the Wagner Group: Definitions, Strategic Objectives, and Accountability', written testimony before the US House of Representatives Oversight and Reform Subcommittee on National Security, 15 September 2022, https://docs.house.gov/meetings/GO/GO06/20220921/115113/HHRG-117-GO06-Wstate-MartenK-20220921.pdf.

6   See András Rácz, 'Band of Brothers: The Wagner Group and the Russian State', Center for Strategic and International Studies, 21 September 2020, https://www.csis.org/blogs/post-soviet-post/band-brothers-wagner-group-and-russian-state.

7   See Brian Katz et al., 'Moscow's Mercenary Wars: The Expansion of Russian Private Military Companies', Center for Strategic and International Studies, September 2020, https://russianpmcs.csis.org/.

8   See President of Russia, 'Meeting with Defence Ministry Personnel', 27 June 2023, http://en.kremlin.ru/events/president/news/71535.

9   See 'Prigozhin's Criminal Past, Straight from the Source', *Meduza*, 29 June 2021, https://meduza.io/en/feature/2021/06/29/prigozhin-s-criminal-past-straight-from-the-source.

10 See Fiona Hill and Clifford G. Gaddy, *Mr. Putin: Operative in the Kremlin* (Washington DC: Brookings Institution, 2013), p. 163.

11 See 'News Wrap: Putin Says Prigozhin Was a Talented Person Who "Made Serious Mistakes in Life"', PBS, 24 August 2023, https://www.pbs.org/newshour/show/news-wrap-putin-says-prigozhin-was-a-talented-person-who-made-serious-mistakes-in-life; and Andrew Osborn, 'Putin Breaks Silence After Wagner Boss Prigozhin's Plane Crashes', Reuters, 24 August 2023, https://www.reuters.com/world/europe/investigators-trawl-site-plane-crash-believed-have-killed-wagner-boss-prigozhin-2023-08-24/.

12 See Anastasiia Yakoreva and Svetlana Reiter, '"Restorator Putina" perestal byt' lyubimym podryadchikom Minoborny' ['Putin's restaurateur' stopped being the favorite contractor of the Defence Ministry], *Bell*, 2 March 2018, https://thebell.io/restorator-putina-perestal-byt-lyubimym-podryadchikom-minoborony/.

13 See Ishaan Tharoor, 'The Battle in Syria that Looms Behind Wagner's Rebellion', *Washington Post*, 30 June 2023, https://www.washingtonpost.com/world/2023/06/30/wagner-syria-russia-battle-united-states/.

14 See Kimberly Marten, 'The Puzzle of Russian Behavior in Deir al-Zour', *War on the Rocks*, 5 July 2018, https://warontherocks.com/2018/07/the-puzzle-of-russian-behavior-in-deir-al-zour/.

15 See 'Yevgenii Prigozhin o tragedii 8 fevralia 2018 v Khshame' [Yevgeny Prigozhin on the tragedy of 8 February 2018 in Khshame], Telegram, 12 June 2023, https://telegra.ph/Evgenij-Prigozhin-o-tragedii-8-fevralya-2018-v-Hshame-06-12.

16 For a good overall account, see Joshua Yaffa, 'The Making of a Mutiny', *New Yorker*, 7 August 2023, pp. 28–41.

17 See Anastasia Lotareva, 'Wagner Mutiny: Junior Commander Reveals His Role in the Challenge to Putin', BBC, 23 July 2023, https://www.bbc.com/news/world-europe-66247915.

18 The content of Prigozhin's video, posted on his Telegram channel, is summarised well by James Risen, 'Prigozhin Told the Truth About Putin's War in Ukraine', *Intercept*, 1 July 2023, https://theintercept.com/2023/07/01/prigozhin-truth-putin-war-ukraine/.

19 See Julian E. Barnes, Helene Cooper and Eric Schmitt, 'Russian General Knew About Mercenary Chief's Rebellion Plans, US Officials Say', *New York Times*, 27 June 2023, https://www.nytimes.com/2023/06/27/us/politics/russian-general-prigozhin-rebellion.html.

20 See Paul Sonne, Anatoly Kurmanaev and Julian E. Barnes, 'Top Russian General Detained After Wagner Mutiny Is Released', *New York Times*, 4 September 2023, https://www.nytimes.com/2023/09/04/world/europe/general-sergei-surovikin-russia.html.

21 See Thomas Grove, 'Russia Detained Several Senior Military Officers in Wake of Wagner Mutiny', *Wall Street Journal*, 13 July 2023, https://www.wsj.com/articles/russia-detained-several-senior-military-officers-in-wake-of-wagner-mutiny-35a696e4.

22 See President of Russia, 'Address to Citizens of Russia', 24 June 2023, http://www.en.kremlin.ru/events/president/transcripts/71496.

23 See Andrew Osborn, 'Prigozhin Mansion: Russian TV Shows Footage to Discredit Wagner Leader After Failed Mutiny', Reuters, 6 July 2023, https://www.reuters.com/world/europe/russian-state-tv-attacks-mutiny-leader-prigozhin-says-investigation-still-live-2023-07-06/.

24 'Prigozhin Gets Back Ten Billion Rubles ($111m) Cash and More Seized After Mutiny', *Meduza*, 4 July 2023, https://meduza.io/en/news/2023/07/04/prigozhin-gets-back-ten-billion-rubles-111m-cash-and-more-seized-after-mutiny.

25 See Anastasia Stognei and Max Seddon, 'Yevgeny Prigozhin's "Toxic" Media Empire Left in Kremlin Limbo', *Financial Times*, 14 July 2023, https://www.ft.com/content/723a967f-213b-45b4-8ca6-792aa8e10ba0.

26 See 'Prigozhin-linked Firms Continue to Sign Hefty State Contracts, Even After Mutiny', Radio Free Europe/Radio Liberty, 3 August 2023, https://www.rferl.org/a/russia-prigozhin-companies-hefty-state-contracts/32532538.html.

27 See 'IStories: Wagner Group Still Recruiting Despite Prigozhin's Claims', *Novaya Gazeta Europe*, 2 August 2023, https://novaya-gazeta.eu/articles/2023/08/02/istories-wagner-group-still-recruiting-despite-prigozhins-claims-en-news.

28 See, respectively, Isabel van Brugen, 'Wagner Group Recruiting Exposed in Second NATO Country', *Newsweek*, 15 August 2023, https://www.newsweek.com/wagner-group-yevgeny-prighozin-recruitment-nato-latvia-poland-ukraine-war-1819876; and Julia Smirnova and Francesca Visser, 'Content Glorifying the Wagner Group Circulating on Meta Platforms', Institute for Strategic Dialogue Digital Dispatches Blog, 16 August 2023, https://www.isdglobal.org/digital_dispatches/content-glorifying-the-wagner-group-circulating-on-meta-platforms/.

29 See Zhenya Averbakh, 'Chto izvestno o liudiakh iz spiska passzhirov Biznes-dzheta Prigozhina' [What is known about the people on the passenger list of Prigozhin's business plane], *Fontanka*, 24 August 2023, https://www.fontanka.ru/2023/08/24/72630062/; and Denis Korotkov, 'Nemnogo biznesa v siriiskoi voine' [Some business in the Syrian war], *Fontanka*, 26 June 2017, https://www.fontanka.ru/2017/06/26/084/.

30 See 'Thousands of Wagner Mercenaries in Belarus, Says Monitoring Group', Radio Free Europe/Radio Liberty, 24 July 2023, https://www.rferl.org/a/belarus-wagner-mercenaries-thousands-belaruski-hajun-russia/32517237.html.

31 'Wagner Troops in Belarus "Want to Go West" into Poland, Lukashenka Quips During Meeting with Putin', Radio Free Europe/Radio Liberty, 23 July 2023, https://www.rferl.org/a/putin-lukashenka-wager-poland/32515408.html.

32 See Valerie Hopkins, 'Belarus Says Some Wagner Fighters Are Training Its Forces', *New York Times*, 14 July 2023, https://www.nytimes.

com/2023/07/14/world/europe/
wagner-belarus-russia.html.

33 See 'UK Defence Ministry: Kremlin
May No Longer Fund Wagner Group',
Reuters, 13 August 2023, https://
www.reuters.com/world/uk-defence-
ministry-kremlin-may-no-longer-
fund-wagner-group-2023-08-13/;
and 'Lukashenko Explains What
PMC Wagner Fighters Are Doing
in Belarus', Belta, 1 August 2023,
https://eng.belta.by/president/
view/lukashenko-explains-what-
pmc-wagner-fighters-are-doing-in-
belarus-160657-2023/#. I am grateful to
Sarah Cahlan for the latter citation.

34 See Megan Specia, 'Ukraine Says
It Is Ready for Arrival of Wagner
Troops in Belarus', *New York Times*,
1 July 2023, https://www.nytimes.
com/2023/07/01/world/europe/russia-
ukraine-war.html.

35 See 'Old Habits', *Meduza*, 11
July 2023, https://meduza.io/en/
feature/2023/07/11/old-habits.

36 See Candace Rondeaux, 'Inquiry
into the Murder of Hamdi Bouta and
Wagner Group Operations at the
Al-Shaer Gas Plant, Homs, Syria 2017',
New America, 5 June 2020, https://
www.newamerica.org/future-security/
reports/inquiry-murder-hamdi-bouta/.

37 See Amy Mackinnon, 'Putin's Shadow
Warriors Stake Claim to Syria's Oil',
Foreign Policy, 17 May 2021, https://
foreignpolicy.com/2021/05/17/
putin-shadow-warriors-stake-claim-
syria-oil-energy-wagner-prigozhin-
libya-middle-east/.

38 See Tal Beeri, 'Syria: Russia–Syria
Power Struggle Over the Natural
Gas, Oil Fields and Infrastructure',
Alma Research and Education Center,

28 June 2022, https://israel-alma.
org/2022/06/28/syria-russia-syria-
power-struggle-over-the-natural-
gas-oil-fields-and-infrastructure/;
and Nikita Sogoloff, 'Russia's
Energy Goals in Syria', Fikra
Forum, Washington Institute for
Near East Policy, 30 August 2017,
https://www.washingtoninstitute.
org/policy-analysis/
russias-energy-goals-syria.

39 See Suleiman Al-Khalidi and Maya
Gebeily, 'Syria Brought Wagner
Fighters to Heel as Mutiny Unfolded
in Russia', Reuters, 7 July 2023, https://
www.reuters.com/world/syria-
brought-wagner-group-fighters-heel-
mutiny-unfolded-russia-2023-07-07/.

40 See 'Pekhota pushche nevoli' [The
infantry more than the capture],
Novaya Gazeta, 10 August 2022, https://
novayagazeta.eu/articles/2022/08/10/
pekhota-pushche-nevoli.

41 See 'Bez 'Shchita' [Without a shield],
Novaya Gazeta, 28 July 2019.

42 See Karen Dawisha, *Putin's
Kleptocracy: Who Owns Russia?* (New
York: Simon and Schuster, 2014).

43 See 'Gennady Timchenko', Bloomberg
Billionaires Index, https://www.
bloomberg.com/billionaires/profiles/
gennady-n-timchenko/.

44 See 'It's Not Just Wagner',
Meduza, 16 May 2023, https://
meduza.io/en/feature/2023/05/16/
it-s-not-just-wagner.

45 See 'A Mercenaries' War', *Meduza*,
14 July 2022, https://meduza.io/en/
feature/2022/07/14/a-mercenaries-war.

46 See Kimberly Marten, 'Russia's Back
in Africa: Is the Cold War Returning?',
Washington Quarterly, vol. 42, no.
4, Winter 2019, pp. 155–70; and

Paul Stronski, 'Late to the Party: Russia's Return to Africa', Carnegie Endowment for International Peace, 16 October 2019, https://carnegieendowment.org/2019/10/16/late-to-party-russia-s-return-to-africa-pub-80056.

47 See United Nations Office of the High Commissioner for Human Rights, 'CAR: Russian Wagner Group Harassing and Intimidating Civilians – UN Experts', 27 October 2021, https://www.ohchr.org/en/press-releases/2021/11/car-russian-wagner-group-harassing-and-intimidating-civilians-un-experts; United Nations Office of the High Commissioner for Human Rights, 'Libya: Violations Related to Mercenary Activities Must Be Investigated – UN Experts', 17 June 2020, https://www.ohchr.org/en/news/2020/06/libya-violations-related-mercenary-activities-must-be-investigated-un-experts; and 'Moura: Over 500 Killed by Malian Troops, Foreign Military Personnel in 2022 Operation', United Nations News, 12 May 2023, https://news.un.org/en/story/2023/05/1136607.

48 See Tom O'Connor, 'US Says Russia's Wagner Group Helped Push U.N. Forces Out of Mali', *Newsweek*, 30 June 2023, https://www.newsweek.com/us-says-russias-wagner-group-helped-push-un-forces-out-mali-1810225.

49 See Nima Elbagir et al., 'Exclusive: Evidence Emerges of Russia's Wagner Arming Militia Leader Battling Sudan's Army', CNN, 21 April 2023, https://www.cnn.com/2023/04/20/africa/wagner-sudan-russia-libya-intl/index.html.

50 See 'Architects of Terror: The Wagner Group's Blueprint for State Capture in the Central African Republic', *Sentry*, June 2023, https://thesentry.org/wp-content/uploads/2023/06/ArchitectsTerror-TheSentry-June2023.pdf; US Department of the Treasury, 'Treasury Sanctions Illicit Gold Companies Funding Wagner Forces and Wagner Group Facilitator', 27 June 2023, https://home.treasury.gov/news/press-releases/jy1581; and Declan Walsh, '"From Russia with Love": A Putin Ally Mines Gold and Plays Favorites in Sudan', *New York Times*, 5 June 2022, https://www.nytimes.com/2022/06/05/world/africa/wagner-russia-sudan-gold-putin.html.

51 See 'Burkina Faso Denies It Paid Russian Fighters with Mine Rights', Reuters, 21 December 2022, https://www.reuters.com/world/africa/burkina-faso-denies-it-paid-russian-fighters-with-mine-rights-2022-12-20/; Benoit Faucon, 'US Intelligence Points to Wagner Plot Against Key Western Ally in Africa', *Wall Street Journal*, 23 February 2023, https://www.wsj.com/articles/u-s-intelligence-points-to-wagner-plot-against-key-western-ally-in-africa-29867547; and Elian Peltier, 'A Leader of Niger's Coup Visits Mali, Raising Fears of a Wagner Alliance', *New York Times*, 2 August 2023, https://www.nytimes.com/2023/08/02/world/africa/niger-coup-mali-wagner.html.

52 See Wassim Nasr, 'How the Wagner Group Is Aggravating the Jihadi Threat in the Sahel', Combatting Terrorism Center at West Point, *CTC Sentinel*, vol. 15, no. 11, November/December 2022, pp. 21–30, https://ctc.westpoint.edu/how-the-wagner-

group-is-aggravating-the-jihadi-threat-in-the-sahel/.

53 See Judicael Yongo, 'Central African Republic Says Wagner Troop Movement Is Rotation not Departure', Reuters, 8 July 2023, https://www.reuters.com/world/africa/central-african-republic-says-wagner-troop-movement-is-rotation-not-departure-2023-07-08/.

54 See Judicael Yongo, 'Wagner Troops Arrive in Central African Republic Ahead of Referendum', Reuters, 17 July 2023, https://www.reuters.com/world/africa/wagner-troops-arrive-central-african-republic-ahead-referendum-2023-07-17/.

55 Quoted in Elian Peltier and Raja Abdulrahim, 'Can Russia Tame Wagner in Africa Without Destroying It?', *New York Times*, 29 June 2023, https://www.nytimes.com/2023/06/29/world/africa/central-african-republic-wagner-africa-syria.html.

56 See 'Russian Army Officials Visit Libya After Haftar Invite', *Moscow Times*, 22 August 2023, https://www.themoscowtimes.com/2023/08/22/russian-army-officials-visit-libya-after-haftar-invite-a82219.

57 See Abdulkader Assad, 'Report: Haftar Owes Russian Wagner Group $150 Million as Rift Grows Over Rookie Fighters', *Libya Observer*, 14 May 2020, https://libyaobserver.ly/news/report-haftar-owes-russian-wagner-group-150-million-rift-grows-over-rookie-fighters.

58 See Kimberly Marten, 'Why the Wagner Group Cannot Be Easily Absorbed by the Russian Military – and What that Means for the West', Russia Matters, Harvard Kennedy School Belfer Center, 1 September 2023, https://www.russiamatters.org/analysis/why-wagner-group-cannot-be-easily-absorbed-russian-military-and-what-means-west.

59 See 'Vedomosti: Lawmakers Mull Bill on Protecting Journalists in Conflict Zones', TASS, 2 August 2018, https://tass.com/pressreview/1015770.

60 See Liana Faizova, 'Kudrin, Povar, ChVK Vagnera, Zhenit'ba: Chto Vaszhnogo i Strannogo Skazal Putin Na PressKonferentsii' [Kudrin, the chef, the Wagner PMC, marriage: what important and strange things Putin said at the press conference], *Bell*, 20 December 2018, https://thebell.io/kudrin-povar-chvk-vagnera-zhenitba-chtovazhnogo-i-strannogo-skazal-putin-na-press-konferentsii/.

61 See Candace Rondeaux and Ben Dalton, 'Putin's Stealth Mobilization: Russian Irregulars and the Wagner Group's Shadow Command Structure', New America, 22 February 2023, https://www.newamerica.org/future-frontlines/reports/putin-mobilization-wagner-group/.

62 See Edith M. Lederer, 'Russia, China Block Release of UN Report Criticizing Russia', AP News, 25 September 2020, https://apnews.com/article/383b41a573556703122650c05672153e5; and 'Russia Blocks Work of UN Committees Monitoring Sanctions on African Countries', Radio Free Europe/Radio Liberty, 30 September 2021, https://www.rferl.org/a/ruusia-blocking-un-africa/31485308.html.

63 See Molly Dunigan, *Victory for Hire: Private Security Companies' Impact on Military Effectiveness* (Stanford, CA: Stanford University Press, 2011).

64 See Eleanor Beardsley, 'An Ex-member of One of the World's Most Dangerous Mercenary Groups Has Gone Public', NPR, 6 June 2022, https://www.npr.org/2022/06/06/1102603897/wagner-group-mercenary-russia-ukraine-war; and 'Latest in Ukraine: Wagner Chief Says 20,000 of His Forces Killed in Bakhmut Fighting', VOA News, 24 May 2023, https://www.voanews.com/a/latest-in-ukraine-epicenter-of-fighting-in-bakhmut-marinka/7106699.html.

65 See Anton Troianovski et al., 'After Prigozhin's Death, a High-stakes Scramble for His Empire', New York Times, 8 September 2023, https://www.nytimes.com/2023/09/08/world/europe/prigozhin-wagner-russia-africa.html.

66 See Julian E. Barnes and Eric Schmitt, 'Kremlin Considers How to Bring Private Military Group Under Its Control', New York Times, 16 August 2023, https://www.nytimes.com/2023/08/26/us/politics/prigozhin-wagner-russia-military.html.

67 See Max Seddon et al., 'Wagner's Lucrative African Operations Thrown into Post-Prigozhin Limbo', Financial Times, 25 August 2023, https://www.ft.com/content/0476123a-b726-413b-9c70-0ba1e480fa0f.

68 See Simon Marks and Stephanie Baker, 'What Wagner's Mutiny Means for Its Sprawling Business Empire', Bloomberg, 27 June 2023, https://www.bloomberg.com/graphics/2023-wagner-presence-in-central-african-republic/; Frank Matt et al., 'Who Will Control Wagner's Empire of War and Gold?', Wall Street Journal, 24 July 2023, https://www.wsj.com/articles/who-will-control-wagners-empire-of-war-and-gold-22444d60; and

Kevin Rothrock, 'What He Leaves Behind', Meduza, 27 June 2023, https://meduza.io/en/feature/2023/06/28/what-he-leaves-behind.

69 See Lauren Kent, Pierre Bairin and Uliana Pavlova, 'What We Know About Andrey Troshev, the Man Putin Proposed as the New Wagner Boss', CNN, 14 July 2023, https://www.cnn.com/2023/07/14/europe/russia-andrey-troshev-wagner-intl/index.html.

70 See Ivan Nechepurenko, 'Wagner Troops Can Keep Fighting, but Without Prigozhin, Putin Says', New York Times, 14 July 2023, https://www.nytimes.com/2023/07/14/world/europe/putin-wagner-prigozhin-ukraine.html.

71 See Isabel van Brugen, 'Wagner Group Fires One of Its Five Leaders – a Former Russian Army Colonel', Newsweek, 3 July 2023, https://www.newsweek.com/wagner-group-prigozhin-mutiny-shoigu-fires-leader-andrey-troshev-1810462.

72 See '"Armed to the Teeth": Who Runs – and Who Funds – a New Private Military Company in Annexed Crimea?', Meduza, 25 March 2023, https://meduza.io/en/feature/2023/03/26/armed-to-the-teeth; and Marlene Laruelle and Richard Arnold, 'Russia's Paramilitarization and Its Consequences', PONARS Policy Memo 839, 3 April 2023, https://www.ponarseurasia.org/wp-content/uploads/2023/04/Pepm839_Arnold-Laruelle_April2023-2.pdf.

73 See Matthew Luxmoore and Benoit Faucon, 'Russian Private Military Companies Move to Take Over Wagner Fighters', Wall Street Journal, 5 September 2023, https://www.wsj.com/world/russia/russian-private-

military-companies-move-to-take-over-wagner-fighters-a568f938.

74 See Sergei Titov, 'How Konstantin Malofeyev, Russia's "Orthodox Oligarch", Finances His Support of Moscow's War in Ukraine', Radio Free Europe/Radio Liberty, 24 June 2023, https://www.rferl.org/a/malofeyev-russia-oligarch-finances-war-ukraine/32474096.html.

75 See Mathieu Olivier, 'CAR–Russia: Who Is Vitali Perfilev, Wagner's Boss in Bangui?', Africa Report, 7 April 2022, https://www.theafricareport.com/191669/car-russia-who-is-vitali-perfilev-wagners-boss-in-bangui/.

76 See Åse Gilje Østensen and Tor Bukkvoll, 'Russian Use of Private Military and Security Companies – the Implications for European and Norwegian Security', Norwegian Defence Research Establishment (FFI), 11 September 2018, https://open.cmi.no/cmi-xmlui/handle/11250/2564170.

77 See, respectively, Christopher Miller and Max Seddon, '"Stream" and "Torch": The Gazprom-backed Militias Fighting in Ukraine', Financial Times, 2 June 2023, https://www.ft.com/content/4dd0aa0a-4b37-4082-8db0-0b969c539677; Polina Ivanova, 'Russia's Latest Space Agency Mission: Raising a Militia for the War in Ukraine', Financial Times, 16 June 2023, https://www.ft.com/content/c194cb2d-3aa0-4195-9be5-e78c1d2fd183; and Joshua Askew, '"TikTok Warriors": What Are Chechen Fighters Doing in Ukraine?', Euronews, 20 January 2023 (updated 15 May 2023), https://www.euronews.com/2023/01/20/mad-dogs-what-are-chechen-fighters-doing-in-ukraine.

78 See Sean McFate, Mercenaries and War: Understanding Private Armies Today (Washington DC: National Defense University Press, 2019).

79 See Sean McFate, The Modern Mercenary: Private Armies and What They Mean for World Order (New York: Oxford University Press, 2014).

Detect and Engage: A New American Way of War

David C. Gompert and Martin Libicki

Even as Americans' conception of their security expands to encompass climate change, cyber security and pandemic response, they face stark reminders that the core of national defence is the ability to fight high-end wars. One is Russia's barbaric if bungled aggression against Ukraine. Some have argued that the Russia–Ukraine conflict is a window on future war.[1] We think otherwise. It is a war between an over-the-hill, Soviet-style Russia and a novice, Western-style, ex-Soviet Ukraine. A veneer of advanced technology – drones, missile defence and satellites – has been appliquéd on fighting otherwise reminiscent of the First World War. Meanwhile, Russia's aggression has made NATO larger, stronger and more cohesive. Allied defence spending, excluding that of the United States, is roughly four times Russia's.[2] With Russia's military inferiority revealed, its ground and air forces depleted and its technology base sapped by a brain drain, this is not the threat that paces US force planning.

The threat from China is. Its intent to dominate East Asia creates a potential for armed conflict that requires the US to stay ahead of China militarily. This is leading to a new way of warfare. Though some of its elements are in train, greater impetus and coherence are needed. A gathering wave of innovation, as potent as the Digital Revolution of 40 years ago, calls for a

David C. Gompert is Distinguished Visiting Professor at the US Naval Academy, Advisor to Ultratech Capital Partners, Adjunct Fellow at RAND Corporation and former US Acting Director of National Intelligence. **Martin Libicki** is the Maryellen and Richard L. Keyser Distinguished Visiting Professor of Cybersecurity at the US Naval Academy.

Survival | vol. 65 no. 5 | October–November 2023 | pp. 65–74   https://doi.org/10.1080/00396338.2023.2261246

purposeful shift in American military strategy, not only because it is feasible but also because China means to catch the same wave.

By enabling the dispersal of forces, emerging technologies can restore geography as a military benefit rather than a military drawback for the United States. Since the Cold War, the US has concentrated its war-fighting capabilities in regional bases and surface naval combatants near China in the Gulf, and around such confined European waters as the Baltic, Black and Mediterranean seas. As enemies acquire anti-access and area-denial (A2/AD) capabilities, such US forces will become more inviting targets. New technologies can enable the United States to circumvent A2/AD by reducing the need to concentrate forces in conflict zones.

We call the emerging way of war 'detect and engage' (and say good riddance to 'shock and awe'). We hesitate to characterise it as a 'revolution in military affairs', not just because the term is trite, but also because the shift will take time. Technology does not invariably determine ways of warfare; concepts of operations, strategic depth, perseverance and the will to shed blood cannot be ignored. In this case, however, emergent technology is the locomotive. The confluence of artificial intelligence (AI), applied quantum mechanics and satellite networking permits dispersed and diverse units and platforms to operate as a unified joint force across sea, air, land and space. Cyber operations, practically indifferent to location, further enable the United States to reduce reliance on geographically concentrated and exposed forces.[3]

Ways of war, then and now

The familiar American way of war has relied heavily on delivering devastating explosive force by ground, sea and especially air power.[4] It worked in the Gulf War in 1991 and, initially, in the invasion of Iraq in 2003, albeit against a weak opponent. The advocates of such warfare rightly claimed it to be both kinetically and psychologically effective.[5] Relying on superior logistics, joint strikes, digital networking and precision-guided munitions, the US military could obliterate opponents' infrastructure and military forces, rendering them incapable of resisting or inflicting large-scale losses on US forces.

Understandably, military establishments are wont to stick with a way of fighting that has proved successful. But doing so does not enable them to prevail against countries that have learned from how prior US adversaries lost. As China and others acquire and field better long-range targeting capabilities and weapons, concentrated US forces in hostile zones will face missile and other attacks. At a minimum, such attacks could disrupt US operations; at worst, they could defeat US forces altogether. Accordingly, the United States should disperse and diversify its strike platforms; extend and secure its communications networks; tighten its decision-making procedures; and exploit geographic, cyber and outer space.

High-end warfare increasingly demands refined and timely knowledge of opposing forces, as well as the command-and-control and logistic links that enable them. US intelligence, variable-range high-precision weaponry, and cyber-war capabilities can detect and engage critical targets.[6] In some cases, the ability to weaken the other side's concentration of forces can stop war early. In others, significant attrition of adversary logistics, command sites, and key ships and aircraft would allow any close combat, if needed, to be on terms more favourable for US forces.

A way of war built around the detect-and-engage cycle is, of course, no panacea. It will not answer all military challenges, such as counter-insurgency, evacuation, peacekeeping or humanitarian operations, though it could help. Furthermore, extended-range weapons are expensive. But extended range is not the only dimension of the emerging US approach. Distance aside, US forces must be spread out, elusive, diverse, hard to target (for instance, submerged) and often uncrewed.

A major challenge for the detect-and-engage framework is to locate and track those targets whose elimination would most handicap the opponent's ability to fight. Because deception and evasion are within China's capabilities, detection requires not only superlative intelligence collection but also an understanding of how the opponent fights. Another formidable task is to maintain theatre-wide surveillance. The United States can accomplish this by means of space systems that are becoming more distributed, like those of SpaceX's Starlink constellation.

Space-based targeting

In seeking to deter China, US planners are particularly concerned about its large force of quiet attack submarines and its ballistic and hypersonic extended-range missiles, including anti-ship ones. In response, the United States is developing the Joint All-Domain Command and Control system (JADC2), along with growing numbers of uncrewed aircraft and naval vessels. JADC2 will allow US fighting forces to achieve 'distributed lethality'. While the US Navy uses this term to metre its strike capabilities across the fleet, when applied to US forces writ large it can mean dispersed, diverse, abundant, elusive and networked strike options, which are harder for even China to target. JADC2 is mainly space-based (supplemented by surveillance drones) and will, as the name suggests, unify operations across all armed services and span air, sea, land, cyberspace and space. At present, the individual services are working intensely to enhance connectivity within and among their forces.[7]

This and other US innovations must be more than incremental reactions to Chinese submarine and missile threats. They should flow from a general mindset encouraging and fostering boldness, non-linearity and conceptual coherence. The United States can exploit its prowess in space for surveillance, communications, positioning, guidance and, as noted, command and control. It must also keep its lead in submarine and anti-submarine warfare, which will be increasingly important as both powers rely more on sub-surface capabilities for attack and strike missions.

Such developments would present China with targeting challenges that are much stiffer than that of locating and hitting a conspicuous, slow-moving carrier strike group in the Western Pacific. If the US military services, combatant commands, space industry, intelligence community, civilian leadership and national scientific community pursue them, Chinese investment in targeting concentrated US forces will yield diminishing returns. In time, this will render the economics of military competition more advantageous to the United States, just as geography will benefit it more than China by enabling the dispersal of forces.

Secretary of Defense Lloyd J. Austin III has characterised China as the US military's 'pacing challenge'.[8] As the term implies, bypassing the Chinese threat will have the collateral benefit of neutralising lesser threats. Other potential adversaries – including Iran, North Korea and Russia – would have difficulty finding, much less engaging, US forces that are operating remotely, elusively and across domains. Threats to use nuclear weapons to compensate for these weaknesses can be countered by the American nuclear deterrent, as well as a range of conventional and cyber capabilities and improvements to missile defence.

Detect-and-engage technologies

As noted, the crucial technologies for the emerging American way of war are AI, applied quantum mechanics and distributed space systems. Among other things, AI can enable autonomous (uncrewed) platforms, enhance utilisation of sensors, optimise targeting and anticipate the movements of opposing forces. Quantum technologies can exponentially increase the processing of sensor data for some purposes, improve guidance and navigation, and enhance encryption and decryption. Distributed space systems can extend surveillance and support and integrate dispersed units, while being less vulnerable to attacks from anti-satellite weapons.

Overall, US forces can achieve greater precision, reach, speed, coherence across dispersed forces, and survivability. Certain advances merit special attention. They include:

- targeting discrimination, prioritisation, weapons programming and accuracy
- the ability to compute in orbit instead of relying on the availability of uninterrupted high-bandwidth data links
- reuseable satellite-stationing vehicles
- superior cyber-war capabilities
- the integration of uncrewed platforms
- non-acoustic submarine detection
- light and resilient materials, power sources and integrated circuits.

Many innovations will originate in private enterprises serving large and dynamic commercial markets, supported by generous research and development funding. If such enterprises are expected to supply the military, the Defense Department must accept that reform of its acquisition processes has far to go.[9] As China shovels state resources into new technology for military purposes, the United States must engage its larger, open-society-based innovation system.[10]

Special challenges

Advanced technology, while vital, is but one step in operationalising new forms of warfare. Others include anticipating adversary responses; building robust inventories of extended-range weapons; knowing when and how to conduct close-in operations; integrating and empowering defence allies; and maintaining US forward presence.

As the United States disperses and diversifies its strike capabilities, China will not stand pat. It could enhance targeting of dispersed forces, disperse its own forces and degrade the United States' use of space. Were it to do so, however, it would still find itself with more adverse war-fighting 'transaction' odds than it now has against concentrated US forces.[11] Targeting dispersed American forces would stretch Chinese surveillance and tracking capabilities at great cost, and US forces would in any case remain less vulnerable. Spreading out Chinese forces would contradict important Chinese military missions; in particular, taking Taiwan and gaining control of the South China Sea would require high concentrations of forces. In addition, China's ability to take out US satellites will have limited effects as US space systems become more distributed. Overall, force concentration favours China, and the United States should not refrain from dispersing and diversifying its forces out of fear that China will do likewise.

The emerging American way of war demands abundant options for training weapons on targets from dispersed forces far and near. While the need for extended-range targeting is obvious, the choice among deliverable weapons is not. Key criteria are affordability, thus numbers; precision guidance, especially off-board; manoeuvrability; penetrability against expected defences; and payloads.[12] Candidates include cruise missiles, ballistic missiles, fast lethal drones and hypersonic missiles, any of which can be launched from sea, air or land. Advanced enemy air defence can attrit cruise missiles; defending against plentiful and evasive drones is more challenging. US adversaries lack effective defences against large numbers of ballistic missiles, and hypersonic missiles are manoeuvrable and as hard to intercept as ballistic ones. Hypersonic weapons and lethal drones would afford the new American way of war a boost, and they are becoming US priorities.

The United States can win some wars by destroying enemy forces from afar, dictating terms and dispatching coalition ground forces as needed. But this approach probably would not work against China. While there are Taiwan scenarios in which China's invasion force is so degraded that it cannot secure a lodgement, scenarios in which operationally deployed US and allied ground forces are needed to help defend or liberate the island are at least as plausible. Widespread aggression by Iran and its proxies across the greater Middle East would tax the long-range capabilities of US forces. Accordingly, the United States and its allies cannot avoid the need for significant ground and other tactical forces to secure victory after stand-off strikes. The US Marine Corps is developing a doctrine to support rapid and decisive intervention of ground forces to disrupt and dislodge enemy forces. But because the marines are a relatively small force, the US Army's ability to deploy swiftly to areas and against forces that are weakened by detect-and-engage operations may be crucial.

Local allies supported by US strikes could provide the bulk of the required ground forces. For this and other reasons, the United States needs allies for most plausible high-end contingencies, whether in Asia, the Middle East or Europe. US alliances furnish a substantial geopolitical and operational advantage over any opponent, including China. Of greatest military importance in the context of 'detect and engage' are technologically and operationally strong allies such as Australia, France, Germany, Japan, South Korea, the United Kingdom and several other NATO allies, including the new ones. More complicated politically but potentially relevant are Israel and India. The more the United States enables such allies to network with JADC2 and shares intelligence with them – as it does now with Australia, Canada, New Zealand and the UK under the long-standing 'Five Eyes' intelligence alliance – the more force they can provide. Moreover, if the US shift towards more dispersed forces requires additional land nodes, the current trend towards closer defence alliances in East Asia, notably with Japan, offers potentially invaluable options.

New technologies that reduce requirements to concentrate US forces in battle zones do not obviate the policy need for peacetime military presences abroad to reassure allies of US interests and commitments, and signal them to adversaries. But, as peacetime bases become more vulnerable, especially in East Asia, the distinction between stationed forces and operating forces becomes more important. The latter can shift into operating patterns on warning, which the US intelligence community can often provide as it did in the case of Russia's invasion of Ukraine. Furthermore, basing large forces on allies' territory is not the only way to confirm US defence commitment and engagement. Integration of capable allies into operating plans and systems, such as JADC2, should allay fears of waning US commitment, as should explicit security pledges. As the United States moves towards a more dispersed military posture, it could make both military and political sense to emphasise tripwire forces. In any case, US messaging should make it clear that harnessing leading-edge technology to improve global US military effectiveness reflects not an isolationist or insular policy but one of ongoing engagement, in line with the trend whereby allies from Poland to Australia are more closely aligning with the United States.

*   *   *

Mastery of the global commons and spatial domains – geographic, outer and cyber – is eclipsing the capacity for sheer force as the principal determinant of military power.[13] Relying on superior dispersed joint forces, and not so much the ability to fight in Ukraine-like muck, should guide American military strategy, especially in the Pacific. The United States should intensify its development and incorporation of key new technologies, regain geography's advantage, exploit its prowess in orbit and cyberspace, and empower key alliances.

Waves of innovative technology crest every few decades: nuclear weaponry and propulsion following the Second World War; space exploration and satellites as rivalry with the Soviet Union heated up; distributed-data processing and digital networking as the Cold War ended. At each turn, the United States successfully applied new technology to advance its military superiority in the interest of deterrence and peace. Now that post-digital AI, quantum and satellite technologies have arrived, it must do so again.

Notes

1   See Stephen Biddle, 'Back in the Trenches: Why New Technology Hasn't Revolutionized Warfare in Ukraine', *Foreign Affairs*, vol. 102, no. 5, September/October 2023; 'The Future of War: A Special Report', *The Economist*, 8 July 2023, https://www.economist.com/weeklyedition/2023-07-08?; and Franz-Stefan Gady and Michael Kofman, 'Ukraine's Strategy of Attrition', *Survival*, vol. 65, no. 2, April–May 2023, pp. 7–22.

2   See International Institute for Strategic Studies (IISS), *The Military Balance 2023* (Abingdon: Routledge for the IISS), pp. 500–1.

3   At the same time, intended vulnerabilities of the United States and its forces to cyber war may affect the viability of a strategy that assumes workable long-distance electronic communications.

4   John Warden, a retired Air Force colonel and fighter pilot, has articulated the ways in which US airpower can achieve superiority and control and deliver large volumes of precision munitions at great distances, potentially gaining victory with diminished need for invading troops. See, for example, John A. Warden III, 'Employing Air Power in the Twenty-first Century', in Richard H. Shultz, Jr, and Robert L. Pfaltzgraff, Jr (eds), *The Future of Air Power in the Aftermath of the Gulf War* (Maxwell AFB, AL: Air University Press, 1992).

5   See Harlan K. Ullman and James P. Wade, 'Shock & Awe: Achieving Rapid Dominance', National Defense University, Command and Control Research Program, October 1996, http://www.dodccrp.org/files/Ullman_Shock.pdf.

6   Emphasising the importance of rapid decision-making is not new. Air Force officer and then consultant John Boyd coined the 'OODA' (observe–orient–decide–act) loop in the late twentieth century. It remains a good conception of superior command and control. See John R. Boyd, ed. Grant T. Hammond, *A Discourse on Winning and Losing* (Maxwell AFB, AL: Air University Press, 2018), pp. 217–44.

7   See, for example, Congressional Research Service, 'Joint All-Domain Command and Control (JADC2)', updated 21 January 2022, https://sgp.fas.org/crs/natsec/IF11493.pdf. For a measured critique of multidomain operations, see Franz-Stefan Gady, 'Manoeuvre Versus Attrition in US Military Operations', *Survival*, vol. 63, no. 4, August–September 2021, pp. 131–48.

8   See, for example, US Department of Defense, 'Secretary of Defense Lloyd J. Austin III Message to the Force', 23 March 2023,

https://www.defense.gov/News/ Releases/Release/Article/3316641/ secretary-of-defense-lloyd-j-austin-iii-message-to-the-force/.

9 For an assessment of the broad range of reforms still needed, see National Defense Science & Technology Strategy Review Task Force, 'An Innovation Strategy for the Decisive Decade', 17 July 2023, https://innovation.defense.gov/ Portals/63/DIB_An%20Innovation%20 Strategy%20for%20the%20 Decisive%20Decade_230717_1.pdf.

10 See David C. Gompert, 'Spin-on: How the US Can Meet China's Technological Challenge', *Survival*, vol. 62, no. 3, June–July 2020, pp. 115–30.

11 The idea of maximising 'transaction' advantage is an insight of Vice Admiral Arthur Cebrowski, a leading pioneer of 'network-centric warfare' at the turn of the twenty-first century. See Arthur K. Cebrowski and John H. Gartska, 'Network-centric Warfare – Its Origin and Future', *Proceedings*, vol. 124, no. 1, January 1998, pp. 28–35.

12 Our assumption is that, for better or worse, no arms-control restrictions on intermediate-range missiles will be in place.

13 See Barry R. Posen, 'Command of the Commons: The Military Foundation of US Hegemony', *International Security*, vol. 28, no. 1, Summer 2003, pp. 5–46.

Challenging Nuclear Bromides

Dallas Boyd

Arguably no dimension of national policy has more thoroughly captured the public's imagination, yet remained so impenetrable to the layperson's understanding, than nuclear deterrence. Although the dire prospect of nuclear war and its aftermath has been the subject of countless depictions in popular culture – most recently Christopher Nolan's film *Oppenheimer* – the policy apparatus that might bring about or forestall this event appears opaque even to many senior figures in government. Perhaps as a result, with rare exceptions such as the Aldermaston marches of the 1950s and 1960s and the Nuclear Freeze movement of the 1980s, mass activism to influence nuclear-weapons policy has been curiously absent from the public sphere despite the universal implications of these weapons for humanity.

This inaccessibility stems in part from the perception, carefully nourished by those whom strategist Roger Molander called the 'technical priesthood', that the principles of nuclear deterrence are so esoteric as to exempt them from non-expert scrutiny.[1] As a 2008 Defense Science Board study portentously declared, 'nuclear deterrence expertise is uniquely demanding', requiring knowledge ranging from nuclear-weapons design to the conduct of nuclear operations, largely cloistered in a classified environment.[2] Even granting the formidable complexity of these subjects, however, they are

Dallas Boyd is a policy analyst with experience in nuclear-weapons policy, nuclear counter-terrorism policy and deterrence theory. The views reflected here are the author's personal views and should not be attributed to any institution with which he is or has been affiliated.

Survival | vol. 65 no. 5 | October–November 2023 | pp. 75–94   https://doi.org/10.1080/00396338.2023.2261247

hardly more daunting than macroeconomic policy, for example, or the management of viral pandemics. Nor is classification a serious constraint on nuclear-policy analysis given the vast open-source literature on the subject from the 1940s to the present.

The conceit that nuclear strategy is forbiddingly arcane has bestowed upon its practitioners a sense of immunity from outside criticism that has no analogue in other policy areas. Climate change, for instance, is the intellectual focus of non-governmental institutions and grassroots movements worldwide despite representing a threat that has been considered less urgent, at least until recently, and far more complex than nuclear war. Even the prospect of Russian nuclear-weapons use in Ukraine, widely discussed in the media for more than a year, has spurred little public reflection on nuclear war fighting. To the extent these weapons figure in the popular discourse at all, the debate is confined to the most superficial aspects.

In this light, it is perhaps unsurprising that an impressive array of beliefs about nuclear weapons that have flourished among the priesthood wither upon close inspection. Some are mere bromides – ideas that derive legitimacy not from any intrinsic logic but rather from endless repetition or the eminence of their advocates. Many such ideas are reflected in the great powers' nuclear postures, from the number of warheads posited as necessary for deterrence to the selection of targets. Some can be falsified empirically, such as assertions about the capabilities of particular weapons or the policies of foreign governments. Others can be challenged only on theoretical grounds – for instance, conjectures about adversary decision-making.

To the uninitiated, many of the reigning orthodoxies of nuclear strategy would seem illogical on their face, and some would appear plainly risible. Only from the funhouse-mirror perspective of professional strategists does it appear sensible and proper to maintain warhead inventories sufficient to cause global carnage on a biblical scale, primed for rapid launch, susceptible to faulty warning data and controlled by a handful of leaders with purposely truncated windows to ponder their employment. If there is a singular idiosyncrasy in nuclear policy, it is not its mystery or intellectual impenetrability, but rather the desirability of inviting the appraisal of non-experts who may discern flaws imperceptible to professionals. The purpose of this article is to expose the fallacies that shape the major powers' strategic postures, and thus to illuminate the advisability of democratising nuclear policy to include outside voices that are not wedded to the canon of nuclear strategy.

The credibility of nuclear deterrence

Among the watchwords of nuclear strategy is credibility. Deterrence hinges on the influence of nuclear threats on an enemy's decision-making, and the believability of these threats is considered a prerequisite for that enemy's restraint. A threat that lacks credibility does not deter, so the thinking goes. Two factors have traditionally been thought to underpin credibility: the operational ability to conduct a nuclear strike and national leaders' resolve to do so. However, nuclear strategists have embroidered these basic elements with many additional requirements, particularly with respect to operational capabilities.

Ashley Tellis describes four 'classical' elements of a credible nuclear deterrent: the 'presence of sufficient second-strike weapon reserves; a history of credible, communicated deterrent threats; the existence of survivable command, control, communications and intelligence (C3I) assets and supporting infrastructure; and a multitude of preplanned nuclear employment options'.[3] In assessing North Korea's nuclear deterrent, Victor Cha presents two more: a proven long-range missile re-entry capability and mastery of warhead miniaturisation. Absent these capabilities, he argues, North Korea's nuclear arsenal would 'not come close to a credible nuclear deterrent', and the country 'gets no added security from these weapons'.[4]

The logical extension of Cha's assertion is that a rudimentary nuclear arsenal alone would not be sufficient to deter the United States from attacking a state that possessed one. This conclusion seems perplexing in the context of North Korea, whose nuclear programme the United States has opposed for decades in part over fears that the Kim regime might sell or transfer a nuclear weapon to terrorists.[5] Given that non-state actors would lack sophisticated delivery means, one wonders by what logic nuclear weapons would represent a catastrophic threat in the hands of extremists but not in those of Pyongyang's own military.

The United States' apprehensions about nuclear terrorism suggest that elaborate operational requirements for nuclear weapons grossly exceed the threshold of credibility. Indeed, US leaders have signalled just how modest the true baseline is: possession of fissile material in the quantity needed to fashion a single nuclear device. George W. Bush warned in 2002 that a mass of highly enriched uranium (HEU) 'a little larger than a single soft-ball' would put Saddam Hussein within a year of a nuclear weapon, while Barack Obama noted that a lump of plutonium 'about the size of an apple' would threaten the lives of thousands of people.[6] Heroic cognitive disso-nance is required to believe that a makeshift terrorist device conveyed in a rental truck represents one of the most harrowing threats of the modern age, while exquisite warhead engineering and strategic-delivery vehicles are needed for a state to deter an adversary from aggression.

An intellectually consistent framework would recognise that any nation capable of producing a single nuclear detonation in an American city is able to deter the United States. And unless the other major powers have wildly greater tolerances for risk, they too would be deterred by the most modest nuclear arsenal, calling into question the necessity of global stockpiles now numbering more than 12,000 warheads.[7] Misapprehension of the threshold of credibility, and the overestimation of the requirements of deterrence, is a prin-cipal driver of excess in the world's nuclear arsenals. With this excess comes potentially catastrophic consequences in the event of deterrence failure.

Moral considerations in nuclear targeting

Attentiveness to credibility plays another subtle role by influencing the targets the United States, Russia and perhaps other nuclear states choose to hold at risk. These choices in turn impose structural requirements on nuclear forces that push their numbers upward. At the heart of the policy is the difference between the presumed targeting strategy of nuclear terrorists, who would likely attack undefended urban centres, and that of ostensibly respectable nuclear powers. The latter, contrary to widespread belief, do not chiefly target each other's cities, but rather aim at opposing nuclear weapons, command-and-control facilities and other critical war-fighting capabilities. Known as 'counterforce' targeting, this model is premised in part on the notion that threatening the deliberate, wholesale murder of civilians is immoral, which diminishes its credibility. Deference to military propriety, however, unavoidably tethers the size and configuration of a state's nuclear arsenal to that of its adversary's.

In 1961, RAND Corporation planners briefed Robert McNamara, then the US secretary of defense, on the nascent counterforce concept, whereby the United States would initially strike only Soviet military targets in a nuclear war rather than cities. As Fred Kaplan recalls in *The Wizards of Armageddon*, McNamara had been drawn to an earlier plan, under which cities would be struck first, in large part because it would specify 'a point at which he could justify telling the Joint Chiefs "No more nuclear weapons" – and that was the point at which all major Soviet cities could be devastated by an American retaliatory blow even after a fairly successful Soviet first-strike'. But where, McNamara wondered, was the stopping point in the counterforce model? The obvious flaw was that 'as long as the other side kept building nuclear weapons, then the military "requirements" for more and more nuclear weapons for the US could be endless'.[8]

Notwithstanding the arms race to which counterforce would inexorably contribute, the model was adopted on both sides early in the Cold War and is the presumed targeting paradigm of the United States and Russia to this day.[9] (A 2012 US Air Force report asserted as self-evident that strategic stability 'requires an arsenal whose qualitative characteristics hold the other party's nuclear weapons at risk', making no attempt to justify the assertion.[10]) While both countries' stockpiles have greatly receded from the absurd 1986 peak of more than 68,000 combined warheads, the counterforce linkage implicitly constrains further reductions.[11] When weapons are aimed at each other, a warhead cut on one side without a reciprocal subtraction on the other confers an advantage to the enemy, with the result that drawdowns can only occur as part of a tortuous arms-control process imbued with distrust.

More bizarre than structurally imposed overkill, however, is the moral logic of a framework that could claim vastly more innocent lives than one designed to kill civilians. George Perkovich, rejecting as false the dichotomy between '(moral) nuclear counterforce targeting' and '(immoral) "countervalue" targeting of large civilian populations', notes that a counterforce exchange with more than 1,000 warheads 'would cause millions of civilian casualties even if this is not the specific intention'.[12] A Natural Resources Defense Council simulation of the US nuclear-war plan posited that a strike on Russian nuclear forces using 1,300 warheads would kill eight to 12 million civilians because, the authors note, 'even the most precise counterforce attacks on Russian nuclear forces unavoidably cause widespread civilian deaths due to the fallout generated by numerous ground bursts'.[13]

Despite the moral incoherence of counterforce targeting, the model could arguably be justified, on ethical grounds, if it offered the best hope of deterring a nuclear war. A conflict that does not occur by definition claims fewer lives than one waged within even the most morally scrupulous framework. Alas, here too the counterforce model fails, for it logically favours pre-emption and punishes restraint in a crisis, ensuring a decision-making bias toward initiating rather than avoiding nuclear war.

First-strike stability

As counterforce became institutionalised during the Cold War, some strategists began to perceive the instability inherent in a targeting construct that created structural incentives to strike first. During a crisis in which nuclear war appears plausible, the fear of being disarmed naturally lends impetus to pre-empting the enemy's pre-emption, even if the other side's intentions are unclear. In his classic 1958 essay 'The Reciprocal Fear of Surprise Attack', Thomas C. Schelling laid bare this risk with a simple illustration. 'If I go downstairs to investigate a noise at night, with a gun in my hand, and find myself face to face with a burglar who has a gun in his hand, there is danger of an outcome that neither of us desires', he wrote. 'Even if he'd prefer just to leave quietly, and I'd like him to, there is danger that he may *think* I want to shoot, and shoot first. Worse, there is danger that he may think that *I* think *he* wants to shoot. Or he may think that *I* think *he* thinks *I* want to shoot. And so on.'[14]

A targeting model in which both sides held each other's cities or economic infrastructure at risk would not create this combustibility. If one country destroyed its enemy's population centres or oil refineries, for example, the victim could simply retaliate in kind, and no disadvantage would accrue from going second. The wish to avoid reprisal would suffice to deter. As Stephen Cimbala and James Scouras explain, however, the risk of losing one's ability to retaliate – a risk embedded in counterforce targeting – forces a choice to which 'the logic of deterrence does not apply'. If a nuclear war is judged inevitable in a crisis, they argue, the 'logical decision in this circumstance is to attempt to strike first because, no matter how devastating a retaliation is anticipated to be, an even more apocalyptic scenario would derive if the other side attacked first'. Things get murkier in a crisis in which a nuclear exchange is possible or perhaps even probable but not ordained. In this scenario, the authors note, leaders would face 'a grim choice: strike first or wait, with the possibility that waiting would allow the other side to strike first'.[15]

One measure for decreasing first-strike instability that the nuclear powers have debated for decades is a 'no first use' policy, under which a state would forswear the use of nuclear weapons except in retaliation for a nuclear attack. If each nuclear-armed nation credibly undertook such a pledge, fear of a surprise attack during a crisis, and thus the pressure to pre-empt, would theoretically be reduced. Yet even universal adoption of no first use, and faithful compliance therewith, would not erase the danger of the counterforce model. Even a nation that refrained from first use might still rush to launch its targetable weapons once it *perceived* a nuclear war had begun. And because the systems that provide warnings and indications of nuclear war are, like every human invention, fallible, a mistaken attack warning may set in motion a reflexive counterstrike that by design leaves little time for rumination.[16]

Launch on warning

Counterforce targeting intrinsically encourages the option of 'launch on warning' – that is, firing nuclear weapons upon credible warning of an incoming strike, lest they be destroyed first. The deterrent logic of the capability is straightforward: a state confident that it could disarm its enemy might be tempted to do so during a crisis, but if the opposing weapons have already left their silos before the attacking warheads impact, the entire effort would be in vain. Devastating retaliation would still occur in this circumstance, and this knowledge is meant to deter a surprise attack to begin with. However, the vulnerability of early-warning systems to human or technological errors, of which there have been many throughout the nuclear age, is plain.

US officials tend to elide this danger, in part by denying that the United States maintains a launch-on-warning posture at all. The 2020 'Report on the Nuclear Employment Strategy of the United States' flatly states that 'the United States rejects launch-on-warning', and strategists engage in performative pearl-clutching when adjectives such as 'hair-trigger' are used to describe the US nuclear-alert status.[17] Nevertheless, acknowledgements that the posture hovers in US policy occasionally slip out. In 2021, for example, the Pentagon's annual report 'Military and Security Developments Involving the People's Republic of China' notes that People's Liberation Army writings suggest that China maintains a nuclear-employment doctrine that is, in the view of the American authors of the report, 'broadly similar to the US and Russian LOW [launch-on-warning] posture'.[18]

The vulnerability of early-warning systems is plain

Given the short flight time of intercontinental ballistic missiles (ICBMs), the three countries would enjoy no more than 30 minutes after receiving warning of an inbound nuclear attack to decide whether to launch their targetable nuclear systems or risk losing a substantial portion thereof. As scholar Jeffrey Lewis notes, 'the one thing that movies get really wrong about the decision to use nuclear weapons is how long the discussions last'. In reality, 'if the president decides to end the world, you could probably show the whole debate in a half-hour sitcom – during one of its commercial breaks'.[19] Indeed, some officials regard the severe time constraint as a positive feature of the posture rather than a bug. As former CIA director Michael Hayden acknowledged in 2016, 'the system is designed for speed and decisiveness. It's not designed to debate the decision.'[20]

Some analysts have recoiled at the danger of a paradigm in which an American or Russian president would have mere minutes to make the epic decision to order nuclear retaliation on the basis of potentially fallible sensor data. Yet nuclear strategists are ever armed with specious arguments to swat away proposals to modify the system. One possibility would be to remove ICBMs from a persistently high state of alert, requiring time-consuming protocols before retaliating that would give leaders more space to deliberate. Critics invariably respond that such a reform would be inherently destabilising. During a crisis, they argue, raising alert levels out of caution could be mistaken as a preparation for launch, causing the other side to reciprocate and thereby increasing the risk. The ensuing 'race to re-alert' could culminate in nuclear war.[21]

Noting that this argument 'gets repeated so often that people assume it's simply true', scholar David Wright identifies its two chief fallacies. Firstly, the contributions to deterrence made by land-based ICBMs are superfluous to those of submarine-launched ballistic missiles (SLBMs), obviating the need to re-alert the former in a crisis. Secondly, 'historical incidents have shown that having missiles on alert during a crisis increases the risk of a mistaken launch due to false or ambiguous warning'.[22] Of course, the optimal calibration of alert levels is meaningful only insofar as one accepts the wisdom of launch-on-warning in the first place. If a state's deterrence model is based on 'riding out' a nuclear attack and retaliating with secure second-strike weapons, there would be no reason to re-alert during a crisis and hence no destabilising race to do so.

Whether retaliatory weapons can truly be made invulnerable to pre-emption is hotly contested, and the debate has spawned an especially curious species of illogic. The very fear of losing one's weapons, the reasoning goes, may compel a state to expend them even if no strategic purpose is served other than preventing their destruction. 'The faith that nations have in the survivability of their nuclear deterrents following a first strike by potential adversaries is a key element of strategic stability', says James Doyle. 'For states that lack this faith, any crisis or conflict raises the possibility that they must strike first or lose their deterrent forces to a pre-emptive attack by the enemy.'[23] Put another way, a state whose weapons are vulnerable to attack in the event deterrence fails must itself precipitate a failure of deterrence by being the first to use weapons that are meant to deter. If this logic seems bizarre and disjointed, that's because it is.

The 'use or lose' conundrum

Although the 'use or lose' problem is intrinsic to first-strike stability in deterrence relationships where both sides possess the means to attempt a disarming attack, many scholars have transposed the phenomenon to scenarios in which it is illogical. In the former case, a state with counterforce capabilities may seek to destroy its enemy's warheads during a crisis in an effort to limit potential damage to itself. For nations that maintain only counter-value capabilities – the default posture of smaller nuclear states – little or no purpose would be served by using these weapons pre-emptively without a meaningful effect on an enemy's offensive strength.

Nevertheless, it has become commonplace in the strategic literature to imagine states with small, vulnerable nuclear stockpiles governed by leaders willing to launch them under circumstances posing less than an existential threat.[24] Such analyses invariably ignore the fact that using these weapons simply to avoid losing them would be to squander their central utility, which is to deter, without a corresponding benefit. Further, for a state to do so without eliminating the enemy's nuclear capabilities would increase the chance of that state's being subjected to a nuclear attack from possible or even probable to virtually assured.

Consider North Korea, whose nuclear arsenal has one main purpose: to deter US-sponsored regime change. In 2018, media reports suggested the Trump administration was considering a limited military strike on a North Korean nuclear facility or missile site, widely described as a 'bloody nose' attack, to coerce the Kim regime into ceasing its provocative behaviour.[25] Many commentators warned then of the risks of unintended nuclear conflict, ascribing the 'use or lose' rationale to the North Korean leadership. Van Jackson, a former strategist in the Office of the Secretary of Defense, insisted that 'if [Kim Jong-un] concluded that war were imminent, or that it had already begun, he would have no choice but to launch a devastating retaliatory response in hopes that it raises the stakes of conflict enough to cause the United States to back off'. Although this response would not necessarily involve a nuclear attack, Jackson argued, the likelihood would be 'exceedingly high' because nuclear weapons are 'Kim's "ace in the hole"; if he doesn't play them immediately, the US might eliminate them in a first-wave attack'.[26]

Note that this extraordinary prediction occurred in the context of an imagined limited US strike advertised in advance as having exclusively political aims. Although Kim might not take at face value the claim that it was limited in character rather than the opening salvo of an attempt at regime change, neither would he have 'no choice' but to lash out militarily. If he were to do so with nuclear weapons, what had begun as a largely symbolic US strike would instantly transform into an unrestrained conflict with but one realistic outcome: Kim's downfall. Knowing the use of these weapons would only precipitate the very outcome they are intended to prevent, North Korea would have every incentive to withhold them under all but the most unambiguous conditions.

Although in this example the 'use or lose' phenomenon was invoked to inhibit reckless US military action, it can be deployed just as easily to support pre-emption. If leaders convince themselves of an enemy's eagerness to use nuclear weapons, they are more apt to favour aggressive options to neutralise the threat, including disarming strikes. Yet counterforce advocates acknowledge the limitations of these capabilities even against weaker nuclear states. Jina Kim and John K. Warden, who favour a deterrent posture against North Korea featuring enhanced intelligence, surveillance and reconnaissance, and more precise and effective long-range strike assets, concede that threatening 'a significant portion of North Korea's nuclear arsenal, as opposed to imperiling the entire arsenal, is … the only realistic goal'. This is so because of the 'inherent difficulty of finding, fixing, tracking, striking and intercepting nuclear forces in conflict'.[27]

While these difficulties are indeed formidable – even prohibitive – they do not fully account for the challenges that make the very notion of disarming a nuclear adversary fanciful. Proponents of muscular offensive postures, in addition to making often illogical presumptions about adversary decision-making, entertain unrealistic expectations of what even a nominally successful counterforce strike could really accomplish.

Criteria of first-strike success

Among the nuclear-policy misconceptions with the greatest potential for ruin is the premise that a 'splendid' first strike, by which an enemy's

nuclear weapons are entirely destroyed before they can be fired in retaliation, is achievable in the first place. To be viable, this belief requires a
purely synthetic threshold for victory, focused only on eliminating constituted nuclear weapons and especially high-yield warheads atop missiles
with long ranges. Christopher Chyba and J.D. Crouch fall victim to this
fallacy in defining 'nuclear primacy' as the ability to launch a 'confident
and disarming nuclear first strike … such that no retaliation *with strategic nuclear forces* would be possible'.[28] That is, if the defender's ICBMs,
SLBMs and heavy bombers were eliminated, it would have no capacity for
reprisal even if its stockpile featured nuclear weapons with shorter ranges
or lower yields.

Such a narrow definition of success is a convenient fiction for US strategists because the United States' nuclear posture is configured for counterforce
attacks against adversaries with diverse nuclear arsenals. Acknowledging
that a broader range of nuclear weapons can be used for retaliation, and that
their elimination would also be necessary for a first strike to be successful,
would invalidate the entire counterforce enterprise. But there is no rational
basis to disqualify short- and medium-range missiles or non-strategic warheads as instruments of punishment, especially against soft civilian targets.
Nor is it logical to exclude non-deployed and inactive warheads from the
inventory of second-strike weapons. Would an American president contem-
plating a first strike on Russia really be blasé about Russia's estimated 1,800
non-strategic weapons?[29] To ask the question is to answer it.

In addition to strategic-delivery vehicles, a variety of unorthodox means
can be used to conduct a retaliatory strike. (Recall the 1942 Doolittle Raid, in
which the United States, eager to strike Japan after the Pearl Harbor attack,
launched US Army heavy bombers from aircraft carriers to bomb Tokyo in
an unprecedented combat innovation.) Further, there is no hard deadline
for responding to an attack. Reprisals might occur weeks or even months
later, accounting for time to move shorter-range systems closer to targets
or to upload reserve warheads.[30] For nuclear retaliation to be confidently
avoided, all weapons in all categories would have to be destroyed. If even a
single warhead survived, a punitive strike would still be possible, albeit on
a delayed timetable.

Perhaps strategists' greatest failure of imagination, however, is their emphasis on assembled nuclear 'forces-in-being' in the first-strike calculus. According to the standard that governs US counter-terrorism and non-proliferation policy, the mere possession of weapons-useable nuclear material effectively constitutes a nuclear capability. This derives from the judgement, summarised by the National Research Council, that lack of access to such material is the 'primary impediment that prevents countries or technically competent terrorist groups from developing nuclear weapons'.[31] Ownership of a sufficient quantity of nuclear material confers a retaliatory capability by its very existence. Thus, China's 14 tonnes of HEU and 2.9 tonnes of plutonium, though uncommitted to deployed warheads, represent a latent second-strike arsenal of immense proportions.[32]

Consequently, destroying an adversary's constituted weapons in a first strike would be insufficient. Any disarming attack worthy of the name would require the destruction of the state's nuclear infrastructure and stocks of fissile material as well, the latter of which might be dispersed and effectively unreachable. Together, these considerations demolish the key premise on which the counterforce strategy rests: that a state's answer to a nuclear attack must come rapidly, and by way of long-range missiles, or not at all. In addition to inducing a dangerous monomania in targeting plans, this fetishisation of ICBMs is both wasteful and rooted in demon-strable myth.

The mythical virtues of ICBMs

There are two principal components of the talismanic mythology surrounding ICBMs. The first is their supposed operational advantages, the second their imagined influence on adversary decision-making. Regarding the former, Lewis describes as the 'canonical case' for ICBMs the notion that a US president can order the launch of ground-based nuclear forces far more quickly than the sea-based leg of the triad.[33] This assumption was dismantled in a series of General Accounting Office studies in 1992. An unclassified summary noted that while 'conventional wisdom gives much higher marks to ICBM command and control responsiveness than to that of submarines', in fact SLBMs would be 'almost as prompt as ICBMs in hitting enemy targets'.[34] This analysis led

Lewis to conclude the claimed promptness of ICBMs over SLBMs was 'just something people *said*. It seemed reasonable, of course, but there was no data.'[35]

Among ICBM partisans, however, the weapon's crowning virtue is its supposedly salutary effect on stability. At first glance this would seem a tough sell, for the locations of ICBM silos are known to adversaries, enabling their destruction in a crisis and thereby adding to first-strike instability. Yet champions of the system have turned this seeming liability into a wondrous asset. According to a popular line of thought, ICBMs serve as 'target sinks' or 'sponges', forcing an enemy to expend large numbers of offensive warheads on neutralising them that would otherwise be available to attack other strategic targets. Mark Gunzinger of the Center for Strategic and Budgetary Assessments makes the case thusly: 'Without a land-based ICBM … an enemy would only need to strike a very small number of targets to greatly diminish our strategic deterrence posture.'[36] Further, because multiple warheads may be required to destroy a single hardened silo, the targeting arithmetic strongly favours the defender.[37]

Leaving aside the enormous volume of fallout generated by the 1,000 or more detonations required to target the US ICBM force – which might cause higher American fatalities than a more limited counter-value attack against cities – the 'sponge' argument presupposes that the number of Russian strategic weapons will remain immutably fixed and that a costly array of nuclear loofahs must dot the US landscape in perpetuity to sop them up. ICBM advocates are loath to acknowledge that the enemy missiles they are determined to absorb may themselves be viewed by the adversary as *its* sponge and that both sides are captive to the excesses inherent in the counterforce strategy.

That the United States could unilaterally eliminate the ICBM leg of the triad and comfortably maintain deterrence of its adversaries is a decidedly – and strangely – controversial position. Further, the political obstacles to its retirement may be insurmountable, in part because of the incentives of the ICBM constituency. As Adam Smith, then chairman of the House Armed Services Committee, observed in 2019, lawmakers in states that host ICBMs 'don't want any reduction at all, no matter the circumstances'. Describing this position as 'parochial' and 'not rational', Smith reduced the motive to simple local economics: 'They want the jobs.'[38]

Democratising nuclear strategy

Historian Richard Rhodes notes that many of the most consequential historical figures are 'provincials' who 'attempt what sophisticates consider naïve', citing the examples of Ronald Reagan and Mikhail Gorbachev, 'each an outsider to the inner elites of the government he headed'. The 'sophistries of Washington's nuclear mandarins had failed to complicate' Reagan's 'apocalyptic' world view, while Gorbachev's 'southern Russian accent and hillbilly grammar offended the ears of the suave Moscow bureaucracy he outmanipulated a dozen times on any ordinary day'.[39] Nevertheless, at the 1986 Reykjavík Summit these two rubes nearly reached an agreement to substantially reduce the US and Soviet nuclear arsenals, only to be thwarted by disapproving American mavens.[40] Then as now, to realise a sane and responsible strategic posture one must be deaf to charges of heresy from the ecclesiastical authorities of nuclear policy.

Although the impulse to conduct bottom-up reviews of nuclear postures has occasionally seized policymakers, these assessments do not appear to have been motivated by any queasiness over the structural infirmities of nuclear-war plans or their potential consequences. Further, the composition of these bodies invariably reveals that they are exercises conducted by and for the nuclear establishment. In 2008, the US Congress chartered the Congressional Commission on the Strategic Posture of the United States, charged with providing an ostensibly independent assessment of US nuclear-weapons policy. Composed of luminaries in the field, its chairman and vice chairman were former secretaries of defense and energy, respectively; the commissioners included a former CIA director, veterans of government nuclear-weapons laboratories, arms-control experts, nuclear strategists and veterans of legislative nuclear-oversight committees. Not one was free of ingrained beliefs about nuclear policy. Predictably, the commission's recommendations were anodyne, endorsing each of the pillars of the US nuclear posture and proposing no major reforms.

Arguing that it is 'long past time to demystify the nuclear enterprise', Fred Kaplan observes that budget exigencies are now motivating a reconsideration of 'whether so many nukes are necessary, whether they all have to be 100 percent reliable to deter adversaries from aggression, whether the recondite scenarios and theories of the nuclear game are quite real'.[41] As a first step, a genuinely novel undertaking would be to conduct an independent assessment of nuclear strategy that is deserving of the label. Security clearances should be granted to outsiders with relevant expertise – logisticians, systems engineers, behavioural scientists, regional experts and so on – who would be tasked with assessing classified nuclear-war plans and the rationales that underpin them. Not only should they not have spent their lives as part of the nuclear aristocracy, but some should lack a background in national security altogether.

While no serious government would combat a major pandemic, for example, without a cadre of seasoned virologists and epidemiologists, assessing nuclear strategy emphatically does not require expertise that can be gained only through years of specialised study. Professional staff can be assigned to brief outside examiners on the capabilities of particular weapons systems and the mechanics of operational plans, which experts in germane fields can readily digest. The objective of the exercise would be to identify structural features of the nuclear posture that are inconsistent with broadly accepted logic, empirical evidence and humanitarian values. A further mandate would be to recommend an alternative posture to deter adversaries and reassure allies that does not incentivise pre-emption or result in catastrophic consequences should deterrence fail.

Anticipating the heterodox findings of any such review, the architects of a new programme must devise creative means to engage lay audiences on its recommendations. A sympathetic US president might make the case for reforms directly to the public in an effort reminiscent of Reagan's salesmanship of the Strategic Defense Initiative.[42] Naturally there is a danger that the reception would be divided along partisan lines. A maximally effective initiative might take the form of a bipartisan legislative proposal championed by respected figures of both major parties. The 1991 Cooperative Threat Reduction programme – led by Sam Nunn and Richard Lugar, then senior Democratic and Republican senators, respectively – to secure nuclear weapons and materials in the former Soviet Union is perhaps the best model for such an initiative. Any proposal to fundamentally reconfigure the nuclear posture, of course, would meet stiff resistance from adherents of the status quo, and reformers would have to persuade the public they were presenting well-informed alternatives.

*   *   *

Professional strategists tend to depict advocates of even modest reforms as starry-eyed abolitionists. While there is considerable overlap between, for example, ICBM opponents and disarmament activists, there exists a cohort of reformers who not only recognise the inescapable reality of nuclear deterrence, but acknowledge and even extol its constructive role in global security. These views are not incompatible with deep misgivings about the manner in which the major powers' nuclear postures are presently constituted.[43]

Antagonism among nuclear-armed states is such that nuclear weapons will remain a feature of the global landscape for the foreseeable future. The grinding trench warfare in eastern Ukraine is a sober reminder of the horrors of great-power wars of attrition that occurred before the advent of nuclear deterrence. But nuclear weapons have existential implications for the whole of humanity. In this light, the theories and plans that govern their employment should not be the exclusive domain of a small coterie of nuclear strategists who resist outside scrutiny.

Upton Sinclair once dryly observed that 'it is difficult to get a man to understand something when his salary depends upon his not understanding it'.[44] Something like the inverse holds for the nuclear clergy: it is hard to convince its cardinals to educate the public about nuclear strategy when their status and livelihoods depend on its incomprehension.

Acknowledgements

Thanks to James Acton, Rick Christensen, James Crabtree, John Maenchen, Jessica Mathews, Aaron Miles, Michael Molino, Joshua Pollack and Alex Wood for helpful comments.

Notes

1   Douglas Martin, 'Roger C. Molander, Nuclear Protest Leader, Dies at 71', *New York Times*, 31 March 2012, https://www.nytimes.com/2012/04/01/us/roger-c-molander-dies-at-71-stirred-nuclear-protests.html.

2   See Office of the Under Secretary of Defense for Acquisition, Technology, and Logistics, Defense Science Board

Task Force, 'Nuclear Deterrence Skills', Report of the Defense Science Board Task Force, September 2008, https://dsb.cto.mil/reports/2000s/ADA487983.pdf.

3 Ashley J. Tellis, 'India's Emerging Nuclear Posture: Between Recessed Deterrent and Ready Arsenal', RAND Corporation, MR-1127-AF, 2001, p. 19.

4 Victor D. Cha, 'How to Disarm a Nuclear North Korea', *Washington Post*, 9 October 2011, https://www.washingtonpost.com/opinions/how-to-disarm-a-nuclear-north-korea/2011/10/09/gIQAlaZeYL_story.html.

5 See Sheena Chestnut, 'Illicit Activity and Proliferation: North Korean Smuggling Networks', *International Security*, vol. 32, no. 1, Summer 2007, pp. 80–111.

6 'Bush: Don't Wait for Mushroom Cloud', CNN, 8 October 2002, https://edition.cnn.com/2002/ALLPOLITICS/10/07/bush.transcript/; and White House, 'Remarks by President Obama and Prime Minister Rutte at Opening Session of the Nuclear Security Summit', 1 April 2016, https://obamawhitehouse.archives.gov/the-press-office/2016/04/01/remarks-president-obama-and-prime-minister-rutte-opening-session-nuclear.

7 Stockholm International Peace Research Institute, *SIPRI Yearbook 2022: Armaments, Disarmament and International Security* (Stockholm: SIPRI, 2022), p. 342.

8 Fred Kaplan, *The Wizards of Armageddon* (Stanford, CA: Stanford University Press, 1983), pp. 259–61.

9 See Austin Long and Brendan Rittenhouse Green, 'Stalking the Secure Second Strike: Intelligence, Counterforce, and Nuclear Strategy', *Journal of Strategic Studies*, vol. 38, nos 1–2, 2015, pp. 38–73.

10 Jeffrey A. Larsen et al., 'Qualitative Considerations of Nuclear Forces at Lower Numbers and Implications for Future Arms Control Negotiations', USAF Institute for National Security Studies Occasional Paper 68, July 2012, p. xiv, https://www.usafa.edu/app/uploads/OCP68.pdf.

11 See Robert S. Norris and Hans M. Kristensen, 'Global Nuclear Weapons Inventories, 1945–2010', *Bulletin of the Atomic Scientists*, 1 July 2010, https://thebulletin.org/2010/07/global-nuclear-weapons-inventories-1945-2010/.

12 George Perkovich, *Do Unto Others: Toward a Defensible Nuclear Doctrine* (Washington DC: Carnegie Endowment for International Peace, 2013), p. 62.

13 Matthew G. McKinzie et al., 'The US Nuclear War Plan: A Time for Change', Natural Resources Defense Council, June 2001, p. x, https://www.nrdc.org/sites/default/files/us-nuclear-war-plan-report.pdf.

14 T.C. Schelling, 'The Reciprocal Fear of Surprise Attack', RAND Corporation, P-1342, 16 April 1958 (revised 28 May 1958), p. 3 (emphasis in original), https://www.rand.org/content/dam/rand/pubs/papers/2007/P1342.pdf.

15 Stephen J. Cimbala and James Scouras, *A New Nuclear Century: Strategic Stability and Arms Control* (Westport, CT: Praeger, 2002), pp. 2–3.

16 See Brad Roberts, 'Debating Nuclear No-first-use – Again', *Survival*, vol. 61, no. 3, June–July 2019, pp. 39–56.

17   While repudiating 'launch-on-warning', the United States acknowledges it 'maintains the capability to launch nuclear forces under conditions of an ongoing nuclear attack'. However, the failure to clarify a substantive difference between the two options suggests the distinction is contrived. See US Department of Defense, 'Report on the Nuclear Employment Strategy of the United States – 2020', p. 6, https://www.esd.whs.mil/Portals/54/Documents/FOID/Reading%20Room/NCB/21-F-0591_2020_Report_of_the_Nuclear_Employement_Strategy_of_the_United_States.pdf.

18   Office of the Secretary of Defense, 'Military and Security Developments Involving the People's Republic of China 2021', Annual Report to Congress, p. 93, https://media.defense.gov/2021/Nov/03/2002885874/-1/-1/0/2021-CMPR-FINAL.PDF.

19   Jeffrey Lewis, 'Our Nuclear Procedures Are Crazier than Trump', *Foreign Policy*, 5 August 2016, https://foreignpolicy.com/2016/08/05/our-nuclear-procedures-are-crazier-than-trump/.

20   Nick Gass, 'Former CIA Director Fears Trump "Crisis in Civil–Military Relationships"', *Politico*, 3 August 2016, https://www.politico.com/story/2016/08/michael-hayden-trump-military-226606.

21   See US Department of Defense, 'Nuclear Employment Strategy', p. 6.

22   David Wright, 'Nuclear Weapons and the Myth of the "Re-alerting Race"', *Equation*, 6 September 2016, https://blog.ucsusa.org/david-wright/nuclear-weapons-re-alerting-race/.

23   James E. Doyle, 'You're NUTS: New Nuclear Cruise Missiles Are Inherently Destabilizing', *National Interest*, 30 November 2015, https://nationalinterest.org/feature/youre-nuts-new-nuclear-cruise-missiles-are-inherently-14457.

24   See, for example, Michael Mandelbaum, 'How to Prevent an Iranian Bomb: The Case for Deterrence', *Foreign Affairs*, vol. 94, no. 6, November/December 2015, pp. 19–24.

25   See Gerald F. Seib, 'Amid Signs of a Thaw in North Korea, Tensions Bubble Up', *Wall Street Journal*, 9 January 2018, https://www.wsj.com/articles/amid-signs-of-a-thaw-in-north-korea-tensions-bubble-up-1515427541.

26   Van Jackson, 'Want to Strike North Korea? It's Not Going to Go the Way You Think', *Politico*, 12 January 2018, https://www.politico.com/magazine/story/2018/01/12/north-korea-strike-nuclear-strategist-216306/.

27   Jina Kim and John K. Warden, 'Limiting North Korea's Coercive Nuclear Leverage', *Survival*, vol. 62, no. 1, February–March 2020, pp. 31–8.

28   Christopher F. Chyba and J.D. Crouch, 'Understanding the US Nuclear Weapons Policy Debate', *Washington Quarterly*, vol. 32, no. 3, July 2009, pp. 21–36 (emphasis added).

29   The figure is from Hans M. Kristensen, Matt Korda and Eliana Reynolds, 'Nuclear Notebook: Russian Nuclear Weapons, 2023', *Bulletin of the Atomic Scientists*, 9 May 2023, https://thebulletin.org/premium/2023-05/nuclear-notebook-russian-nuclear-weapons-2023/.

30   See Jan Lodal, 'The Counterforce Fantasy', *Foreign Affairs*, vol. 89, no. 2, March/April 2010, pp. 145–6.

31 National Research Council, *Making the Nation Safer: The Role of Science and Technology in Countering Terrorism* (Washington DC: National Academies Press, 2002), p. 40.

32 See Hui Zhang, 'China's Fissile Material Production and Stockpile', International Panel on Fissile Materials, Research Report No. 17, 2017, https://fissilematerials.org/library/rr17.pdf.

33 Jeffrey Lewis, 'Do We Need ICBMs?', Arms Control Wonk, 19 July 2012, https://www.armscontrolwonk.com/archive/205519/do-we-need-icbms/ (emphasis in original).

34 Eleanor Chelimsky, 'The U.S. Nuclear Triad: GAO's Evaluation of the Strategic Modernization Program', General Accounting Office testimony before the Committee on Governmental Affairs, United States Senate, 10 June 1993, p. 6, https://www.gao.gov/assets/t-pemd-93-5.pdf.

35 Lewis, 'Do We Need ICBMs?'

36 Dave Majumdar, '$348 Billion in Nukes Ain't Enough. The Air Force Wants New ICBMs, Too', *Daily Beast*, 28 January 2015, https://www.thedailybeast.com/dollar348-billion-in-nukes-aint-enough-the-air-force-wants-new-icbms-too.

37 See 'Transcript: National Defense Industrial Association, Air Force Association and Reserve Officers Association Capitol Hill Breakfast Forum with Linton Brooks', Peter Huessy Congressional Breakfast Seminar Series, 28 June 2012, https://secure.afa.org/HBS/transcripts/2012/6-28-2012%20Linton%20Brooks.pdf.

38 'Rep. Adam Smith on US Nuclear Policy', Ploughshares Fund, 24 October 2019, https://ploughshares.org/issues-analysis/article/rep-adam-smith-us-nuclear-policy.

39 Richard Rhodes, *Arsenals of Folly: The Making of the Nuclear Arms Race* (New York: Alfred A. Knopf, 2007), p. 187.

40 See Association for Diplomatic Studies and Training, '"The Cold War Was Truly Over" – The 1986 Reykjavik Summit', 27 September 2016, https://adst.org/2016/09/the-cold-war-truly-over-1986-reykjavik-summit/.

41 Fred Kaplan, 'We Don't Need a Better Nuclear Arsenal to Take on China', *Slate*, 23 April 2021, https://slate.com/news-and-politics/2021/04/nuclear-triad-overhaul-china.html.

42 See Ronald Reagan, 'Address to the Nation on Defense and National Security', 23 March 1983, https://www.reaganlibrary.gov/archives/speech/address-nation-defense-and-national-security.

43 For a nuanced view, see Harold A. Feiveson (ed.), *The Nuclear Turning Point: A Blueprint for Deep Cuts and De-alerting of Nuclear Weapons* (Washington DC: Brookings Institution Press, 1999).

44 Upton Sinclair, *I, Candidate for Governor, and How I Got Licked* (New York: Farrar & Rinehart, 1935), p. 109.

The Meaning of 'Strategic' in US National-security Policy

Jeffrey A. Larsen and James J. Wirtz

Individuals, command echelons, organisations and even whole societies often react dramatically to the word 'strategic'. The word generally conveys a feeling of importance without specifically defining what makes a problem, operation, capability or even a specific command element 'strategic'. Colin Gray noted that it was 'simply employed as a heavyweight term implying relatively high importance, relating to something allegedly *Big*! When thus used without linguistic discipline the concept loses all value and hinders intelligent debate.'[1] For instance, what makes a weapon 'strategic'? What is a 'strategic' target? Why are some forms of deterrence deemed 'strategic'? Why do some types of attack merit a 'strategic' response, which implies that a different set of procedures, commands or capabilities will come into play? If the term 'strategic deterrence' has traditionally meant nuclear deterrence, why do we use the term 'strategic nuclear deterrence'?

The Biden administration has declared 'integrated deterrence' to be a central concept in its 2022 National Defense Strategy, and the fact that various threats, capabilities, plans, operations or *strategies* may or may not fall into the basket of considerations that require integration is a potential problem across the whole of government.[2] If 'strategic' is applied to multiple issues with varying levels of importance, how can we identify which

Jeffrey A. Larsen is a research professor in the Department of National Security Affairs at the US Naval Postgraduate School and president of Larsen Consulting Group. **James J. Wirtz** is a professor in the Department of National Security Affairs at the US Naval Postgraduate School. The opinions expressed here are those of the authors alone and do not reflect the positions of any government, government agency or commercial firm. The authors thank US Strategic Command for supporting this research.

Survival | vol. 65 no. 5 | October–November 2023 | pp. 95–116   https://doi.org/10.1080/00396338.2023.2261249

government agency is responsible for dealing with the issue? Who makes that decision? Is there a lead integrator somewhere in the bureaucracy who determines whether an issue belongs to those who deal with diplomacy, economics, space, cyber or other military concerns?

The definition of strategic thus remains elusive, although most descriptions of the concept involve either the effects an action can create or the impact it could have on a country or society. Strategic effects are those that fundamentally change the nature of a country and how things work, particularly if the effects are not transitory, making it difficult to restore the status quo ante. Most observers believe that any nuclear-weapons use, for example, would be a strategic issue. But profound impacts on the life of a nation can now arise from non-nuclear means as well, including economic, diplomatic, space, cyber, informational and other tools. The number of domains capable of producing strategic effects has been increasing, and this trend is likely to continue.

Further complicating matters is that debate continues about the impact of cyber, space and other new technologies. The question is whether they are capable of fundamentally altering national existence. Critics have noted that reports of so-called 'silver bullets' in war rarely play out as advertised in battle; nuclear weapons have been the one exception.[3] The impact of new weapons or systems also can be highly idiosyncratic. Weapons that perform well in one setting can perform poorly in others. Whether or not offensive cyber operations, for instance, should be considered as 'strategic' in their effect as a nuclear attack remains unclear. Because many new capabilities are under development, uncertainties linger about which weapon or system might have a 'strategic' impact.

Why does the definition of 'strategic' matter? The linguistic consider-ations are interesting in themselves, but the more important reasons are the bureaucratic and institutional ramifications, compounded by the new US strategy of integrated deterrence that is central to the 2022 National Defense Strategy. The lack of a proper grand strategy and the ambigu-ity surrounding the meaning of the term have put the United States in a position where there is no lead integrator, no true whole-of-government approach to deterrence, and uncertainty within the organisations that must carry out that mission about their roles. The responsibility is shared among too many players, and the rule book is vague about who is in charge of what. This bodes poorly for a concerted, well-defined approach to the more dangerous world we face today.

From the interwar period to the end of the Cold War, anything strategic presumptively fell into the Strategic Air Command's purview. Later, the need arose to integrate the activities that can produce strategic effects of various commands, capabilities and operations across the Department of Defense. Several issues might emerge due to a lack of integration and synchronisation across the US defence establishment. The Pentagon had best establish greater clarity in defining strategic threats, operations, systems, command relationships and deterrence.

Interwar through the Cold War

Lawrence Freedman, the eminent historian of strategy, links the contemporary use of the term 'strategic' to interwar developments in the realm of airpower.[4] In the 1920s, the Italian theorist Giulio Douhet suggested that airpower could produce strategic effects if bombers armed with chemical munitions were sent to attack an opponent's urban areas in wartime, leading the terrorised citizenry to force their government to end an ongoing war.[5] Airpower could be strategic if used wisely because it could directly shape politics by reducing the will of the opponent to continue to prosecute a conflict. American airpower enthusiasts, such as Billy Mitchell, suggested a different target set for conventional munitions: critical industrial sectors. Precision bombardment could halt logistical flows, leading to the collapse of the opponent's war effort.[6] British Air Marshal Hugh Trenchard also identified the key characteristic of the bomber that made it a strategic weapon: it could sidestep the bulk of the opponent's military while striking directly at the heart of a nation.[7] While some airpower theorists used the term 'strategic' to suggest that aircraft could serve in more than a tactical role as mobile artillery to support the infantry, their use of the term still highlighted the war-winning potential of long-range aerial bombardment. Long-range bombers could fly over the forward edge of the battle area to attack critical industrial or political nodes, making it possible to defeat an opponent without defeating its forces in the field in gruelling attritional warfare. It is easy to understand how the idea of strategic airpower appealed to veterans of the Great War.

Although variations of Douhet's approach to strategic bombardment were attempted during the Second World War with mixed results, the Allied bombing campaigns solidified the distinction between tactical and strategic airpower in popular culture, force structure and strategy.[8] This conceptual framework came in handy on 6 August 1945 when elements of the US Army Air Corps' 393rd Bombardment Squadron dropped an atomic bomb on Hiroshima, Japan. Airpower enthusiasts immediately embraced nuclear weapons because they exponentially increased the firepower that could be delivered from the air. A single aircraft could now carry an explosive payload that previously required hundreds of planes. A strategic (that is, long-range) bomber finally had a strategic (that is, nuclear) weapon worthy of the name. Within five years, a true revolution in military affairs had taken place. The word 'strategic' was now linked to a new deterrent strategy based on long-range bombers and nuclear weapons, and implemented by a new air force headquartered at a former cavalry outpost in Omaha, Nebraska: Strategic Air Command.

As the nuclear age unfolded, the importance of the strategic deterrent and the inherent risk of nuclear war attracted much scholarly and public interest. Soviet and US acquisition of massive numbers of fusion weapons, land-based and submarine-based intercontinental ballistic missiles, and bombers capable of intercontinental missions led to a situation of mutual assured destruction (MAD), whereby each side maintained a secure second-strike capability. If deterrence failed, many of these forces would survive nuclear attack, which guaranteed that the opponent could not win the nuclear war in any politically or militarily meaningful way. In practice, this led to a de facto division of the US military into conventional war-fighting units that occasionally engaged in active hostilities, and deterrent forces, mostly controlled by Strategic Air Command, which were held in reserve to deter nuclear attack on the United States, its allies and US forces worldwide. If nuclear deterrence failed, the Strategic Air Command's surviving units would guarantee the destruction of the adversary. This secure second-strike capability constituted the *ultima ratio regum* of the nuclear age.

The concept of strategic deterrence took on additional emotional content and political meaning as it spanned new conceptual space and nuclear arsenals grew. Strategic deterrence was alternatively depicted as mitigating the risk of a global nuclear catastrophe and as the potential source of that catastrophe.[9] The Strategic Air Command and the strategic deterrent it provided allowed the United States to dominate any potential opponent except for the similarly armed Soviet Union. Friend and foe alike increasingly acknowledged the so-called nuclear revolution. The threat of nuclear annihilation moderated the behaviour of the great powers, setting the stage for one of the longest periods of great-power peace in the history of the nation-state system.[10] At the same time, issues deemed 'strategic' now conjured images of nuclear holocaust; the word indicated that national, even human, survival was at risk.[11]

By the 1980s, only historians associated the US strategic bomber force with attacks on ball-bearing plants or railroad yards. Nevertheless, some of the ideas that early airpower theorists had championed did manage to carry over to the nuclear age, albeit in a slightly different form. Thomas C. Schelling articulated the notion of the 'diplomacy of violence', whereby states could execute nuclear counter-value attacks without first defeating the opponent's military. He added that states could also launch counter-value attacks even after their societies were in ruins and their conventional forces were destroyed, an idea that had not been entertained in the interwar years.[12] By the end of the Cold War, the word 'strategic' evoked a kaleidoscope of imagery revolving around nuclear deterrence, national survival and the Strategic Air Command.

The contemporary era

On 1 June 1992, US Strategic Command was established to replace Strategic Air Command. The new command absorbed the Joint Strategic Target Planning Staff, the office with responsibility for nuclear-war planning. The idea for this new command was actually suggested by officers of the Strategic Air Command's J5 Plans and Policy Division, who were encouraged by General Colin Powell, then chairman of the Joint Chiefs of Staff, via General George Butler, then the commander of Strategic Air

Command, to think creatively about adapting to a post-Soviet future.[13] The result was a significant reduction in the size of the US nuclear arsenal and a reduced emphasis on nuclear weapons in US defence policy. The creation of Strategic Command also reflected the 1986 Goldwater–Nichols Act. In keeping with the intent of this legislation, one joint command was created to take charge of all US strategic nuclear forces.[14] Strategic Command led the effort to integrate a nascent conventional global-strike capability with the US strategic deterrent.

Within ten years, however, a process of accretion occurred whereby Strategic Command became the locus of multiple emerging domains and operational capabilities.[15] The first new element to merge with Strategic Command was US Space Command in 2002. The leadership of Strategic Command attributed this move to recognition that US space capabilities, in terms of command, control and communications, along with intelligence, surveillance and reconnaissance, provided the basis for the tactical and operational reconnaissance-strike complex that was becoming a new American way of war. Space Command was 'strategic' in the sense that it provided capabilities that supported the entire Department of Defense. When Strategic Command was formed in 1992, the only real experts in cyber were computer scientists and futurists.[16] That situation changed quickly. For a short time, in 2009–10, US Cyber Command operated as a sub-unified command under Strategic Command. The impetus for this temporary migration of cyber to Strategic Command seemed to be cyber's novelty and uniquely wide

Ways to think about 'strategic':

- Geographic location of target
- Geographic location of delivery vehicle
- Type of weapon, warhead or delivery vehicle
- Size of attack
- Use of nuclear weapons
- Attack on US or allies' homeland
- Attack on US nuclear forces or nuclear command, control and communication assets
- Attack on critical infrastructure or continuity of government
- Attack that causes major damage to the economy or societal structures

applicability. According to US Cyber Command, 'the information age and its technologies changed the way the world functioned, creating global networks and allowing adversaries to access strategic centers of national power'.[17]

It may appear that by briefly including the space and cyber domains, Strategic Command gave them 'strategic' cachet. Nevertheless, space and cyber operations did not need a brief stay with Strategic Command to gain truly strategic qualities. Space and cyber operations are not bound by geography; are not limited to the forward edge of the battle area; support an entire defence establishment; enable a broad range of operations; and can produce strategic effects on a routine basis by undertaking or enabling global operations that shape the battlespace and an opponent's politics.

For a time, the consensus within the Defense Department was that Strategic Command was the logical headquarters to manage a basket of capabilities (global strike) and operations in new domains (cyber, space) that shared certain characteristics with the strategic nuclear force. Strategic Command retained control of all strategic forces, including those in new domains. By 2010, though, clarity about the term 'strategic' was beginning to deteriorate as capabilities emerged that provided new ways to produce strategic-deterrent or operational effects, or provided critical services to the entire US defence establishment. These new capabilities enabled a new American way of war based on the development of reconnaissance-strike complexes in a variety of tactical, regional and even global settings. In common parlance, the term 'strategic' was still used to euphemise Strategic Command's nuclear-deterrence mission, but other domains, operations and commands now described their contribution to national defence as also capable of producing strategic effects. As the Cold War faded into increasingly distant memory, these new capabilities' potential to achieve strategic effects without the destructiveness of nuclear weapons tended to overshadow the US nuclear deterrent.[18]

Where you stand depends on where you sit

From their vantage point in Omaha, officers in US Strategic Command have noted that the contemporary use of the word 'strategic' in a variety of contexts hints at a deeper issue permeating the US defence establishment. They are not exactly sure what that issue is or even if others have taken notice, but, like blind men touching an elephant, they are describing the part of the creature within reach. They do not know if others in the Defense Department have also touched it, or if anyone has seen the whole beast.

Strategic Command is not alone in noting that changes are afoot within the Department of Defense. Higher command echelons have also observed that complexity is increasing and that efforts at integration and synchronisation of policy, operations and routine activity on a global scale create growing challenges. Following one of the best-known adages of organisational behaviour – where you stand depends on where you sit – different organisations see a different manifestation of the problem – or, to use the previous metaphor, they each have taken hold of a different part of the elephant. Officers and officials sitting in echelons above Strategic Command understand why the headquarters staff in Omaha is concerned about the proliferation of commands, capabilities and operations potentially capable of producing strategic effects, because responsibility for global integration of the strategic effects they produce is no longer solely Strategic Command's. It is now a whole-of-government matter, with ultimate responsibility lying somewhere among the Joint Staff, the National Military Command Center, the Office of the Secretary of Defense, the State Department, other cabinet agencies, the National Security Council and the Oval Office itself. The lead agency is not predetermined, but rather situation-dependent. Given this relative uncertainty, integration is clearly a work in progress, which explains why questions are arising about the contemporary meaning of the word 'strategic'. Insiders agree that context and organisational setting drive how the term is used within the Defense Department. There is also a tendency for observers from other organisations to describe their responsibilities and activities as truly strategic, and to view others as lacking strategic roles.

Despite these various perspectives, there are some consistent points of agreement. For instance, the term strategic is usually applied to operations, policies or commands that transcend regional commands or produce effects that alter the military, economic or political status quo – typically with little or nothing to do with altering the situation along the forward edge of a battle area. Many officers, including liaisons from key allies, identify a strategic threat as one that could potentially alter the American or allied homelands in fundamental ways, such that they would not be the same if they suffered a strategic attack.[19] Such a prospect, to most observers, would merit a strategic (probably nuclear) deterrent threat. The Office of the Secretary of Defense, the National Military Command Center and even the Joint Staff note their contribution to the 'global integrator' task, but all admit that in a crisis, practical considerations in command relationships would prevail. Officials at the National Military Command Center, for example, note that practical solutions to a given task are typically worked out 'on the fly', through conferencing among the commands.[20]

Nevertheless, officials interviewed for this article also acknowledge that it is uncertain exactly when Strategic Command would or should play a more significant role in the integration and synchronisation effort, given Omaha's responsibility for the nuclear force. They agree that it is important never to lose sight of an overriding goal of US defence policy: to deter strategic threats to the United States, its allies and US forces stationed overseas. There is general agreement that the issue reflects the fact that new domains, capabilities and command relationships are emerging faster than the concepts, theories and organisational relationships to deal with them are developing.

Owing to their unique perspectives, two organisations have managed to get a look at the 'global integration' beast (with its 'strategic' tail) in its entirety. One is the Office of the Assistant Secretary of Defense for Space Policy. While that name is congressionally mandated, the organisation's purview – space, cyber, nuclear forces countering weapons of mass destruction, and space and missile defence – crosses most of the capabilities, domains and operations that involve strategic effects. Nevertheless, members of this office readily admit that the relationships and interactions among the various elements of their newly reorganised office are a work in progress. They also note that it is not clear how the various elements of their office will interact with the activities of the Assistant Secretary of Defense for Strategy, Plans and Capabilities, which has responsibility for strategy and force development. They say with some irony that the office charged with developing strategy is not part of the office that is responsible for capabilities that produce strategic effects.[21]

Members of US Cyber Command, the other organisation, have suggested that traditional strategic concepts and organisations are being overtaken by new capabilities and operations. They see the need for a fundamental change in the US approach to strategy and policy along several dimensions of the emerging political–military–technological landscape. They note, for instance, that the time has arrived to abandon the traditional American characterisation of war and peace as a dichotomy and the related notion that peace is the natural state of things in international affairs. Instead, they suggest that American foreign and defence policy should aim to shape the peacetime environment, and that some forces and capabilities have a greater role in peacetime than they might in wartime. They also observe that traditional notions of command are outmoded because no one organisation is capable of exercising control over the different resources needed to accomplish a given mission. Instead, a more collaborative approach to managing the force needs to arise. Disparate entities might come together on an ad hoc basis to collaborate on novel solutions to emergent challenges. They consider it unlikely that traditional approaches to organising defence can cope with nascent warfare domains while integrating and synchronising long-standing capabilities.[22]

Problems of linguistic imprecision

Several immediate and practical issues are linked to the increase in the number of organisations and capabilities that can – at least in theory – produce strategic effects. While officers and officials suggest that they can be integrated and synchronised on an ad hoc basis, there are at least three issues involving the nebulousness of the 'strategic' concept that might bedevil these efforts: accidental or inadvertent escalation; dysfunctional command relationships; and the integration of deterrent postures and policies.

Accidental or inadvertent escalation

Escalation from peace to war, or from conventional to nuclear operations, can occur as a matter of deliberate strategy and policy. NATO's policy of flexible response, for instance, was a deliberate effort to link conventional and nuclear deterrence along the inner-German border during the Cold War, while Russia's current strategy of 'escalate to de-escalate' is based on the idea that the use of nuclear weapons could promptly halt a deteriorating situation on some conventional battlefield. The two strategies are from the same mould, attempting to end fighting on terms favourable to the side willing to escalate to the next level of violence to regain the initiative. Inadvertent escalation, by contrast, occurs in the absence of political control, or even control by higher-level military commands. It can arise for a variety of reasons. Opposing units operating near each other might exchange fire through miscalculation, accident or panic. Local incentives and opportunities could replace those of higher authorities, such that line soldiers take matters into their own hands. For example, some eyewitness reports suggested that the first shot of the American Revolution was fired at British regulars not by the American militia withdrawing from the field but from Buckman Tavern, which overlooked Lexington Common.[23]

For US Strategic Command, the risk of inadvertent escalation increases when other commands undertake operations with strategic effects, especially those involving deterrent red lines or the infrastructure associated with an opponent's nuclear forces. This well-known problem was best articulated by Barry Posen in his work *Inadvertent Escalation*.[24] Posen suggested that an opponent could interpret conventional attacks against dual-use command, control, intelligence, reconnaissance and surveillance systems and logistical networks as the opening move in a conventional counterforce attack against strategic nuclear forces, or even an opening move in a nuclear counterforce attack. The gradual erosion of an opponent's ability to use non-nuclear systems that were also key to employing nuclear weapons might put an opponent in a 'use it or lose it' situation. Given the growing number of capabilities and commands that can create strategic effects, officials in Omaha are rightfully concerned that a successful use of some non-kinetic or extraterrestrial capability might begin to degrade an opponent's confidence in its deterrent capabilities, inadvertently raising the spectre of nuclear-weapons use in a less-than-existential conflict. Furthermore, US operations and capabilities might not involve the use of nuclear weapons but could be perceived by adversaries as signalling prospective US nuclear use.

Another potential path of escalation is more directly related to the liberal use of the term 'strategic'. Non-nuclear operations could take on unwanted nuclear connotations because they somehow end up falling into Strategic Command's span of control as 'strategic' referents. This might best be thought of as accidental escalation caused by the miscommunication or mischaracterisation of a threat. Not everything called 'strategic' really is strategic – that is, a threat that will change America or its way of life. While mischaracterising a situation along these lines would be unlikely to lead to the immediate use of nuclear weapons, it could cause Strategic Command to initiate alert measures that could subvert overall US political objectives by ratcheting up an opponent's nuclear-alert status.[25] The probability of such unintended consequences would increase if such moves were not coordinated with other parts of the US government, such as the State Department or White House.

One such mischaracterisation occurred during NATO's *Able Archer* nuclear command-and-control exercise in 1983, when Soviet officers and officials for a time believed that the exercise constituted real preparations to initiate nuclear hostilities against the Warsaw Pact. In the early 1980s, the Kremlin assessed that the likelihood of war with the West was growing and initiated a collection and analysis effort – *Operation RYaN (Raketno-Yadernoe Napadenie)* – to determine indications and warnings of an impending nuclear offensive. *Operation RYaN* utilised unique communication channels, so when information about the *Able Archer* exercise was transmitted through these channels, receivers tended to treat it as indicating a genuine impending nuclear attack. In turn, NATO commanders noticed an increase in the alert level of Soviet nuclear units, recognised what was happening and decided not to order a similar alert. Communicating about a routine and benign event in 'strategic' reporting channels led decision-makers to act on the messenger rather than the message.[26]

While these concerns might sound far-fetched, Strategic Command's involvement in a future crisis could be seen as a red flag to an opponent suggesting that nuclear weapons might be somehow involved. Officials and policymakers therefore need to be aware that Strategic Command's involvement in 'strategic' matters could appear to introduce a nuclear element into an ongoing crisis even when it is not intended to do so.

Command relationships

The most recent US Unified Command Plan (UCP) simultaneously creates and attempts to alleviate the problem of overlapping missions between major commands within the Department of Defense.[27] For example, the UCP gives the mission for parts of the electromagnetic spectrum to three separate commands – Cyber Command, Space Command and Strategic Command. Strategic Command is responsible for strategic nuclear-weapons delivery and strategic deterrence. This terminology is not clearly defined in the UCP, but is easily extrapolated from that document's mission statement for the command, as well as the command's name. Accordingly, it would be reasonable to conclude that strategic deterrence is Strategic Command's sole mission. Additionally, most people still assume that strategic deterrence means nuclear deterrence, even if that is not an accurate view of what integrated deterrence and whole-of-government approaches to deterrence imply today.

The UCP recognises that there will be overlap between command areas of responsibility. It stipulates that each commander may operate his or her forces in other areas of responsibility when necessary, without asking permission first. If the operation is significant, however, the affected commanders are expected to form a task force to coordinate their efforts. This is the case for functional combatant commands, like Strategic Command, as well as regional ones, though the UCP focuses on coordination among regional commands. Further muddying the waters, the commander of each functional command is responsible for 'detecting, deterring, and preventing threats and attacks against the United States; its territories, possessions, and bases; and employing appropriate force across the full spectrum of competition and conflict to defend the nation'.[28] This means that Strategic Command does *not* have an exclusive role in deterrence, merely the lead role at the presumed strategic level. But what does that encompass? All strategic issues, or just those involving nuclear weapons? Would Strategic Command become the global integrator once hostilities escalated to the nuclear level? That seems unlikely, given that its focus is on nuclear weapons and long-range strike capabilities, but not the myriad other possible strategic challenges to the United States.

A notional scenario highlights the challenges facing combatant commanders in a real-world situation. Suppose an adversary conducts a 'strategic strike' against ground-based space-communication and -command centres in Indo-Pacific Command's area of responsibility. Further assume that this appears to be part of a larger attack by a nuclear-armed adversary on an ally to which the United States has offered extended-deterrence guarantees. Who is in charge of dealing with this scenario? Do multiple commands have responsibility? Which command is ultimately responsible for deterring adversary nuclear use? Would it be Indo-Pacific Command, since the incident took place in its area of responsibility? Or would it be in Space Command's bailiwick, since, according to the UCP, its forces and facilities remain assigned to it even when they are serving in other commands' areas of responsibility? Or would Strategic Command have responsibility, given the nuclear implications of an attack against a critical dual-use facility?

Most officials see the regional combatant command as the most likely lead for responses and regional deterrence, with the transregional and functional commands (Strategic Command, Cyber Command, Space Command and US Special Operations Command) in supporting roles.[29] Nevertheless, there are no obvious good answers to this problem, and the time to sort them out is not after an attack has occurred. While there has been little public discussion of this challenge, General David H. Berger, until July 2023 commandant of the US Marine Corps, recently expressed his concern over the secretary of defense's broad span of control in dealing with combatant commands and their disparate missions, potentially creating a situation where 'getting the right perspectives on the table becomes really difficult'.[30]

Such issues may be easier to resolve in the European theatre, since US European Command and NATO have been closely intertwined since 1949. Furthermore, the Alliance has long experience in thinking about nuclear war. Still, there are uncertainties. Current US national-security documents assess that the greatest likelihood of nuclear use would arise from a regional conflict.

In that case, European Command would probably already be involved in a war in Europe at the conventional level. Nuclear deterrence, and potentially nuclear use, are the responsibilities of US Strategic Command. However, European Command controls dual-capable aircraft with tactical nuclear weapons that are based in-theatre. Furthermore, although the US president has ultimate authority for launching any US nuclear weapon, the US Air Force and key NATO allies have aircraft and nuclear weapons forward-deployed in the European area of responsibility that are not under the direct control of either US Strategic Command or European Command. So at what point does the fight become 'strategic', whereupon Strategic Command would take over from European Command? What role would European Command's commander retain in his or her dual-hatted authority as the NATO Supreme Allied Commander Europe (SACEUR) if US strategic forces were involved? Would Strategic Command simply be used to backstop European Command's prosecution of the war, even if that conflict escalated to nuclear use? And what of the US Air Force's and NATO allies' dual-capable aircraft, supposedly controlled by the NATO secretary-general and the North Atlantic Council, with advice from SACEUR? Which of a multitude of commanders is the president listening to?[31]

In the early years of the post-Cold War era, the United States tried to lend clarity to the cluttered decision-making situation by according responsibility for regional or theatre nuclear strikes to the geographic commands. By virtue of the so-called 'silver books', the regional combatant commands would plan and conduct nuclear-strike missions in their respective areas of responsibility, presumably using non-strategic nuclear weapons. US Strategic Command was involved only as a supporting command in planning the mission.[32] By the end of the 1990s, however, the silver books were closed or sent back to Omaha. As far as is publicly known, the regional commanders no longer had, and do not have today, the authority to plan and potentially use nuclear weapons.[33]

Integrated deterrence

The Biden administration's new term 'integrated deterrence' seems to make sense as part of a holistic, whole-of-government approach to dealing with multiple adversaries coming from different directions, across the spectrum of conflict, with many types of weapons, in all domains. In fact, the concept says everything and nothing, and in some ways further confuses issues. Integrated deterrence appears to be little more than an aspirational goal.

According to the National Security Strategy, due to 'more capable competitors and new strategies of threatening behavior below and above the traditional threshold of conflict', the United States 'cannot afford to rely solely on conventional forces and nuclear deterrence'.[34] This would seem to imply a reduced role for US Strategic Command, or at least a broadening of the responsibilities for deterrence and strategic security to some of the new functional commands that are no longer under its purview.

Furthermore, the concept of integrated deterrence assumes a whole-of-government approach that includes integration across domains, regions, the spectrum of conflict, the US government, and allies and partners. This is a much broader mandate than the senior leadership in Omaha can or should be expected to handle. Integrated deterrence logically involves the State Department and other cabinet departments, as well as the Defense Department, at multiple levels and every combatant command. The UCP may simply be reflecting the reality of modern threats when it gives overlapping responsibilities for strategic deterrence to multiple commands. That is the world we live in today. Arguably, the UCP provides a general solution in describing those relationships. But it does not adequately clarify organisational relationships for all scenarios.

Nor is the lead integrator for integrated deterrence defined in any of the public US national-security documents. According to officials in Washington, the Office of the Secretary of Defense was largely behind the development of the concept of integrated deterrence, which could imply a role for the secretary of defense. Senior officials mentioned these organisations as possible lead integrators: the Office of the Secretary of Defense, the secretary of defense himself, the Joint Chiefs of Staff or its chairman, the J3 (operations), the J5 (plans and policies) divisions and the National Military Command Center. Others have suggested that responsibility for integrating deterrence should fall on the supported regional commander, or possibly the operations directorate of US Strategic Command. State Department officials suggested that the White House or the National Security Council would make the final decisions and determine who the supported commander and lead integrator would be for a specific scenario.[35] That is a reasonable default position. At present, however, the National Security Council does not have a senior director or a directorate for deterrence. Bureaucratic uncertainty thus remains, with an ad hoc response to a crisis the most likely way deterrence would be integrated in a future contingency.

Dealing with the conundrums

It is unlikely that a single military command could field the wide variety of strategic attacks and strategic effects – different systems, operational effects and domains – noted in this article. Strategic means more than nuclear, and the Defense Department is slowly adjusting to this fundamental change in the international security environment. US Strategic Command's role remains primarily to provide the 'big stick' of nuclear deterrence and retaliation, which backstops all operational approaches and scenarios managed by other commands.

Some Washington insiders have suggested an organisational change to resolve or at least ameliorate the challenge of overlapping command responsibilities. Several offices in the Defense and State departments asked, 'Why doesn't US Strategic Command change its name?' Admittedly, their remarks were somewhat tongue-in-cheek, but they were also based in reality, which suggests their ideas might just merit some consideration. The general view is that the word 'strategic' now covers a mission set that has become too broad for a single military command and tends to obscure Strategic Command's predominant nuclear responsibilities. The Defense Department could conceivably create a 'Nuclear Command' that would perform the missions that the Strategic Air Command had during its Cold War heyday. In the past decade, Space Command and Cyber Command have dispersed from their former short-term home in Omaha. Nearly all missions the UCP now assigns to Strategic Command are related to strategic deterrence: nuclear operations; global strike; nuclear command, control and communications; missile defence; analysis and targeting; and missile threat assessment.[36]

Perhaps US Strategic Command could become US Deterrence Command, or US Global Strike Command (it already has command authority over Air Force Global Strike Command). This is not a new idea. A former head of Strategic Command said that he considered changing the name when he was ordered to absorb some of these new missions into US Strategic Command in the early 2000s. After reflection, however, he chose to leave the name as it was.[37]

As suggested, the civilian component of 'strategic deterrence' could benefit from the establishment of a senior director for integrated deterrence (and supporting directorate) within the National Security Council. This office would deal with the key players in an inter-agency, whole-of-government approach to deterrence, addressing the survival of those strategic elements of America's economy, governance, critical infrastructure and military capabilities. The senior director would be formally designated the lead integrator for deterrence matters.

While a new position on the National Security Council staff would facilitate policy and operational coordination, precisely what capabilities need to be integrated to produce tomorrow's strategic effects remains to be determined. Because nuclear weapons and issues involving strategic deterrence lost much of their salience between the fall of the Berlin Wall and the annexation of Crimea, strategists and theorists were slow to develop concepts and organisational schemes that synchronised new warfare domains and new technologies with existing strategic capabilities and concepts.[38] The Russian invasion of Ukraine has illuminated this shortcoming. Without more up-to-date theory to define and contextualise key concepts – in particular, the term 'strategic' – the integration effort could become mired in endless debates about first principles. Accordingly, some organisation within the US government should be tasked with concept development for integrated deterrence.

A revamped definition of what constitutes a truly strategic threat, interest, effect, deterrent or capability for the United States is also required. This is not a pedantic call to revisit fundamental concepts. There is no need, for instance, to endlessly refine ideas such as deterrence by denial, assured destruction, deterrence credibility, first strike, secure second strike or other Cold War-era parameters. Instead, the priority should be to develop new ideas and theories that capture technically driven strategic changes that have occurred since the end of the nuclear-focused, bipolar setting of the Cold War. Equipped with tighter theory, it would be easier for the organisations identified as critical to advance the integration effort in practice.

*   *   *

The definition of strategy is well understood. Strategy is about ends, ways and means. It is about the art of devising a plan to use the resources at one's disposal to achieve objectives, often while facing an opponent that embraces a competing strategy to obtain different goals. In conflict and in competitions short of war, strategy unfolds in a dialectical setting. The meaning of 'strategic', however, is not so clear. The word is overused and has multiple definitions, leading to potentially dangerous organisational confusion. It reflects the institutional perspectives of each organisation that has a role in managing strategic affairs, including integrated deterrence. Uncertainty about the lead integrator for US defence and deterrence requirements reflects a traditional American reliance on common sense and ad hoc solutions. Until a more rigorous approach yielding greater clarity on leadership responsibilities and missions for each element of the military structure arises, all government entities will remain uncertain as to who is in charge when a truly strategic issue arises.

US Strategic Command will continue to be the strategic nuclear command, the holder of the ultimate deterrence guarantee. But it does not have comprehensive authority in strategic matters; it is not the same one-stop strategic shop that Strategic Air Command was during the Cold War. It will serve as a supporting command for most scenarios below the level of nuclear preparation or conflict, including those that may be cavalierly labelled 'strategic' but are not in fact existential. To better define the contemporary organisational roles of Strategic Command and interacting authorities, the US government should consider creating a think tank for conceptualising and designing a truly integrated deterrent, as well as a new grand strategy for confronting the fresh strategic challenges America faces in the twenty-first century.

Notes

1   Colin S. Gray, *The Future of Strategy* (Cambridge: Polity Press, 2015), p. 26, emphasis in original.

2   See White House, 'National Security Strategy', October 2022, https://www.whitehouse.gov/wp-content/uploads/2022/11/8-November-Combined-PDF-for-Upload.pdf; and US Department of Defense, '2022 National Defense Strategy', 27 October 2022, https://media.defense.gov/2022/Oct/27/2003103845/-1/-1/1/2022-NATIONAL-DEFENSE-STRATEGY-NPR-MDR.PDF.

3   See Gray, *The Future of Strategy*, p. 22.

4   See Lawrence Freedman, *The Evolution of Nuclear Strategy*, 4th ed. (New York: Palgrave Macmillan, 2019), pp. 1–15; and Lawrence Freedman, *Strategy: A History* (Oxford: Oxford University Press, 2013), pp. 3–9.

5   See Giulio Douhet, *Command of the Air* (Maxwell AFB, AL: Air University Press, 2019).

6   See Michael E. Brown, *Flying Blind: The Politics of the US Strategic Bomber Program* (Ithaca, NY: Cornell University Press, 1992), pp. 35–62; and John T. Correll, 'Daylight Precision Bombing', *Air & Space Forces Magazine*, 1 October 2008, https://www.airandspaceforces.com/article/1008daylight/.

7   See George Quester, *Deterrence Before Hiroshima: The Influence of Airpower on Modern Strategy* (New York: John Wiley, 1966), p. 52.

8   See Brown, *Flying Blind*, pp. 61–5.

9   This paradox is known to undergraduates from the 'Sagan–Waltz Debate'. See Scott D. Sagan and Kenneth N. Waltz, *The Spread of Nuclear Weapons: An Enduring Debate*, 3rd ed. (New York: W. W. Norton & Co., 2012).

10   See Robert Jervis, *The Meaning of the Nuclear Revolution: Statecraft and the Prospect of Armageddon* (Ithaca, NY: Cornell University Press, 1989).

11   Jonathan Schell, *The Fate of the Earth* (New York: Alfred A. Knopf, 1982).

12   See Thomas C. Schelling, *Arms and Influence* (New Haven, CT: Yale University Press, 1966), pp. 1–34.

13   See Gregory S. Gilmour, 'From SAC to STRATCOM: The Origins of Unified Command Over Nuclear Forces', MA Thesis, Naval Postgraduate School, June 1993, pp. 60–2, https://apps.dtic.mil/sti/pdfs/ADA268609.pdf.

14   Some theatre commanders also retained the authority for tactical nuclear-weapons planning in their areas of responsibility.

15   See US Strategic Command, 'History', https://www.stratcom.mil/About/History/.

16   See James J. Wirtz, 'The Cyber Pearl Harbor Redux: Helpful Analogy or Cyber Hype?', *Intelligence and National Security*, vol. 33, no. 5, April 2018, pp. 771–3.

17   See US Cyber Command, 'Our History', https://www.cybercom.mil/About/History.

18   See Harald Müller and Annette Schaper, 'US Nuclear Policy After the Cold War', PRIF Reports No. 69, Peace Research Institute Frankfurt, 2004, https://www.hsfk.de/fileadmin/HSFK/hsfk_downloads/prif69.pdf.

19   Author interviews with senior officials from Australia and the United Kingdom, October 2022.

20 Author interviews with senior officials, Washington DC, December 2022.

21 *Ibid.*

22 *Ibid.*

23 See David Hackett Fischer, *Paul Revere's Ride* (Oxford: Oxford University Press, 1995), p. 402.

24 Barry Posen, *Inadvertent Escalation: Conventional War and Nuclear Risks* (Ithaca, NY: Cornell University Press, 1991).

25 See Bruce G. Blair, *The Logic of Accidental Nuclear War* (Washington DC: Brookings Institution, 1993).

26 See Gordon Barrass, '*Able Archer 83*: What Were the Soviets Thinking?', *Survival*, vol. 58, no. 6, December 2016–January 2017, pp. 7–30; and Nate Jones (ed.), *Able Archer 83: The Secret History of the NATO Exercise that Almost Triggered Nuclear War* (New York: New Press, 2016).

27 For more on Unified Command Plans, see Andrew Feickert, 'The Unified Command Plan and Combatant Commands: Background and Issues for Congress', CRS Report R42077, Congressional Research Service, 3 January 2013, https://sgp.fas.org/crs/natsec/R42077.pdf.

28 White House, 'Unified Command Plan', 13 January 2021, p. 3, para 10a.

29 Author interviews with officials in Washington DC, and Omaha, NE, autumn 2022.

30 Quoted in Justin Katz, 'Berger: Time to Look at Changing Combatant Command Structure', *Breaking Defense*, 24 May 2023, https://breakingdefense.com/2023/05/berger-time-to-look-at-changing-combatant-command-structure/.

31 According to a recent study, 'current military doctrine does not clearly assign responsibility for planning nuclear operations for regional contingencies, which is necessary for effective conventional-nuclear integration at the operational level. JP [Joint Publication] 3-72 states that the "geographic combatant commander (GCC), supported by USSTRATCOM" is prepared "to perform nuclear targeting to generate desired effects and achieve objectives," while JP 3-35 states that "specialized planning is typically conducted by USSTRATCOM in coordination with the supported GCC."' Adam Mount and Pranay Vaddi, 'An Integrated Approach to Deterrence Posture: Reviewing Conventional and Nuclear Forces in a National Defense Strategy', Federation of American Scientists, 2020, https://docslib.org/doc/8927812/an-integrated-approach-to-deterrence-posture-reviewing-conventional-and-nuclear-forces-in-a-national-defense-strategy.

32 See Hans M. Kristensen, 'The Role of Nuclear Weapons in Regional Counterproliferation and Global Strike Scenarios', Presentation to the New Mexico Nuclear Study Group Workshop 'What Role, If Any, For Nuclear Weapons?', Center for Science, Technology, and Policy, University of New Mexico, 11–12 September 2008, https://programs.fas.org/ssp/nukes/publications1/UNMbrief2008.pdf.

33 One exception to this general observation may be European Command's nuclear-contingency planners supporting NATO's nuclear-planning office at Supreme Headquarters Allied Powers Europe.

[34] White House, 'National Security Strategy', p. 22.

[35] Author interviews in Washington DC, December 2022.

[36] See Feickert, 'The Unified Command Plan and Combatant Commands'.

[37] Author interview, February 2023.

[38] The regrettable lack of attention paid to nuclear matters (and to Russian studies) by the generation following the end of the Cold War has been quite noticeable to the small cohort that remained in these fields. See Bryan Bender, 'The Dangerous and Frightening Disappearance of the Nuclear Expert', *Politico*, 28 July 2023, https://www.politico.com/news/magazine/2023/07/28/nuclear-experts-russia-war-00108438.

The Consequences of Generative AI for Democracy, Governance and War

Steven Feldstein

Generative artificial intelligence (AI) models have exploded onto the public scene, with profound implications for governance, politics and war. The potential range of its effects in these areas is enormous, but it remains subject to considerable speculation and little hard fact. This article focuses on four areas posing major challenges: democratic governance; autocratic regimes; cyber capabilities; and war planning and military operations.

This article examines short- and medium-term risks stemming from generative-AI applications, focusing on threats that are concrete and identifiable. Given the novelty of the technology and the immense disruptions that are already ensuing, there is value in assessing how these changes will impact society today and in the near future. The article does not address more speculative or long-term existential risks in light of the challenges of predicting and evaluating such outcomes. But the piece does consider a wide range of issues, including battlefield transformations from generative AI as well as democratic disruptions and authoritarian enhancement. The reason is that AI technology is helping to precipitate a new age of geopolitics. Its effects therefore are not easily severable by topic or issue. AI's impact on war will inevitably shape the functioning of democracy and governance. Many military applications linked to AI will also extend to the civilian domain.

Steven Feldstein is a senior fellow in the Democracy, Conflict, and Governance Program at the Carnegie Endowment for International Peace and the author of *The Rise of Digital Repression: How Technology Is Reshaping Power, Politics, and Resistance* (Oxford University Press, 2021). From 2014 to 2017, he served as US Deputy Assistant Secretary of State for Democracy, Human Rights, and Labor.

Survival | vol. 65 no. 5 | October–November 2023 | pp. 117–142 https://doi.org/10.1080/ 00396338.2023.2261260

What is generative AI and how does it work?

Generative AI is a general term describing AI systems whose main function is to create new content, from images and text to videos and data. Its applications are based on foundation models – AI systems trained on a large quantity of data that can be used for a wide range of downstream tasks. Researchers deem them 'foundational' to emphasise their central yet incomplete character. Developers can build on foundational models to create specialised systems tailored for specific purposes.[1]

Large language models (LLMs) are specifically designed to analyse language and create text through predictive patterns. This article focuses primarily on the implications of LLMs because they are the basis for most of the foundational models in use today. But that does not presuppose that other types of foundational models – such as DeepMind's Gato, which performs tasks not restricted to language – will not become more relevant in the future. While this field has been in development for decades, it has leaped forward in the past couple of years. The latest systems use what are known as transformers: neural-network architectures – computer systems modelled on the human brain and nervous system – that allow for analysis of entire sentences at once rather than examining words one at a time.[2] They include OpenAI's ChatGPT-4, Google's PaLM and DeepMind's Gopher, all of which have been applied to millions of texts, books and articles to generate full-text answers to natural-language prompts and questions.

A model's structure is defined by the amount and quality of its training data and what is called its parameter count; parameters are numerical values that represent the statistical patterns learned by the model, which function as clues to help the model predict missing words in text.[3] As computing power and techniques have improved, the size of datasets has increased. An important aspect of the training process is for models to predict the next part of a large body of text. If the model predicts incorrectly, it is penalised; if it predicts correctly, it is rewarded. Through continual trial and error, models start to generate accurate outcomes. Models trained with more parameters on larger datasets can learn significantly more relationships and patterns, and thus generate more accurate outputs. OpenAI's GPT-3 model, for instance, vastly exceeded earlier models, incorporating an estimated 175 billion parameters trained on 300bn tokens (tokens being basic units of text, such as characters or words, that are fed into the model and used to process and generate language).[4]

While users largely rely on natural-language prompts to operate chatbots or image generators, AI personal assistants or 'autonomous AI agents' have recently emerged. Instead of requiring a continuous series of natural-language prompts to guide the completion of a task, these agents come up with a multi-step sequence of tasks that the system works on until it has achieved its goal.[5] For example, if a user wants to eat Thai food for dinner, rather than guide a chatbot step by step through identifying a suitable restaurant, perusing the menu, ordering and paying for the meal, the user can simply ask the agent to order a four-star Thai dinner that will be delivered to their home in an hour. The algorithm breaks down this task into a series of steps.

While ChatGPT requires continued prompting from a human user, it is now widely presumed that AI agents can take the output from GPT and feed it back into its memory to improve its performance and help it become more accurate for future iterations. Autonomous agents can already perform a variety of tasks, such as conducting basic internet research, writing code or generating task lists. But they are still in their infancy and remain fairly clunky. They are prone to 'hallucinate' – tech jargon for making things up.[6] Or they may get fixated on peripheral details. One developer related how he asked an agent to carry out market research on waterproof shoes only for the agent to get stuck in an endless loop regarding shoelaces.[7] There is also the problem of 'drift': attempts to modify one part of the model can inadvertently affect the performance of another part; for example, research-ers at Stanford University and the University of California at Berkeley have observed the deterioration of ChatGPT in completing certain mathematical operations.[8] Still, technologists argue that advances in the autonomy of AI systems might enable them to serve a range of critical functions, from oper-ating as 'data brokers' to facilitate transactions with health providers, file taxes or obtain government services, to serving as personal tutors, career coaches or researchers.[9]

While the cost efficiencies and creative potential stemming from genera-tive AI are auspicious, the technology also brings significant risks.

Undermining democracy

Experts warn about the potential for chatbots powered by LLMs to advance unscrutinised narratives with major impacts for society. According to Gary Marcus, 'chatbots can clandestinely shape our opinions, in subtle yet potent ways, potentially exceeding what social media can do. Choices about datasets may have enormous, unseen influence.'[10] In practice, this means that questions posed in ChatGPT can generate biased or flawed responses unknown to the user, which are not well understood by the model's engineers and could bring about unintended and even anti-democratic outcomes. A Berkeley professor got ChatGPT to write code specifying that only white or Asian men would make good scientists.[11] Some dubious qualities may be inadvertent. An example is so-called 'value lock', whereby LLMs reinforce outdated social values due to old training data, making it subsequently difficult to foster changes in public opinion.[12]

As millions of people begin to rely on chatbots to search for basic information, guide how they vote and perhaps refine their political beliefs, some will bestow enormous political power to opaque algorithms nominally under the control of a handful of unaccountable private companies. While individuals can exercise agency in choosing sources of information or deciding whether to trust news generated by chatbots, the emergence of LLMs as platform mediators poses a new and potentially harmful wrinkle to mass information consumption. The worry, says Hannes Bajohr, is that a 'new oligopoly' will control the future of 'political opinion-forming', in which a handful of private companies enjoy wide discretion to shape values and discourse, and are not subject to control or oversight aside from the preferences of their shareholders.[13]

Countering sexist, racist or other types of biased content generated from LLMs involves censoring outputs, filtering unwelcome components from the training data to render the algorithm more benign, or limiting access to the model. But as Bajohr observes, when companies put their thumbs on the scale to determine what content is toxic, this 'necessarily involves formulating a social vision'.[14] It is, in itself, a political act. This raises a crucial question: who gets to define this social vision? Does giving this type of gatekeeping power to AI companies subvert an essential element of democracy, which vests such power in a wider group of stakeholders, including civil society, journalists, elected public officials, regulatory agencies and ordinary citizens?

For democratic societies, one approach to mitigating the platform oligopoly problem is to pass laws that require adherence to the public interest and establish direct regulatory oversight for generative-AI applications. European decision-makers are pursuing this option. The Artificial Intelligence Act requires regulators to determine acceptable risks and ethical boundaries of emerging technologies.[15] But Europe remains the exception. Other jurisdictions – including the United States, where most of the leading AI companies are located – lag far behind. While it is possible that over time the European Union's legislation will have a global influence in shaping generative-AI products and services, this is far from a certainty.

LLMs also have the potential to disseminate industrial levels of propaganda and disinformation. In March 2023, numerous deepfake images of Donald Trump's arrest spread across social-media platforms. One doctored image that went viral came from Eliot Higgins, founder of the open-source investigative group Bellingcat, who was experimenting with generative-AI visualisation applications.[16] In April, the Republican National Committee issued a 30-second ad, generated entirely with AI tools, which projected a dystopian scenario involving China's invasion of Taiwan, US economic collapse, and the quarantining of San Francisco due to crime and fentanyl abuse.[17] In May, fake images of an explosion at the Pentagon briefly went viral, stoking panic and even causing a dip in the stock market before being debunked.[18] The unique degrees of useability, accuracy and scaleability make AI-generated propaganda singularly problematic.[19] While some experts contend that creating high-quality deepfakes 'still requires a fair degree of expertise', including post-production skills to touch up outputs generated from AI, the available know-how will likely improve over time, lowering barriers to entry.[20] Machine-generated content will probably become increasingly indistinguishable from human text.

The biggest propaganda advantage of LLMs could be their capacity to generate a nearly unlimited supply of false or untrustworthy information to poison public discourse and manipulate the views of those who consume it, whether for mercenary or ideological purposes. Novel tactics unique to generative AI are already emerging. LLMs potentially enable personally customised real-time content generation through individual interactions with chatbots.[21] Josh A. Goldstein and Girish Sastry warn that 'given access to fine-grained data on U.S. communities from polls, data brokers, or social media platforms, future language models might be able to develop content for a coherent persona, allowing propagandists to build credibility with a target audience without actually knowing that audience'.[22] That said, empirical studies of microtargeting show inconsistent results. One such study found that while microtargeting strategies generally outperformed alternative messaging campaigns, there was no evidence that subsequent personalised interactions yielded additional gains.[23]

More broadly, however, generative AI could challenge traditional forms of democratic engagement. Sarah Kreps and Douglas Kriner found that legislators did not distinguish between letters generated from ChatGPT and almost identical human messages. Thus, an enterprising individual seeking to influence policymakers could programme an LLM to send mass quantities of letters to congressional offices or regulatory agencies on specific issues. Indeed, there is clear precedent. Back in 2017, in response to US Federal Communications Commission proposals for regulations on net neutrality, at least one million automatically drafted comments were submitted to the agency's public-comment system.[24] Generative-AI models like ChatGPT allow users to deliver finely tuned messages at an accelerated pace. Over time, these interventions could sway congressional votes and shift political positions, undermining the process of democratic deliberation.[25]

Authoritarian enhancement

Generative-AI models permit authoritarian governments to supercharge existing surveillance and propaganda efforts.[26] Certain governments, notably China's, employ data-management strategies for social control. The goal of the Chinese Communist Party (CCP) is to create a self-perpetuating feedback loop.[27] Technology is used to automate the social-management process through the mass surveillance of citizens, monitoring their online communications, geo-tracking their locations and building genomic databases through mandatory DNA sampling. At least 97 countries or territories are using AI technology for public-surveillance purposes.[28]

To date, AI-surveillance systems used by authoritarian regimes have focused on classification (for instance, facial identification of individuals) or prediction (identification of suspected dissenters based on behavioural traits or activity). LLMs can enhance these efforts by aggregating data trails to generate profiles of potential dissenters. A major constraint with existing systems is the siloing of databases, which makes it difficult for authorities to integrate information. Countries like China have launched 'data fusion' initiatives to remedy the problem, but entrenched bureaucracies have barred comprehensive data access.[29] Generative-AI applications can use chatbots to access multiple databases, develop reports from threat-intelligence data and devise detection rules or threat hunts to optimise searches. LLMs can also enhance an authoritarian state's ability to generate persuasive propaganda and disinformation to manipulate its own population and to keep rival democracies off-balance through election-interference campaigns and related efforts.

Authoritarian regimes such as China also face a conundrum. LLMs derive much of their power from massive amounts of uncensored data, most of which comes from Western sources. This makes generative-AI models from OpenAI, Google or Anthropic threats to Chinese control. For example, when given the prompt, 'What happened in Tiananmen Square in 1989?', ChatGPT generated an inconveniently thorough and even-handed account of the Tiananmen Square episode (see Figure 1).

Such a response would obviously alarm Beijing's censors. Unsurprisingly, Chinese citizens are unable to access ChatGPT services in China except through virtual private networks (VPNs).[30] But even Chinese LLMs have generated responses that veer into sensitive political realms. ChatYuan, a chatbot created by Chinese AI company Yuan Yu, generated numerous problematic responses, such as listing China's economic problems and naming Russia as an aggressor in the Russia–Ukraine war.[31] Unsurprisingly, Chinese authorities shut down ChatYuan within days of its release.[32]

Chinese authorities could limit how Chinese LLMs are trained, restricting their training data to censored material or party-approved datasets. But this

Figure 1: **ChatGPT's response to the query, 'What happened in Tiananmen Square in 1989?'**

Source: ChatGPT, https://chat.openai.com

approach would undermine the effectiveness of Chinese AI models by circumscribing the amount of data and information that can be used to improve their performance.[33] In August 2023, the Cyberspace Administration of China (CAC) issued final guidelines for generative-AI platforms that hold companies offering public-facing services responsible for any problems or inappropriate content generated by the models.[34] The CAC's rules likely make it difficult for smaller companies that lack censorship or compliance systems to offer services. The rules could generally hinder Chinese firms' ability to assemble large datasets required to stay competitive with foreign companies.[35] Chinese AI companies have struggled to roll out LLMs comparable to US models. According to one recent study, they 'trail years, not months' behind international competitors when it comes to developing LLMs.[36]

If authoritarian states allow their citizens unfettered access to Western platforms like OpenAI, they run the risk of losing control of their information ecosystems and undermining their censorship regimes. Alternatively, they could follow China's lead and mandate that their citizens only use state-approved LLMs. Another option would be for countries to develop their own restricted AI models, but the cost of doing so is high (though not insuperable).[37] The emirate of Abu Dhabi's Technology Innovation Institute's (TII), for example, recently unveiled an open-source LLM with 40bn parameters trained on one trillion tokens that compares favourably to rival models.[38] While all but a few countries would be priced out of developing their own LLMs, many developers, such as TII or Meta, are opting to make their models open-source, thus allowing their code to be 'freely copied, modified, and reused' for generative-AI applications.[39] Presumably, this presents an opportunity for authoritarian countries, allowing them to avoid the high cost of developing their own LLMs while giving their companies the ability to fine-tune customisable apps based on these open-source models. Another possibility for autocratic leaders would be to reach an agreement with OpenAI, Google or similar Western platforms using closed foundational models to implement customised controls and surveillance capabilities in exchange for market access. While an LLM provider could not mathematically guarantee that its product would never violate the kinds of strict rules enacted by China for its generative-AI companies, it would be technically feasible for a company to develop a base LLM that could be fine-tuned or calibrated according to country-specific guidelines. Such a dispensation, while unfortunate, would resemble the existing practices of social-media companies, many of which tweak their community standards and content-moderation policies to reflect different governmental preferences and local laws – even if they conflict with international human-rights standards.[40]

Hacking and cyber attacks

LLMs raise the possibility of much larger, more sophisticated and more frequent hacking operations. Fraud and impersonation are especially acute threats, as generative AI can create text, audio or video that perfectly mimics other sources. In March 2023, con artists used AI to impersonate a CEO's voice demanding the transfer of $243,000.[41] US Federal Trade Commission head Lina Khan warns that AI tools are increasingly being used to 'turbocharge' fraud and scams.[42] While LLMs like ChatGPT have built-in safeguards to assess the potential for text input to generate sexual, hateful, violent or self-harming content, users can easily circumvent these protections. Common manipulation techniques include 'prompt engineering' or 'jailbreaking', whereby users tailor how they ask a question to influence what the AI system generates.[43] This can involve pretending to be a fictional character or replacing trigger words in the prompt and changing the context later.[44]

LLMs can also rapidly produce malware for cyber attacks in several different programming languages. ChatGPT already makes it possible to create simple tools, such as phishing pages or malicious versions of VBA scripts (code widely used with Microsoft Office products).[45] As models improve, they will doubtless enhance their code-generation capabilities, allowing attackers to produce code faster and with more complexity. Generative AI can equally benefit cyber defences, however, by helping firms discover software or network vulnerabilities and permitting higher rates of testing to facilitate patching.[46]

Here obvious parallels to the spyware market arise, particularly for secondary vendors who are selling commercial means of exploitation. A burgeoning ecosystem of malware suppliers that includes boutique spyware firms, hacker-by-night operations and exploit brokers are relying on a range of unconventional techniques, such as open-source malware from GitHub, to mount attacks.[47] While experts like Ronald J. Deibert describe these groups and tools as the 'surveillance equivalent of strip-mall phone repair shops', it would be logical for them to turn to AI chatbots to boost their business.[48]

Finally, LLMs can help individuals quickly gain information required to commit crimes.[49] They can subsequently use this information to launder money, perpetrate financial crimes or commit terrorist acts. Information acquisition is, of course, just one of several prerequisites of successful exploitation. ChatGPT, for instance, doesn't seem to provide the scientific steps needed to go from material acquisition to developing and distributing a pathogen. Nevertheless, there are malign uses that law enforcement should monitor, such as the ability of LLMs to generate shopping lists for weapons or to source hard-to-find elements of terrorist devices by searching through hundreds of websites simultaneously.[50]

Military planning and war

AI technology is already reshaping how war is planned and fought. The Russia–Ukraine war has produced some early real uses of AI in direct conflict.[51] Commanders are using AI-powered software to consolidate different streams of commercial data, thermal imaging of artillery fire and related intelligence to assist with the selection of targets.[52] AI is helping military tacticians game out war-planning scenarios and project potential enemy manoeuvres. Loitering munitions, which hover in designated areas to identify targets, have operated semi-autonomously, including in the 2020 Nagorno-Karabakh war as well as the Russia–Ukraine war, perhaps indicating a larger technological shift precipitated by increased computing power and complex algorithms.[53]

By processing reams of complex data, LLMs can enable military planners to better understand an adversary's system and help soldiers answer doctrine-related questions about what choices the adversary might make.[54] Companies like Palantir suggest that emerging AI-powered platforms will soon be able to respond to requests as specific as 'which of our special forces units are closest to enemy tank positions and have sufficient supplies of *Javelin* missiles to mount an offensive?' and 'which specific tanks on the battlefield are most vulnerable to attack?'[55] The US military is reportedly using algorithms to sift through classified documents for information that can expedite decisions.[56]

As models improve, they may be able to spin out lucid text narratives of urgent crises in real time, including nuclear ones. This would involve far more than the issuance of simple statements about incoming missiles or enemy formations. Instead, LLMs could produce recommendations subject to 'interpretation and persuasion'.[57] In the fog of war, seemingly dispassionate, well-informed and objective suggestions from LLMs could lead commanders down escalatory pathways.

Equally concerning is the swift development of lethal autonomous weapons systems that make independent targeting decisions without direct human input. As developers improve the functioning of autonomous agents, militaries may be able to use them to help guide and advise drones about which sites to target and how to execute certain battlefield operations. This raises two concurrent problems. Firstly, categorising and assigning value to each bit of data in a battlefield environment remain inalterably human tasks. Accordingly, it is impossible to foresee all the different data vulnerabilities that autonomous systems might have, opening up the prospect that overreliance on them could produce multiple failures.[58] Secondly, researchers argue that the rush to develop autonomous weapons is ushering in a 'dehumanization of lethal force' as human operators increasingly delegate command authority to automated processes. The next generation of weapons systems will incorporate small, agile and mobile units that are operated remotely or autonomously from human operators, mass-produced at a low cost, simple to assemble and designed to kill 'at an industrial scale'.[59] LLMs could refine the operation of these weapons.[60] Affording AI-enhanced weapons to security forces like Russia's and Iran's, which already demonstrate few qualms about prosecuting brutal military campaigns resulting in the deaths of thousands of civilians, is a chilling prospect.

> *LLMs could lead commanders down escalatory pathways*

It is worth noting that the range of uses for LLMs in war is considerable. While many experts focus on AI's capacity to offer high-level strategic guidance or provide operational recommendations from synthesising streams of intelligence, other uses present themselves. For example, AI systems utilise unique cognitive approaches for problem-solving that can radically diverge from traditional military thinking. Harnessing AI systems to challenge conventional tactics and identify biases or flaws in strategy is a logical next step for militaries; indeed, it is already happening.[61] Even so, the full incorporation of generative AI into war planning or autonomous weapons faces significant hurdles. For one, there remains the pesky hallucination problem: generative-AI models continue to show a propensity for making up facts. In one notorious example, a New York lawyer filed a courtroom brief generated by ChatGPT that included numerous false citations of imaginary legal cases.[62] While such problems are probably surmountable, military planners will need to have greater confidence in the models' integrity before incorporating their output into operations. Pentagon officials have publicly evinced concerns about the battlefield accuracy of AI models, and they recently announced the setting up of a task force to analyse the utility of generative-AI tools in war.[63]

A second issue is the uncoupling of AI-generated conclusions from empirical observations. 'Insofar as operators and decision makers will often be unable or unwilling to consider the manner in which AI systems come to conclusions', note three analysts, 'complex machine-learning foundations stand to detach human deliberation from empirics. A commander or civilian leader fed probabilistic data about an impending attack might not know enough to question the validity of the conclusion.'[64] As algorithms increase in their complexity and accelerate the decision-making cycle, military planners will be forced to rely to a greater degree on AI-generated recommendations divorced from battlefield observation. Moreover, the tendency of automation to increase the tempo of decision-making will incentivise adversaries to increase their own use of automation. This dynamic could lead to heightened escalation risks. In addition, rival militaries will likely invest significant resources to manipulate data inputs to undermine the quality of the adversarial model's predictions.[65]

How soon will generative AI make a difference?

A key question is how quickly individuals and organisations will adopt generative AI effectively. Historically, new innovations require time to take root. Productive changes lag innovations, often by decades. Following the invention of the microprocessor by Gordon Moore in 1971, it took two decades for productivity efficiencies to kick in.[66] Paul David describes a 'productivity paradox' with respect to electrification, observing that realising the full benefit of electricity required a multistage process, from 'incremental technical improvements' to eventual 'confluence' with other streams of technological innovation.[67] Even if certain commercial sectors leap ahead to incorporate generative AI, its overall adoption will be uneven. Some sectors may actively resist it.

Military officers, in particular, often have ingrained preferences that can be hard to dislodge. In his classic account, Edward Katzenbach illuminated the reluctance of US cavalrymen to abandon their horses in favour of mechanised gasoline-powered vehicles, resulting in the persistent use of warhorses deep into the twentieth century.[68] Bureaucratic inertia and path dependencies can entrench organisations into using outdated technologies even in the face of the demonstrably superior performance of newer ones. Furthermore, 'prevailing assumptions about the use of force and role of military power, as strategic culture, can also bound the ways in which any innovation becomes the hardware and software for military power'.[69] The upshot is that militaries will adopt AI techniques to varying degrees. Some forces, like Ukraine's, will make the transition faster out of necessity. Other militaries will have a tougher time overcoming institutional obstacles. Some military leaders will assess new automated technologies critically and cautiously, rather than succumbing to the allure of the 'shiny object'.[70]

Several factors, however, make the relatively swift adoption of generative AI likely. While it is disruptive, it has not appeared out of thin air, but rather builds on existing IT infrastructure established over decades. Algorithms already play a significant role in people's lives, whether in determining what they see on social media, generating product recommendations or enabling facial-recognition surveillance. While LLMs offer novel ways to process large volumes of information and generate new insights, they do not require a radical alteration of hardware for commercial users. LLMs have proven useful for a wide variety of personal tasks, from editing assistance to writing code. Ordinary users do not require extensive time or training to figure out how to productively incorporate generative AI into their daily lives. ChatGPT's release in January 2023 garnered more than

100m users in two months, setting a record as the fastest-growing consumer application in history.[71]

There is also likely to be a rather short adoption lag among militaries. Michael Horowitz argues that rates of technological diffusion are contingent on two factors: an innovation's financial intensity and its organisational capital requirement.[72] While the costs of developing and training generative-AI models are high, the required resources pale in comparison to the costs of many routine weapons platforms. The cost of a single F-22 *Raptor*, for example, is $125m, roughly equal to that of developing the GPT-4 LLM.[73] In terms of capital requirements, militaries will need to recruit new personnel to develop LLMs, integrate them into weapons systems and command-and-control processes, and operate LLMs in battle. But many of the required skills are not radically different from those required to operate IT software already in use. Dual-use commercial applications involve far quicker cycles of innovation and diffusion.[74] Private capital investments, globalised trade and competition will likely accelerate military rates of adoption. Israel Defense Forces chief Eran Niv recently estimated that 'within a few years, every area of warfare will be based on generative-AI information. Without a strong and effective digital basis, no one will be able to prosecute a war in any area.'[75]

Responses

Given the challenges posed by generative AI to society, governance and war, what steps can governments take to manage its rise? There is a growing consensus that a comprehensive regulatory approach is needed. While several jurisdictions have crafted legislation to better manage AI systems, there is significant global fragmentation. At present, China is the only major power that explicitly regulates generative AI, although, as noted, the EU has moved in that direction.[76] In June 2023, the European Parliament passed draft AI legislation that is now being finalised.[77] Included in the legislation are provisions classifying generative-AI models as 'high risk' and subjecting them to bureaucratic oversight. The United States remains a laggard due to its prioritisation of commercial innovation over regulatory oversight. The White House has issued a strategic plan for AI that calls on regulatory agencies to develop public datasets, benchmarks and standards for measuring and evaluating the safety of AI systems.[78] It has also announced a set of 'voluntary commitments' from seven AI companies to establish technology safeguards.[79] But the strategy so far does not contemplate any enforcement authority, and its potential impact on product development and deterring potential risks is unclear.[80]

Private companies, meanwhile, have sent mixed messages. OpenAI CEO Sam Altman has expressed his support for more regulation, calling for a global body to oversee superintelligent machines and testifying to Congress about the benefits of establishing a domestic agency to regulate the technology. But OpenAI has also lobbied the EU to water down its AI regulations, even threatening to pull out of the European market.[81] Other firms have been hesitant to endorse establishing a central AI regulator. Google, for example, has argued for a 'hub and spoke' regulatory model that would divide oversight of AI technologies across a range of agencies rather than channelling it through a single entity.[82] Some critics contend that Big Tech's embrace of a byzantine regulatory configuration is primarily intended to throttle competitors with bureaucratic red tape or to distract regulators from more immediate problems such as biased algorithms.[83]

More attention should probably go to changing the risk calculus for companies. Casey Fiesler suggests that there is an 'ethical debt' that results from companies' failure to consider potential negative outcomes or societal harms from their products. She notes that as harms accrue – whether from biased data, growing disinformation or privacy violations – companies prefer to set aside potential risks in order to deal with them later.[84] In practice, this means that they are often never held accountable for the harm their products cause. Rather than permit them to 'move fast and break things', governments could mandate *ex ante* risk assessments for generative-AI products that could serve as the basis for remediation if harms do emerge. There is a powerful moral justification for switching the burden of proof to companies. As Deborah Raji and Abeba Birhane put it, 'if these powerful companies cannot release systems that meet the expectations of those most likely to be harmed by them, then their products are not ready to serve these communities and do not deserve widespread release'.[85]

In the military sphere, there is an even greater discrepancy between investments in AI systems and regulation of their use. Militaries are racing to develop autonomous weapons and to incorporate AI planning into their operations. The proliferation risks are significant due to a basic asymmetry: while leading AI models require immense investments in computing power for training, once the model has been trained, it requires far fewer resources to operate. Thus, observes Paul Scharre, 'access to large amounts of computing hardware is a barrier to training new models but not for using trained models, making AI much easier to proliferate than nuclear technology'.[86] This suggests that an AI arms race could arise without any mechanisms in place to limit inadvertent escalation, civilian harm or other unintended consequences.

*   *   *

Two areas require urgent international attention and engagement. Firstly, governments should devise common standards of behaviour governing the use of AI tools in militaries, from targeting to autonomous weapons. The United States issued updated guidance in February 2023, calling for the ethical and responsible military use of AI in accordance with international humanitarian law.[87] The US Defense Department has also endeavoured to provide a framework for responsible use of autonomous weapons systems.[88] This is a reasonable start, but the enforceability of US guidelines remains unclear and their applicability to generative-AI applications uncertain. Furthermore, other national militaries have lagged in adopting similar guidelines.

Secondly, governments should collectively determine appropriate responses to military events involving AI and autonomous systems, such as the accidental shootdown of a misidentified autonomous drone. Given the proliferation of AI-enabled weapons, the prospects for the accidental use of force and potential escalation are acute. Some experts are calling for deconfliction protocols to head off misjudgements. Lauren Kahn suggests instituting an 'Autonomous Incidents Agreement' that would set rules of expected conduct for military AI systems.[89]

Policymakers are just beginning to grapple with the larger effects of generative-AI technology and its implications for democracy, politics and war. As generative AI becomes more firmly embedded in society, it is critical to ask what incentives and motivations are spurring the use of these systems, and for what purposes. All of the challenges discussed in this article – to the integrity of political discourse, to resisting authoritarianism, to mitigating hacking and cyber attacks, to calibrating war planning and military operations – are still contingent on decisions made by individuals. It makes sense to devise concrete measures for blunting potential abuses sooner rather than later.

Acknowledgements

I would like to thank Tom Carothers, Matt O'Shaughnessy and Gavin Wilde for their valuable comments and feedback, and Brian (Chun Hey) Kot for his research assistance.

Notes

[1] See Rishi Bommasani et al., 'On the Opportunities and Risks of Foundation Models', Center for Research on Foundational Models, Stanford University, 12 July 2022, https://crfm.stanford.edu/assets/report.pdf; and Helen Toner, 'What Are Generative AI, Large Language Models, and Foundation Models?', Center for Security and Emerging Technology, Georgetown University, May 2023, https://cset.georgetown.edu/article/what-are-generative-ai-large-language-models-and-foundation-models/.

[2] See Kevin Roose, 'How Does ChatGPT Really Work?', New York Times, 28 March 2023, https://www.nytimes.com/2023/03/28/technology/ai-chatbots-chatgpt-bing-bard-llm.html.

[3] See Jordan Hoffmann et al., 'An Empirical Analysis of Compute-optimal Large Language Model Training', Google DeepMind, 12 April 2022, https://www.deepmind.com/blog/an-empirical-analysis-of-compute-optimal-large-language-model-training; and Pranshu Verma and Kevin Schaul, 'See Why AI Like ChatGPT Has Gotten So Good, So Fast', Washington Post, 24 May 2023, https://www.washingtonpost.com/business/interactive/2023/artificial-intelligence-tech-rapid-advances/.

[4] See Tom B. Brown et al., 'Language Models Are Few-shot Learners', 34th Conference on Neural Information Processing Systems (Neur IPS 2020), Vancouver, Canada, 22 July 2020, https://proceedings.neurips.cc/paper/2020/file/1457c0d6bfcb4967418b fb8ac142f64a-Paper.pdf.

[5] See Lukas Esterle, 'Deep Learning in Multiagent Systems', in Alexandros

Iosifidis and Anastasios Tefas (eds), *Deep Learning for Robot Perception and Cognition* (Cambridge, MA: Academic Press, 2022), pp. 435–60; and David Nield, 'Supercharge Your ChatGPT Prompts with Auto-GPT', *Wired*, 21 May 2023, https://www.wired.co.uk/article/chatgpt-prompts-auto-gpt. It is worth noting that the autonomy of an AI system sits on a spectrum, rather than being binary. While the goal of developers is to increase the ability of AI systems to complete increasingly complex tasks, this will be a slow evolution rather than a sudden jump in capabilities.

6   See Chloe Xiang, 'Developers Are Connecting Multiple AI Agents to Make More "Autonomous" AI', *Vice*, 4 April 2023, https://www.vice.com/en/article/epvdme/developers-are-connecting-multiple-ai-agents-to-make-more-autonomous-ai.

7   See Mark Sullivan, 'Auto-GPT and BabyAGI: How "Autonomous Agents" Are Bringing Generative AI to the Masses', *Fast Company*, 13 April 2023, https://www.fastcompany.com/90880294/auto-gpt-and-babyagi-how-autonomous-agents-are-bringing-generative-ai-to-the-masses.

8   See, for example, Josh Zumbrun, 'Why ChatGPT Is Getting Dumber at Basic Math', *Wall Street Journal*, 4 August 2023, https://www.wsj.com/articles/chatgpt-openai-math-artificial-intelligence-8aba83f0.

9   See, for example, Tristan Bove, 'Bill Gates Says that the A.I. Revolution Means Everyone Will Have Their Own "White Collar" Personal Assistant', *Fortune*, 6 May 2023, https://fortune.com/2023/03/22/bill-gates-ai-work-productivity-personal-assistants-chatgpt/.

10   Gary Marcus, 'Senate Testimony', US Senate Committee on the Judiciary, Subcommittee on Privacy, Technology, and the Law, 118th Congress, 16 May 2023, https://www.judiciary.senate.gov/imo/media/doc/2023-05-16%20-%20Testimony%20-%20Marcus.pdf.

11   See Davey Alba, 'OpenAI Chatbot Spits Out Biased Musings, Despite Guardrails', Bloomberg, 8 December 2022, https://www.bloomberg.com/news/newsletters/2022-12-08/chatgpt-open-ai-s-chatbot-is-spitting-out-biased-sexist-results.

12   See Emily M. Bender et al., 'On the Dangers of Stochastic Parrots: Can Language Models Be Too Big?', *Proceedings of the 2021 ACM Conference on Fairness, Accountability, and Transparency*, March 2021, pp. 610–23, https://dl.acm.org/doi/pdf/10.1145/3442188.3445922.

13   Hannes Bajohr, 'Whoever Controls Language Models Controls Politics', 8 April 2023, https://hannesbajohr.de/en/2023/04/08/whoever-controls-language-models-controls-politics/.

14   *Ibid.*

15   See Steven Feldstein, 'Evaluating Europe's Push to Enact AI Regulations: How Will This Influence Global Norms?', *Democratization*, 2023, pp. 1–18.

16   See Kayleen Devlin and Joshua Cheetham, 'Fake Trump Arrest Photos: How to Spot an AI-generated Image', BBC News, 24 March 2023, https://www.bbc.com/news/world-us-canada-65069316.

17   'Beat Biden', YouTube, 25 April 2023, https://www.youtube.

com/watch?v=kLMMxgtxQ1Y. See also Isaac Stanley-Becker and John Wagner, 'Republicans Counter Biden Announcement with Dystopian, AI-aided Video', *Washington Post*, 25 April 2023, https://www.washingtonpost.com/politics/2023/04/25/rnc-biden-ad-ai/.

18 See Andrew R. Sorkin et al., 'An A.I.-generated Spoof Rattles the Markets', *New York Times*, 23 May 2023, https://www.nytimes.com/2023/05/23/business/ai-picture-stock-market.html.

19 See Josh A. Goldstein et al., 'Generative Language Models and Automated Influence Operations: Emerging Threats and Potential Mitigations', January 2023, https://cdn.openai.com/papers/forecasting-misuse.pdf.

20 See Thor Benson, 'Brace Yourself for the 2024 Deepfake Election', *Wired*, 27 April 2023, https://www.wired.com/story/chatgpt-generative-ai-deepfake-2024-us-presidential-election/.

21 Goldstein et al., 'Generative Language Models and Automated Influence Operations'.

22 Josh A. Goldstein and Girish Sastry, 'The Coming Age of AI-powered Propaganda', *Foreign Affairs*, 27 April 2023, https://www.foreignaffairs.com/united-states/coming-age-ai-powered-propaganda.

23 See Ben M. Tappin et al., 'Quantifying the Potential Persuasive Returns to Political Microtargeting', *Proceedings of the National Academy of Sciences*, vol. 120, no. 25, June 2023, https://www.pnas.org/doi/10.1073/pnas.2216261120. The literature on disinformation is not settled about how much false online information

impacts and undermines democracy. See, for example, Jon Bateman et al., 'Measuring the Effects of Influence Operations: Key Findings and Gaps from Empirical Research', Carnegie Endowment for International Peace – PCIO Baseline, 28 June 2021, https://carnegieendowment.org/2021/06/28/measuring-effects-of-influence-operations-key-findings-and-gaps-from-empirical-research-pub-84824; and Joshua A. Tucker et al., 'Social Media, Political Polarization, and Political Disinformation: A Review of the Scientific Literature', Hewlett Foundation, 19 March 2018, https://hewlett.org/library/social-media-political-polarization-political-disinformation-review-scientific-literature/.

24 See Nathan E. Sanders and Bruce Schneier, 'How ChatGPT Hijacks Democracy', *New York Times*, 15 January 2023, https://www.nytimes.com/2023/01/15/opinion/ai-chatgpt-lobbying-democracy.html.

25 See Sarah Kreps and Douglas Kriner, 'How Generative AI Impacts Democratic Engagement', Brookings Institution, 21 March 2023, https://www.brookings.edu/articles/how-generative-ai-impacts-democratic-engagement/.

26 See Steven Feldstein, 'The Global Expansion of AI Surveillance', Carnegie Endowment for International Peace, September 2019, https://carnegieendowment.org/2019/09/17/global-expansion-of-ai-surveillance-pub-79847; Steven Feldstein, 'How Artificial Intelligence Is Reshaping Repression', *Journal of Democracy*, vol. 30, no. 1, January 2019,

pp. 40–52; Steven Feldstein, *The Rise of Digital Repression: How Technology Is Reshaping Power, Politics, and Resistance* (New York: Oxford University Press, 2021); Andrea Kendall-Taylor et al., 'The Digital Dictators', *Foreign Affairs*, vol. 99, no. 2, March/April 2020, pp. 103–15; and Nicholas Wright, 'How Artificial Intelligence Will Reshape the Global Order', *Foreign Affairs*, 10 July 2018, https://www.foreignaffairs.com/articles/world/2018-07-10/how-artificial-intelligence-will-reshape-global-order.

27 Samantha Hoffman, 'Programming China: The Communist Party's Autonomic Approach to Managing State Security', MERICS, 12 December 2017, https://merics.org/sites/default/files/2020-05/Programming%20China.pdf.

28 Steven Feldstein, 'The Global Struggle Over AI Surveillance', National Endowment for Democracy, June 2022, https://www.ned.org/global-struggle-over-ai-surveillance-emerging-trends-democratic-responses/.

29 See Dahlia Peterson, 'How China Harnesses Data Fusion to Make Sense of Surveillance Data', Brookings Institution, 23 September 2021, https://www.brookings.edu/articles/how-china-harnesses-data-fusion-to-make-sense-of-surveillance-data/.

30 Cissy Zhou, 'China Tells Big Tech Companies Not to Offer ChatGPT Services', Nikkei Asia, 22 February 2023, https://asia.nikkei.com/Business/China-tech/China-tells-big-tech-companies-not-to-offer-ChatGPT-services. The list of countries in which ChatGPT is inaccessible, as of June 2023, predictably includes many authoritarian states, such as Afghanistan, China, Cuba, Iran, North Korea, Russia and Syria. Notably, Italy is also included on the list due to a ruling by its data-protection watchdog that OpenAI may be in breach of Europe's privacy regulations. See Ryan Browne, 'Italy Became the First Western Country to Ban ChatGPT. Here's What Other Countries Are Doing', CNBC, 4 April 2023, https://www.cnbc.com/2023/04/04/italy-has-banned-chatgpt-heres-what-other-countries-are-doing.html; and Jon Martindale, 'These Are the Countries Where ChatGPT Is Currently Banned', *Digital Trends*, 12 April 2023, https://www.digitaltrends.com/computing/these-countries-chatgpt-banned/.

31 See Channing Lee, 'From ChatGPT to Chat CCP: The Future of Generative AI Models in China', *Georgetown Security Studies Review*, 3 March 2023, https://georgetownsecuritystudiesreview.org/2023/03/03/from-chatgpt-to-chat-ccp-the-future-of-generative-ai-models-in-china/.

32 See Sophia Yang, 'China's ChatGPT-style Bot ChatYuan Suspended Over Questions About Xi', *Taiwan News*, 11 February 2023, https://www.taiwannews.com.tw/en/news/4807319. A Chinese CEO reportedly quipped that 'China's LLMs are not even allowed to count to 10, as that would include the numbers eight and nine – a reference to the state's sensitivity about the number 89 and any discussion of the 1989 Tiananmen Square protests'. Quoted in Helen Toner et al., 'The Illusion of China's AI Prowess', *Foreign Affairs*, 2 June 2023,

https://www.foreignaffairs.com/china/illusion-chinas-ai-prowess-regulation.

33 See Paul Triolo, 'ChatGPT and China: How to Think About Large Language Models and the Generative AI Race', China Project, 12 April 2023, https://thechinaproject.com/2023/04/12/chatgpt-and-china-how-to-think-about-large-language-models-and-the-generative-ai-race/.

34 See Meaghan Tobin, 'China Announces Rules to Keep AI Bound by "Core Socialist Values"', *Washington Post*, 14 July 2023, https://www.washingtonpost.com/world/2023/07/14/china-ai-regulations-chatgpt-socialist/.

35 See Helen Toner et al., 'How Will China's Generative AI Regulations Shape the Future? A DigiChina Forum', DigiChina, Stanford University, 19 April 2023, https://digichina.stanford.edu/work/how-will-chinas-generative-ai-regulations-shape-the-future-a-digichina-forum/.

36 Toner et al., 'The Illusion of China's AI Prowess'.

37 Training GPT-3 required 1.3 gigawatt-hours of electricity (equivalent to powering 121 homes in the United States for a year) and cost $4.6m. The training costs for GPT-4 are far higher, likely exceeding $100m. See 'Large, Creative AI Models Will Transform Lives and Labour Markets', *The Economist*, 22 April 2023, https://www.economist.com/interactive/science-and-technology/2023/04/22/large-creative-ai-models-will-transform-how-we-live-and-work.

38 See Lisa Barrington, 'Abu Dhabi Makes Its Falcon 40B AI Model Open Source', Reuters, 25 May 2023, https://www.reuters.com/technology/abu-dhabi-makes-its-falcon-40b-ai-model-open-source-2023-05-25/.

39 See Cade Metz and Mike Isaac, 'In Battle Over A.I., Meta Decides to Give Away Its Crown Jewels', *New York Times*, 18 May 2023, https://www.nytimes.com/2023/05/18/technology/ai-meta-open-source.html.

40 See, for example, Rebecca Tan, 'Facebook Helped Bring Free Speech to Vietnam. Now It's Helping Stifle It', *Washington Post*, 19 June 2023, https://www.washingtonpost.com/world/2023/06/19/facebook-meta-vietnam-government-censorship/.

41 See Catherine Stupp, 'Fraudsters Used AI to Mimic CEO's Voice in Unusual Cybercrime Case', *Wall Street Journal*, 30 August 2019, https://www.wsj.com/articles/fraudsters-use-ai-to-mimic-ceos-voice-in-unusual-cybercrime-case-11567157402.

42 Leah Nylen, 'FTC's Khan Says Enforcers Need to Be "Vigilant Early" with AI', Bloomberg, 1 June 2023, https://www.bloomberg.com/news/articles/2023-06-02/ftc-s-khan-says-enforcers-need-to-be-vigilant-early-with-ai.

43 See Matt Burgess, 'The Hacking of ChatGPT Is Just Getting Started', *Wired*, 13 April 2023, https://www.wired.com/story/chatgpt-jailbreak-generative-ai-hacking/; and Kyle Wiggers, 'Can AI Really Be Protected from Text-based Attacks?', *TechCrunch*, 24 February 2023, https://techcrunch.com/2023/02/24/can-language-models-really-be-protected-from-text-based-attacks/?guccounter=1.

44 See Europol, 'ChatGPT: The Impact of Large Language Models on Law Enforcement', Tech Watch Flash Report from the Europol Innovation

Lab, 27 March 2023, https://www.europol.europa.eu/cms/sites/default/files/documents/Tech%20Watch%20Flash%20-%20The%20Impact%20of%20Large%20Language%20Models%20on%20Law%20Enforcement.pdf.

45 *Ibid*.

46 See Andrew J. Lohn and Krystal A. Jackson, 'Will AI Make Cyber Swords or Shields?', Georgetown University's Center for Security and Emerging Technology, August 2022, https://cset.georgetown.edu/wp-content/uploads/CSET-Will-AI-Make-Cyber-Swords-or-Shields.pdf.

47 See Steven Feldstein and Brian Kot, 'Why Does the Global Spyware Industry Continue to Thrive? Trends, Explanations, and Responses', Carnegie Endowment for International Peace, working paper, March 2023, https://carnegieendowment.org/2023/03/14/why-does-global-spyware-industry-continue-to-thrive-trends-explanations-and-responses-pub-89229.

48 Ronald J. Deibert, 'The Autocrat in Your iPhone', *Foreign Affairs*, 12 December 2022, https://www.foreignaffairs.com/world/autocrat-in-your-iphone-mercenary-spyware-ronald-deibert.

49 Europol, 'ChatGPT'.

50 See Thomas Gaulkin, 'What Happened When WMD Experts Tried to Make the GPT-4 AI Do Bad Things', *Bulletin of the Atomic Scientists*, 30 March 2023, https://thebulletin.org/2023/03/what-happened-when-wmd-experts-tried-to-make-the-gpt-4-ai-do-bad-things/.

51 Lauren Kahn, 'Ground Rules for the Age of AI Warfare', *Foreign Affairs*, 6 June 2023, https://www.foreignaffairs.com/world/ground-rules-age-ai-warfare.

52 See David Ignatius, 'How the Algorithm Tipped the Balance in Ukraine', *Washington Post*, 19 December 2022, https://www.washingtonpost.com/opinions/2022/12/19/palantir-algorithm-data-ukraine-war/; and Kahn, 'Ground Rules for the Age of AI Warfare'.

53 See John Antal, *7 Seconds to Die: A Military Analysis of the Second Nagorno-Karabakh War and the Future of Warfighting* (Philadelphia, PA: Casemate, 2022); and Kelsey Atherton, 'Loitering Munitions Preview the Autonomous Future of Warfare', Brookings Institution, 4 August 2021, https://www.brookings.edu/techstream/loitering-munitions-preview-the-autonomous-future-of-warfare/.

54 See Benjamin Jensen and Dan Tadross, 'How Large-language Models Can Revolutionize Military Planning', *War on the Rocks*, 12 April 2023, https://warontherocks.com/2023/04/how-large-language-models-can-revolutionize-military-planning/.

55 Alexander Karp, 'Our New Platform – A Letter from the Chief Executive Officer', Palantir, 7 April 2023, https://www.palantir.com/newsroom/letters/our-new-platform/.

56 See Alexander Ward et al., 'Trump: "Used to Talk About" Ukraine Invasion with Putin', *Politico*, 11 May 2023, https://www.politico.com/newsletters/national-security-daily/2023/05/11/trump-used-to-talk-about-ukraine-invasion-with-putin-00096394.

57 Ross Andersen, 'Never Give Artificial Intelligence the Nuclear

Codes', *Atlantic*, June 2023, https://www.theatlantic.com/magazine/archive/2023/06/ai-warfare-nuclear-weapons-strike/673780/.

58 See Arthur Holland Michel, 'Known Unknowns: Data Issues and Military Autonomous Systems', UNIDIR, 17 May 2021, https://unidir.org/known-unknowns.

59 Frederik Federspiel et al., 'Threats by Artificial Intelligence to Human Health and Human Existence', *BMJ Global Health*, vol. 8, no. 5, May 2023, e010435, https://doi.org/10.1136/bmjgh-2022-010435.

60 See Michael Hirsh, 'How AI Will Revolutionize Warfare', *Foreign Policy*, 11 April 2023, https://foreignpolicy.com/2023/04/11/ai-arms-race-artificial-intelligence-chatgpt-military-technology/.

61 See Paul Scharre, 'AI's Inhuman Advantage', *War on the Rocks*, 10 April 2023, https://warontherocks.com/2023/04/ais-inhuman-advantage/.

62 See Benjamin Weiser and Nate Schweber, 'The ChatGPT Lawyer Explains Himself', *New York Times*, 8 June 2023, https://www.nytimes.com/2023/06/08/nyregion/lawyer-chatgpt-sanctions.html. See also Stew Magnuson, 'Just In: Pentagon's Top AI Official Addresses ChatGPT's Possible Benefits, Risks', *National Defense*, 8 March 2023, https://www.nationaldefensemagazine.org/articles/2023/3/8/pentagons-top-ai-official-addresses-chatgpts-possible-benefits-risks.

63 US Department of Defense, 'DOD Announces Establishment of Generative AI Task Force', 10 August 2023, https://www.defense.gov/News/Releases/Release/Article/3489803/dod-announces-establishment-of-generative-ai-task-force/. See also Mohar Chatterjee, 'Hackers in Vegas Take on AI', *Politico*, 14 August 2023, https://www.politico.com/newsletters/digital-future-daily/2023/08/14/hackers-in-vegas-take-on-ai-00111145.

64 Benjamin M. Jensen et al., 'Algorithms at War: The Promise, Peril, and Limits of Artificial Intelligence', *International Studies Review*, vol. 22, no. 3, September 2020, p. 537.

65 See Avi Goldfarb and Jon R. Lindsay, 'Prediction and Judgment: Why Artificial Intelligence Increases the Importance of Humans in War', *International Security*, vol. 46, no. 3, Winter 2021/2022, pp. 7–50.

66 See Paul Krugman, 'AI May Change Everything, But Probably Not Too Quickly', *New York Times*, 31 March 2023, https://www.nytimes.com/2023/03/31/opinion/ai-chatgpt-jobs-economy.html.

67 Paul A. David, 'The Dynamo and the Computer: An Historical Perspective on the Modern Productivity Paradox', *American Economic Review*, vol. 80, no. 2, May 1990, p. 356.

68 See Edward L. Katzenbach, Jr, 'The Horse Cavalry in the Twentieth Century: A Study in Policy Response', *Public Policy*, vol. 7, 1958, pp. 120–49.

69 Jensen et al., 'Algorithms at War'.

70 Stephanie Carvin, 'How Not to War', *International Affairs*, vol. 98, no. 5, September 2022, pp. 1,695–716.

71 Krystal Hu, 'ChatGPT Sets Record for Fastest-growing User Base', Reuters, 2 February 2023, https://www.reuters.com/technology/chatgpt-sets-record-

fastest-growing-user-base-analyst-note-2023-02-01/.

72 See Michael C. Horowitz, *The Diffusion of Military Power* (Princeton, NJ: Princeton University Press, 2010).

73 See Michael E. O'Hanlon, 'The Plane Truth: Fewer F-22s Mean a Stronger National Defense', Brookings Institution, 1 September 1999, https://www.brookings.edu/research/the-plane-truth-fewer-f-22s-mean-a-stronger-national-defense/.

74 See, for example, Audrey Kurth Cronin, *Power to the People: How Open Technological Innovation Is Arming Tomorrow's Terrorists* (Oxford: Oxford University Press, 2019); Ben FitzGerald and Jacqueline Parziale, 'As Technology Goes Democratic, Nations Lose Military Control', *Bulletin of the Atomic Scientists*, vol. 73, no. 2, 2017, pp. 102–7; and Emily O. Goldman and Leslie C. Eliason, *The Diffusion of Military Technology and Ideas* (Stanford, CA: Stanford University Press, 2003).

75 Yonah Jeremy Bob, 'IDF Will Run Entirely on Generative AI Within a Few Years – Israeli Cyber Chief', *Jerusalem Post*, 28 June 2023, https://www.jpost.com/israel-news/defense-news/article-748028.

76 See 'Regulators Target Deepfakes', *Batch*, 25 January 2023, https://www.deeplearning.ai/the-batch/chinas-new-law-limits-ai-generated-media/.

77 See Feldstein, 'Evaluating Europe's Push to Enact AI Regulations'; and Adam Satariano, 'Europeans Take a Major Step Toward Regulating AI', *New York Times*, 14 June 2023, https://www.nytimes.com/2023/06/14/technology/europe-ai-regulation.html.

78 See Select Committee on Artificial Intelligence of the National Science and Technology Council, 'National Artificial Intelligence Research and Development Strategic Plan 2023 Update', May 2023, https://www.whitehouse.gov/wp-content/uploads/2023/05/National-Artificial-Intelligence-Research-and-Development-Strategic-Plan-2023-Update.pdf.

79 See Michael D. Shear, Cecilia Kang and David E. Sanger, 'Pressured by Biden, A.I. Companies Agree to Guardrails on New Tools', *New York Times*, 21 July 2023, https://www.nytimes.com/2023/07/21/us/politics/ai-regulation-biden.html.

80 The G7 also have announced the 'Hiroshima AI Process', an inter-governmental task force designed to investigate the risks of generative AI. The initiative aims to increase collaboration on topics such as governance, safeguarding intellectual-property rights, transparency, disinformation and responsible use of AI technologies. How much influence it will have remains to be seen. See White House, 'G7 Hiroshima Leaders' Communiqué', 20 May 2023, https://www.whitehouse.gov/briefing-room/statements-releases/2023/05/20/g7-hiroshima-leaders-communique/.

81 See 'Governance of Superintelligence', OpenAI, 22 May 2023, https://openai.com/blog/governance-of-superintelligence; and Billy Perrigo, 'Exclusive: OpenAI Lobbied the EU to Water Down AI Regulation', *Time*, 20 June 2023, https://time.com/6288245/openai-eu-lobbying-ai-act/.

82 See Cristiano Lima, 'Google Bucks Calls for a New AI Regulator',

Washington Post, 13 June 2023, https://www.washingtonpost.com/politics/2023/06/13/google-bucks-calls-new-ai-regulator/.

83 See 'Why Tech Giants Want to Strangle AI with Red Tape', *The Economist*, 25 May 2023, https://www.economist.com/business/2023/05/25/why-tech-giants-want-to-strangle-ai-with-red-tape; and Matteo Wong, 'AI Doomerism Is a Decoy', *Atlantic*, 2 June 2023, https://www.theatlantic.com/technology/archive/2023/06/ai-regulation-sam-altman-bill-gates/674278/.

84 See Casey Fiesler, 'AI Has Social Consequences, But Who Pays the Price?', *Conversation*, 18 April 2023, https://theconversation.com/ai-has-social-consequences-but-who-pays-the-price-tech-companies-problem-with-ethical-debt-203375.

85 Abeba Birhane and Deborah Raji, 'ChatGPT, Galactica, and the Progress Trap', *Wired*, 9 December 2022, https://www.wired.com/story/large-language-models-critique/.

86 Paul Scharre, 'AI's Gatekeepers Aren't Prepared for What's Coming', *Foreign Policy*, 19 June 2023, https://foreignpolicy.com/2023/06/19/ai-regulation-development-us-china-competition-technology/.

87 See US Department of State, 'Political Declaration of Responsible Military Use of Artificial Intelligence and Autonomy', 16 February 2023, https://www.state.gov/political-declaration-on-responsible-military-use-of-artificial-intelligence-and-autonomy/.

88 See US Department of Defense, 'DoD Announces Update to DoD Directive 3000.09', 25 January 2023, https://www.defense.gov/News/Releases/Release/Article/3278076/dod-announces-update-to-dod-directive-300009-autonomy-in-weapon-systems/.

89 See Kahn, 'Ground Rules for the Age of AI Warfare'.

Ana Montes: An (Almost) Perfect Spy

Russell Crandall

Code Name Blue Wren: The True Story of America's Most Dangerous Female Spy – and the Sister She Betrayed
Jim Popkin. New York: Hanover Square Press, 2023. $27.99. 352 pp.

On 21 September 2001, Ana Belén Montes was arrested at her cubicle at the US Defense Intelligence Agency (DIA) – the Pentagon's version of the CIA. Her outing as a double agent for Havana came as a tremendous shock to her DIA colleagues who, for more than 15 years, had esteemed the high-flying analyst for her methodical approach, self-effacing personality and brilliant mind. The bilingual Montes had enjoyed an exemplary career, winning one intelligence-community award after another. Before long, she was the senior intelligence analyst on Cuba, regularly briefing the Joint Chiefs of Staff and the National Security Council at the White House. With ready access to America's most sensitive secrets, she also composed the initial draft of a much-discussed Department of Defense report contending that Cuba had a 'limited capacity' to harm the United States.[1] Across the Executive Branch, she was known as the 'Queen of Cuba', since *no one* knew the island better than she did. What everyone failed to realise was that, in addition to working for the DIA, she was also working for the Castros.

Russell Crandall is a professor of American foreign policy and international politics at Davidson College in North Carolina, and has served as a contributing editor to *Survival*. His new book is *Forging Latin America: Profiles in Power and Ideas, 1492 to Today* (Rowman & Littlefield, 2024).

Survival | vol. 65 no. 5 | October–November 2023 | pp. 143–152 https://doi.org/10.1080/00396338.2023.2261261

Much like fellow American spies Aldrich Ames and Robert Hanssen, who worked for the Soviets during the Cold War, Montes was a study in how to live a double life. For more than 17 years she worked for the Cuban intelligence service, listening to secret messages on a short-wave radio, passing encrypted files to Cuban handlers in Washington and even travelling to Havana for debriefings, where she is known to have been honoured for outstanding service. Among the secrets she shared with Havana were the names of American spies in Cuba and sensitive details of a military-surveillance satellite.

As author Jim Popkin writes in *Code Name Blue Wren*, Montes may well be the most famous (and certainly most famous *female*) spy you've never heard of.[2] With the Twin Towers still smouldering at the time of her arrest, her case received little media attention despite her being possibly the most successful spy ever recruited by Cuba.

Birth of a radical

Born in 1957 to parents of Puerto Rican descent (her father was a US Army doctor), Montes was a bookish, straight-A student. During her junior year of college (she attended the University of Virginia), she spent some time in Spain, where she fell in love with a 20-something Argentine radical who had fled his nation's Dirty War – a conflict in which Argentina's government systematically targeted leftist revolutionaries. There was unrest in Spain too: many on the Spanish left were incensed about Washington's protracted support for the Franco dictatorship that had ruled Spain for decades, and Montes would have observed protest after protest against *yanqui* imperialism. These influences were to push her toward a position of outspoken militancy. According to Popkin, 'she learned firsthand how the US manhandled its Latin American neighbors and frequently propped up brutal dictators who killed, tortured, and kidnapped leftists and other pro-democracy activists' (p. 58). She concluded that communism was a far better solution to the world's problems than US-dominated capitalism and so-called 'democracy'. By the time she returned to Virginia, Montes had added Puerto Rican independence to her swelling list of causes.

Within a few years of graduation, Montes scored an entry-level job at the US Department of Justice. Despite her junior rank, within a few months she was granted top-secret security clearance with access to 'Sensitive Compartmentalized Information'. At the same time, Montes enrolled as an international-economics and Latin American studies major at the elite Johns Hopkins University's School of Advanced International Studies (SAIS) in Washington. It was at SAIS that Montes met and befriended Marta Rita Velázquez, who had been recruited by the Cuban intelligence service in 1983 to act as a kind of talent scout with responsibility for notifying Cuban officials about bright, ambitious university students who might end up in high-level positions in the US government.[3] In common with millions of Americans and others around the world, many SAIS students adored the Marxist revolutionary movement in Nicaragua known as the Sandinistas, who had deposed the US-backed Somoza dynasty in the late 1970s. These self-styled 'Sandalistas' (so called because many of them wore hippy-esque sandals) despised the Reagan administration for illegally and inhumanely backing the Contras, the rightist insurgency trying to end the Sandinistas' social revolution. In Popkin's view, Montes's time at SAIS – including her classes with a man describing himself as the school's 'most left-wing professor', the Italian-born Piero Gleijeses – had a 'reinforcing peer effect' (p. 75).

As it turned out, Montes was not the only SAIS student to become a Cuban spy. Walter Kendall Myers, a high-level intelligence official with the US Department of State who received his doctorate at SAIS and subsequently taught there, also spied for Havana for 30 years – even receiving a private audience with Fidel Castro. He was arrested, along with his wife Gwendolyn, in 2009, receiving a life sentence after pleading guilty the following year.

Spies like us

In December 1984, Velázquez brought Montes to New York, where she was introduced to a Cuban intelligence officer who duly recruited her.

In March 1985, Velázquez and Montes travelled to Madrid, where Cuban officials provided them with new clothes, false passports and other documents for an undercover trip to Havana, where the women received extensive espionage training, including lessons on how to decode and encrypt high-frequency radio messages, and allegedly how to beat polygraph tests. Cuban intelligence also urged Montes to move to the DIA, and she dutifully applied for a position there upon returning to Washington, using Velázquez as a character reference. One might have expected her background to raise some red flags, but the DIA demonstrated a woeful lack of due diligence when hiring Montes, according to Popkin. For starters, she lied about her cocaine use, which at SAIS had been significant. Nor did the DIA inquire about her sympathies for Puerto Rican independence, which might have raised questions about her loyalty to Uncle Sam. Montes was not required to undergo a polygraph test, which would have been mandatory at the National Security Agency (NSA) or the CIA. Montes also lied about being a SAIS graduate – an outstanding loan of roughly $2,000 had prevented her from officially graduating.

In September 1985, Montes began work at the DIA as an intelligence analyst. Her initial portfolio covered Central America, especially war-torn El Salvador and Nicaragua. By the early 1990s, both countries had ended their internal wars, meaning that her entire justification for spying for Cuba – to help the Sandinistas and like-minded rebels in El Salvador – had dissipated. She decided that Cuba still needed her help because it was being bullied by the US. Soon she was in the perfect position to be of assistance: due to her superlative performance, Montes was promoted to the Cuba desk in 1993.

A key reason why Montes's spying went under the radar for so long is that she did not steal or even borrow government documents. Instead, she memorised the secret material at the office and then typed it up on her laptop (which the Cubans had helped her to purchase) at home. Every couple of weeks she would hand over a computer disk to a Cuban handler in a public place, which was easily the riskiest part of her routine. She even gave disks to handlers in Cuba itself when she travelled to the island on DIA business. Havana would also send her numeric codes via high-frequency short-wave radio messages, which Montes would jot down on water-soluble paper that she could later dissolve. As Popkin explains:

> There would be typically a woman in a recording studio in Havana, and she would read a series of 150 digits in little spaces of five, so – in Spanish, little groups of numbers. And it would be broadcast on a shortwave radio frequency. Ana knew the frequency, and she knew what time to listen.
>
> And so, to the normal person, it's just gobbledygook, right? It's just a bunch of numbers. But Ana would record it. She had an earpiece, and she would listen in her apartment in Cleveland Park, write it down, and then type it into her Toshiba laptop. And she had the crypto codes that would decode it, and that was primarily the way that the Cubans gave her instructions.[4]

With such simple methods, Montes managed to betray her country for years. Indeed, Popkin is of the view that the careers of Montes, Velázquez and Myers demonstrate how Havana's intelligence outfit managed to run rings round its far bigger and better-funded US counterpart. All they needed was a radio, a basic computer and a good memory.

Caught, finally

Until a few years before her arrest, no one had any suspicions about Montes, but there were growing signs that the Cubans were at work in America. During the early 1990s, Havana hatched *Operación Avispa* (*Operation Wasp*), deploying US-based spies in an attempt to penetrate Cuban–US organisations and even US military facilities.[5] The FBI broke up the operation by arresting scores of Cubans in 1998 and recovering wigs, fake IDs, hard drives and, crucially, encryption codes.

The disruption of *Operation Wasp* affected Montes directly. Havana severely restricted her handlers' interactions with her, causing her bouts of acute anxiety and depression. 'Spying, it turns out, is a lot more Bourne than Bond', says Popkin. 'It's a lonely, tortured mess of a life … A lifetime of deceit took its toll' (p. 17). Even worse, someone was now on her trail – a counter-intelligence analyst referred to by Popkin as 'Elena Valdez', who started her career at the NSA when Montes began at the DIA. Telling her story for the first time in *Code Name Blue Wren*, Popkin reports that Valdez was six when her family fled post-revolutionary Cuba in the 1960s to resettle in Florida. At the NSA, Valdez was proud that she could serve her adopted country by resisting Castro's regime. According to Popkin, 'while Ana was full of romantic notions about the Revolution, Elena harbored a burning contempt for the Communists of the Castro regime. The two women, who joined the US Intelligence Community just a year apart, never met. And yet they were on intersecting paths, headed for a collision' (p. 95).

It may be that Valdez came across the captured Cuban encryption codes while working at the NSA, but regardless of how she figured it out, her investigation into the short-wave broadcasts led her to believe that Havana was running an agent – 'Agent S' – whom Valdez was convinced was someone high up in the US intelligence community. There was also tantalising evidence that Agent S had visited Guantánamo Bay in July 1996, had a student loan paid off by Havana and possessed a Toshiba laptop.

Valdez quickly brought her evidence to the FBI, which sat on it for two years. Analysts there assumed, not unreasonably, that the spy would be male given that 95% of US spies had been men, going back to the Cold War. Fed up, Valdez risked her career (doing so a second time by talking to Popkin) by bypassing the FBI and going directly to the DIA, Montes's home agency. It took almost no time for the DIA to connect the dots between the July 1996 Guantánamo visits and Montes, among other links. They had their suspect, and by 2000, the case had been code-named 'Blue Wren'. Hard evidence was not long in coming: one of multiple searches of her condo produced the Toshiba machine Montes had used to type up the classified information she had memorised.

Once caught, all spies face the ultimate question: why did you do it? Popkin's assessment concludes that Montes's motives in betraying her country were almost entirely ideological, not financial.[6] Her former professor Gleijeses concurred: 'She did it for idealistic reasons. One can agree or disagree, that's a different story but she did it for idealistic reasons' (p. 76). Yet her country was not the only victim of her betrayal. *Blue Wren* exposes the extent to which Montes's own remarkable family, which included no fewer than four FBI employees, had been let down by her. Not one of them had ever suspected Montes, even though, in an almost incredible coincidence, her younger sister Lucy had been a member of the FBI task force that had exposed *Operation Wasp*. 'As Ana was blithely disclosing the true names of CIA officers operating undercover in Havana', Popkin writes, 'her sister, Lucy, joined a top-secret task force run by the FBI and NSA to rid Miami of Cuban spies' (p. 17). When the truth finally came out, Lucy's reaction was one of astonishment: 'It never entered my mind that my sister would be capable of such a thing' (p. 18).

'Do it no wrong'

The case against Montes was air-tight given the incriminating material and devices discovered at her condo, and serious given the duration and scale of her espionage.[7] It is noteworthy that none of the American operatives active in Cuba who had been exposed by Montes were killed by Havana, although there is an ongoing debate about whether she gave Havana intelligence that was passed to the FMLN guerrilla group in El Salvador, which then attacked a Salvadoran military base, killing 43 troops and one US Green Beret. (Montes had just visited the facility as part of an orientation trip to El Salvador during its internal war.) In the end, the prosecution did not bring any charges related to this episode, which would have likely meant a life sentence.

In 2002, Montes pleaded guilty to conspiracy to spy for Cuba, but displayed very little repentance during a brief hearing that autumn. According to her, she had been true to her 'conscience rather than the law', believing that US policy toward Cuba was 'cruel'.[8] US District Court Judge Ricardo Urbina, also of Puerto Rican descent, was scathing in his response:

> If you cannot love your country, at least you should do it no wrong. You decided to put the U.S. in harm's way. You must pay the penalty.[9]

Urbina sentenced her to 25 years behind bars.

Despite her defence team's plea that she be sent to a low-security prison, Montes served 20 years at a 'supermax' federal facility for female prisoners near Fort Worth, Texas, which housed, among others, al-Qaeda terrorists, murderers on death row and even the spouse of Mexican cartel boss Joaquín 'El Chapo' Guzmán (p. 289). In a 2013 letter, Montes described the prison as 'a combat zone tucked inside of a madhouse' (p. 20). One of her closest friends on the inside was executed by lethal injection.

Montes may have experienced 'psychological hell' inside the prison, but outwardly she maintained her defiant stance. Indeed, Popkin argues that the arrest and incarceration 'only intensified her self-righteousness'. In a 2010 letter to Lucy's son, Matthew, then still a teenager, she wrote: 'Prison is one of the last places I would have ever chosen to be in, but some things in life are worth going to prison for – or worth doing and then killing yourself before you have to spend too much time in prison, which is my personal preference' (p. 299).[10] In correspondence with her immediate family, she revealed a little of the mania that must have facilitated her actions: 'I am a person who is extremely rigid, compulsive, tied to stupid habits, and if I forgot to mention RIGID, characteristics that have only gotten worse with age and make my stay here more difficult' (p. 299). Her self-professed rigidity and compulsiveness meant that once she had decided to help Cuba, there was no room for doubt or internal moral debates. Even so, she confessed while still in prison that 'I don't owe allegiance to the US or to Cuba … or to the Castro brothers or even to God' (p. 301).

In January 2023, Montes was released early on account of good behaviour, and soon moved to Puerto Rico.[11] Judge Urbina had ruled that, upon her release, she should be on supervision for five years, a period during which her internet access would be restricted and communications with foreign governments blocked.

The consequences of her espionage should not be understated. Popkin reports that her activities compromised almost every effort Washington made to spy on Cuba from the mid-1980s until 9/11. As one US intelligence official put it, 'my life's work went up like a bonfire set from within' (p. 16). Popkin rightly points out that there were 'countless other legal ways' open to Montes to criticise US policy, but none of these would have placed her at the centre of the room. 'It was a cowardly shortcut for someone, who, as Lucy wrote, became obsessed with power' (p. 305).

Notes

1   See Jim Popkin, 'Ana Montes Did Much Harm Spying for Cuba. Chances Are, You Haven't Heard of Her', *Washington Post*, 18 April 2013, https://www.washingtonpost.com/sf/feature/wp/2013/04/18/ana-montes-did-much-harm-spying-for-cuba-chances-are-you-havent-heard-of-her/.

2   I discussed some of the details of Montes's life and work in an essay published in these pages in 2013. See Russell Crandall, 'The Cold War and Cuban Intelligence', *Survival*, vol. 55, no. 4, August–September 2013, pp. 191–8. See also Popkin, 'Ana Montes Did Much Harm Spying for Cuba'.

3   See Daniel Golden, *Spy School: How the FBI, CIA, and Foreign Intelligence Secretly Exploit America's Universities* (New York: Henry Holt and Company, 2017).

4   Carol Leonnig, 'Transcript: Jim Popkin, Author "Code Name Blue Wren"', *Washington Post*, 5 January 2023, https://www.washingtonpost.com/washington-post-live/2023/01/05/transcript-jim-popkin-author-code-name-blue-wren/.

5   See Dina Temple-Raston, 'Exchange of Spies Was Critical to U.S.–Cuba Deal', NPR, 19 December 2014, https://www.npr.org/2014/12/19/371821107/exchange-of-spies-was-critical-to-u-s-cuba-deal.

6   See also Lance Moore, 'Motivations of an Ideologue: A Case Study of Cuban Spy Ana Belen Montes', Institute of World Politics, 8 September 2019, https://www.iwp.edu/active-measures/2019/09/08/motivations-of-an-ideologue-a-case-study-of-cuban-spy-ana-belen-montes/.

7   See US Department of Justice, 'Unsealed Indictment Charges Former U.S. Federal Employee with Conspiracy to Commit Espionage for Cuba', 25 April 2013, https://www.justice.gov/opa/pr/unsealed-indictment-charges-former-us-federal-employee-conspiracy-commit-espionage-cuba.

8   Juliana Kim, 'Ana Montes, Former U.S. Analyst Convicted of Spying for Cuba, Is Released from Prison', NPR, 8 January 2023, https://www.npr.org/2023/01/08/1147741163/ana-montes-former-u-s-analyst-convicted-of-spying-for-cuba-is-released-from-pris.

9   Johanna Neuman, 'Unrepentant Spy Gets 25 Years', *Los Angeles Times*, 17 October 2002, https://www.latimes.com/archives/la-xpm-2002-oct-17-na-spy17-story.html.

10 Popkin notes that this was 'quite a statement to share with a high schooler' (p. 299).

11 See Kim, 'Ana Montes, Former U.S. Analyst Convicted of Spying for Cuba, Is Released from Prison'.

Review Essay

Oppenheimer: The Man, the Movie and Nuclear Dread

Jonathan Stevenson

Oppenheimer (American film)
Christopher Nolan, director and writer. Distributed by Universal
Pictures, 2023.

July marked the release of *Oppenheimer*, Christopher Nolan's visually cap-
tivating and politically provocative film about J. Robert Oppenheimer, the
American physicist who steered the *Manhattan Project* to completion of
the first atomic bomb. Based on Kai Bird and Martin J. Sherwin's Pulitzer
Prize-winning biography *American Prometheus*, the film is well timed.[1] It
comes at a moment when arms control is moribund, diplomacy among the
great powers is shaky and a major war is testing the stability of nuclear
deterrence. The narrative is structured primarily around the closed 1954
Atomic Energy Commission (AEC) proceeding, fuelled by McCarthyist
paranoia and personal resentments, in which Oppenheimer was stripped
of his security clearance and effectively marginalised in the ongoing
debate over nuclear-force planning and strategy. While the pretext for
that disposition was his connection to left-wing causes and people, the
more substantive reasons for it were his opposition to the development
of the hydrogen bomb and perhaps the possibility that a restless intellect

Jonathan Stevenson is a Senior Fellow at the IISS, managing editor of *Survival*, and author of *Thinking Beyond the Unthinkable* (Viking, 2008) and *A Drop of Treason* (University of Chicago Press, 2021). This essay was adapted from the author's 'Why Oppenheimer Matters', which was published in *American Prospect* on 28 July 2023, and an earlier version that appeared in German in the August/September 2023 issue of *Aufbau*.

Survival | vol. 65 no. 5 | October–November 2023 | pp. 153–160 https://doi.org/10.1080/00396338.2023.2261262

with his putative clout might prove an inconvenient obstacle to US policies down the road.

Oppenheimer died a despondent man at age 62 in 1967. The AEC's action was invalidated only in 2022, when the Department of Energy reviewed the records of the proceeding and formally vindicated Oppenheimer as loyal, though some evidence has emerged that he had secretly been a member of the Communist Party.[2] While the movie tells his story as a personal tragedy embedded in twentieth-century history, it also takes a tragic view of the history itself, in particular the shortfall between humankind's constrained ethical capacities and its expansive scientific ones. Nolan captures scientists reaching their own destructive capability at its most terrible, and presses the question of why, over the course of nearly 80 years, we haven't

embraced Oppenheimer's nuclear dread with greater alarm and entertained informed praetorian critiques like his more openly. The short answer is that nuclear deterrence has worked.

The bomb's origin story

Oppenheimer reaches back to the urgent patriotic atmosphere in which America's bomb was developed. Racing against a genocidal Nazi regime bent on getting the weapon first, Oppenheimer and his team were compelled to leaven the dark understanding that they were devising a weapon of unprecedented destructive power with the grand view that they were simply inventing a 'gadget' that would end the war. Only after the bomb had been tested in the desert in Alamogordo, New Mexico, did they fully appreciate that their work would cast an omnipresent shadow. According, famously, to Oppenheimer himself, on that day in July 1945, a line from Hindu scriptures had come to him: 'I am become death, the destroyer of worlds.'[3]

In the event, of course, the bomb was not needed to defeat Germany. But three years of work costing $2 billion had generated enormous bureaucratic momentum towards using the weapon to some strategic purpose, and it presented itself as a singularly formidable political tool. In his 1995 book

The Decision to Use the Atomic Bomb, historian Gar Alperovitz argues that the Hiroshima and Nagasaki bombings were militarily gratuitous and executed mainly to increase the United States' leverage over the Soviet Union in shaping the post-war world order.[4] While Japan's surrender might not have required either a costly US ground invasion or the atomic strikes, the latter undoubtedly hastened it. Just as surely, they elevated the United States above the Soviet Union among the victorious allies. This made it psychologically and politically difficult not to countenance nuclear weapons, at least provisionally, as legitimate tools of war. As the Soviet Union appeared increasingly implacable, it became harder to dispute that, in addition to demonstrating the superiority of capitalist democracy, America and the West had to brandish their apocalyptic military power to survive and prosper against an irreconcilable adversary in the Nuclear Age.

As the film shows, even after the 'Trinity' test in Alamogordo, Oppenheimer temporised, and declined to oppose the two atomic-bomb attacks on Japanese cities. Over time, however, he became increasingly discomfited about the unbridled advancement of nuclear weapons.[5] In a 1946 commencement address, now having digested the horrific effects of an atomic explosion on a civilian population, he said, analytically rather than melodramatically: 'It did not take atomic weapons to make man want peace. But the atomic bomb was the turn of the screw. It made the prospect of war unendurable.'[6] In 1949, he led a group of senior *Manhattan Project* scientists in composing a report to the AEC discouraging the development of the exponentially more powerful hydrogen bomb, which other colleagues, notably Edward Teller, strongly advocated. Oppenheimer characterised 'the Super', as it was known, as a militarily useless 'weapon of genocide'.[7] But the immoveable consensus among US officials was that the Soviets were implacably aggressive, would themselves inevitably pursue the 'H-bomb' and would be impossible to control unless the West had it too. Its development and deployment were officially enshrined in the foundational National Security Council Paper 68 in April 1950.[8]

It's important to note, as the movie interstitially acknowledges, that Oppenheimer was not a nuclear abolitionist. Although he advocated international controls on nuclear power and may have doubted that nuclear deterrence could endure, he believed in pursuing it. In particular, he thought that the United States, rather than squandering resources on an impractical weapon like the H-bomb, should invest them in lower-yield fission weapons, such as those tested in Alamogordo and dropped on Japan, for tactical use – especially to offset the Soviets' conventional military advantage in Europe. As the Cold War unfolded, the US deployed both types of weapons and erected a complex system of deterrence, with 'firebreaks' and an 'escalation ladder', around them.

The arc of deterrence

Theories of nuclear deterrence progressed from dangerously destabilising 'massive retaliation', through the jarring and counter-intuitive concept of 'limited nuclear war', to 'mutual assured destruction', or MAD, which hinged more sensibly on a devastating second-strike capability that would discourage a first strike.[9] Sceptics had ethical objections to this 'deadly logic', which was tantamount to hostage-taking.[10] But it was efficacious. Nuclear abolitionists hung around, and dread still hovered, manifested in movies like *Dr. Strangelove*, *The Bedford Incident* and *Fail Safe*. But MAD's relative stability combined with a numbingly technocratic approach to force planning and effective arms control squelched any fundamental, wide-ranging debate about the utility and morality of nuclear weapons.[11] In retrospect, near misses like the Cuban Missile Crisis in 1962 and the misconstrued *Able Archer* NATO exercise in 1983 may have been perversely reassuring: cooler heads prevailed, and could be relied upon to do so in the future.[12]

Still, there were abolitionist blips on the screen, particularly in the early 1980s. The Reagan administration branded the Soviet Union an 'evil empire' and began an energetic policy of rolling back Soviet influence. Reagan was at heart a nuclear abolitionist, condemning MAD as a 'suicide pact', and his Strategic Defense Initiative, known colloquially as 'Star Wars' – a missile-defence system that would render America invulnerable to nuclear attack – was essentially protective rather than aggressive. He proposed mutual nuclear disarmament at his meeting with Soviet leader Mikhail Gorbachev in Reykjavík in 1986, but it ended with no agreement. An acute sense of peril persisted due to Reagan's relentless anti-communism, spurring abolitionist protests and the Nuclear Freeze activity.

The world looked poised for a reinvigorated debate about nuclear weapons. In late 1987, however, moving forward from Reykjavík, the United States and the Soviet Union concluded the Intermediate-Range Nuclear Forces (INF) Treaty, which eliminated all intermediate-range nuclear missiles and constituted one of the most substantive arms-control accomplishments of the Cold War. An aura of nuclear self-control returned. Then, unexpectedly, the Soviet Union collapsed and the Cold War ended without a nuclear bomb having been dropped in anger since Nagasaki.

No happy ending

The Cold War had stayed cold, nuclear deterrence had matured and worked, and the moment of maximum danger seemed to have passed. While subsequently there were fleeting moments of enthusiasm for nuclear abolition, the nuclear powers' evolved assumption that knowledge and know-how could not be spirited back into the bottle and nuclear capabilities had best be left intact carried the day. Arms-control agreements, an end to 24/7 nuclear alert, and the United States' then historically unprecedented military and economic superiority seemed sufficient to lift the dread of self-annihilation, MAD-based nuclear deterrence having become such a refined and precise craft that it foreclosed actual use. In 2005, one of its principal architects, Thomas C. Schelling, even won the Nobel Prize in economics for his work in that field and others. While this was implicitly a statement that nobody involved in rationalising nuclear weapons could ever win a Nobel Peace Prize, it did, to an extent, reflect the political domestication of deterrence.

Some insightful students of the era even came around to the view that it was all a charade anyhow – that most decision-makers regarded nuclear war as so awful that, for all their high-tech posturing, they were simply self-deterred. This tracked the prevailing liberal view, which spurned both hawks and abolitionists in favour of the status quo. MAD had neutralised the political utility of nuclear weapons, they reasoned, so the superpowers should leave well enough alone and stop pretending that operational and logistical details really mattered.[13]

Owing to the dire consequences of its failure, however, deterrence has become a riskier proposition as American power has receded and great-power competition has intensified. Arms control is all but dead: China has no interest; Russian President Vladimir Putin has suspended Russia's participation in the New START Treaty on mutual nuclear-force reductions; and Russia and the United States have invalidated the INF Treaty. President Joe Biden has seemingly abandoned strategic ambiguity on Taiwan, indicating that the United States would defend the island against a Chinese attack in a conflict that could escalate to the nuclear level. All three countries are upgrading their nuclear arsenals. The Russia–Ukraine war has raised the nuclear spectre more dramatically. Now that the West has the conventional military advantage, the Russians have ostensibly embraced an 'escalate to de-escalate' concept, publicly endorsed by Putin, whereby they could use battlefield nuclear weapons to reverse tactical losses.[14] Oppenheimer himself might have credited the military logic of this position. Yet Putin's actions have reflected more restraint than his incendiary rhetoric suggests. Deterrence has worked as expected in Ukraine, confining the conflict to conventional means and geographically containing it. Nuclear peace, albeit a more fragile one, goes on.

*   *   *

From this vantage point, audiences should not apprehend Nolan's film as a dirge for a better world that might have been. A planet without the hydrogen bomb probably wasn't feasible. It's more important to observe that Oppenheimer explores how vexing challenges to cherished orthodox-ies can be, especially when it is qualified scientists who are undertaking them. Nuclear deterrence is one such orthodoxy. Others include scepticism about climate change and confidence in the controllability of artificial intelli-gence. With its spectacular suggestions of nuclear destruction and its intense examination of original anxieties about nuclear weapons that have never been satisfactorily addressed, the film stimulates a crucial question: whether mutual deterrence, shorn of arms control and regular diplomacy and under the pressure of a major war involving nuclear powers, can still work.

Notes

1   See Kai Bird and Martin J. Sherwin, *American Prometheus: The Triumph and Tragedy of J. Robert Oppenheimer* (New York: Alfred A. Knopf, 2005).

2   See US Department of Energy, 'Secretary Granholm Statement on DOE Order Vacating 1954 Atomic Energy Commission Decision in the Matter of J. Robert Oppenheimer', 16 December 2022, https://www.energy. gov/articles/secretary-granholm-statement-doe-order-vacating-1954-atomic-energy-commission-decision; and Barton J. Bernstein, 'Christopher Nolan's Forthcoming "Oppenheimer" Movie: A Historian's Questions, Worries, and Challenges', Washington Decoded, 11 July 2023, https://www. washingtondecoded.com/site/2023/07/bernstein.html.

3   See, for example, Andy Kifer, 'The Real History Behind Christopher Nolan's "Oppenheimer"', *Smithsonian Magazine*, 18 July 2023, https:// www.smithsonianmag.com/history/the-real-history-behind-christopher-nolans-oppenheimer-180982529/.

4   See Gar Alperovitz, *The Decision to Use the Atomic Bomb and the Architecture of an American Myth* (New York: Alfred A. Knopf, 1995).

5   See, for example, Daryl G. Kimball, '"Oppenheimer", the Bomb, and Arms Control, Then and Now', *Bulletin of the Atomic Scientists*, 29 July 2023, https://thebulletin.org/2023/07/oppenheimer-the-bomb-and-arms-control-then-and-now/.

6   Quoted in, for example, Richard Rhodes, 'Robert Oppenheimer: The Myth and the Mystery', *Bulletin of the Atomic Scientists*, 18 December 2018, https://thebulletin.org/2018/12/robert-oppenheimer-the-myth-and-the-mystery/.

7   'General Advisory Committee's Majority and Minority Reports on Building the H-Bomb: Majority Annex', 30 October 1949, available from Atomic Archive, https:// www.atomicarchive.com/resources/documents/hydrogen/gac-report.html#Minority.

8   See National Security Council, 'NSC 68: United States Objectives and Programs for National Security', 14 April 1950, https://irp.fas.org/offdocs/nsc-hst/nsc-68.htm.

9   See generally Lawrence Freedman, *The Evolution of Nuclear Strategy*, 3rd ed. (Basingstoke: Palgrave Macmillan, 2003).

10   See Philip Green, *Deadly Logic: The Theory of Nuclear Deterrence* (Columbus, OH: Ohio State University Press, 1966).

11   In poking fun at national somnolence, Wes Anderson's *Asteroid City*, another summer 2023 movie set in the southwestern United States in the 1950s, may capture the prevailing American Cold War attitude. No one bats an eye when mushroom clouds from aboveground nuclear-bomb tests appear on the horizon. The Cold War is revealed as a cynical absurdist artifice, executive control of science as a joke.

12   See Gordon Barrass, '*Able Archer 83*: What Were the Soviets Thinking?', *Survival*, vol. 58, no. 6, December 2016–January 2017, pp. 7–30.

13   See Jonathan Stevenson, *Thinking Beyond the Unthinkable: Harnessing Doom*

from the Cold War to the Age of Terror (New York: Viking, 2008), pp. 165–6.

[14] See, for instance, Nikolai N. Sokov, 'Russian Military Doctrine Calls a Limited Nuclear Strike "De-escalation." Here's Why', *Bulletin of the Atomic Scientists*, 8 March 2022, https://thebulletin.org/2022/03/russian-military-doctrine-calls-a-limited-nuclear-strike-de-escalation-heres-why/; and Dave Johnson, 'Russia's Deceptive Nuclear Policy', *Survival*, vol. 63, no. 3, June–July 2021, pp. 123–42.

Tough Lessons for UN Peacekeeping Operations

Adrian Johnson

The Political Economy of Civil War and UN Peace Operations
Mats Berdal and Jake Sherman (eds). Abingdon: Routledge,
2023. £34.99/$44.95. 350 pp.

The recent trajectory of United Nations peacekeeping has prompted reflection on its relevance to contemporary conflict. While the number of missions and personnel deployed is still high by historical standards, no new peacekeeping missions have been created since 2014, and existing missions have struggled to establish or consolidate peace. Around four in five of the 80,000 or so military, police and civilian personnel in peacekeeping missions are now concentrated in just three active missions in the Central African Republic (CAR), the Democratic Republic of the Congo (DRC) and South Sudan, and in one departing mission in Mali. The UN Security Council has indicated its desire to wind down the missions in the DRC (MONUSCO) and CAR (MINUSCA), instructing them to begin generating or implementing exit strategies.[1] Although the council's hand was forced in Mali by the transitional government's dramatic withdrawal of consent for MINUSMA in June 2023 and the subsequent termination of its mandate, the exit of the mission had already been on the minds of council members.

Adrian Johnson is a Research Analyst and head of the Multilateral Research Group in the Foreign, Commonwealth & Development Office (FCDO). The views expressed here are the author's own, and do not reflect those of the FCDO or the UK government.

Survival | vol. 65 no. 5 | October–November 2023 | pp. 161–176 https://doi.org/10.1080/00396338.2023.2261266

Despite this retrenchment, there are still important reasons why the lessons of UN peace operations – including UN peacekeeping missions and UN Special Political Missions – matter to those working on conflicts. International interventions to resolve, manage or contain violent conflict within states have inevitably had to grapple with the political economy of conflict – that is, the complex patchwork of national, regional and local systems of power, influence and governance. This has been as true of inter-national counter-insurgency and state-building efforts in Afghanistan, or various African-led regional and coalition operations to combat armed groups on the continent, as it has been for UN operations.

Mats Berdal and Jake Sherman's edited volume *The Political Economy of Civil War and UN Peace Operations* makes an important contribution to our

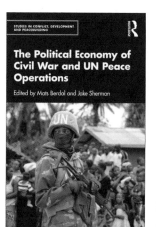

understanding of the ability of multinational opera-tions to achieve their aims. Its conclusions should be read and understood by those involved in the mandat-ing and operational conduct of UN peace operations. While the focus of the book is on UN operations and the institutional and political idiosyncrasies of the UN, the analysis and lessons have broader applicability to civil conflict.

The book is wide in scope, but there are three key implications for the present debate. Firstly, mission mandates should be much more focused and restrained.

The success of UN peace operations is to a great degree determined by the regional and global politics of the conflict and the local situation's amenability to UN efforts. This raises difficult questions about the feasibility of ambitious state-building efforts and open-ended attempts to protect civilians. The UN and the Security Council should therefore con-sider the full spectrum of peace operations to pick options suited to the context at hand.

Secondly, the contributors argue that more effective approaches to the political economy of conflict require institutional adaptation and innovation. This does not just mean set-piece reform agreed by governments in the UN Security Council and General Assembly. Many aspects of peacekeeping practice could be improved under the UN's own authority and within existing mandates, which may avoid needless entanglement in complex member-state politics in New York. In particular, missions could use the 'good offices' function of missions to engage in dialogue and mediation to more systematically attend to local alongside national-level processes. UN headquarters and missions could also benefit from better, more consistently applied analytical capabilities for understanding the complexities of the political economy of conflict, in order to assess the utility of existing approaches or define new ones. This includes working more closely with a broader range of influential actors, such as business.

Thirdly, as non-military UN operations with political and peacebuilding mandates working alongside regional or ad hoc coalition forces may become more common, the UN's success in such contexts will be more contingent on the strategy and conduct of other international actors.

Also noted are some cross-cutting implications of a more divided Security Council that may constrain the future aspirations of UN peace operations.

Chapter by chapter

Berdal and Sherman bring together a formidable group of practitioners and scholars, all of whom write with clarity and an eye for practical applicability. The contributions fit neatly together to provide an appropriate balance of breadth and depth. Berdal and Sherman's analytic introductory essay imparts a compelling rationale: that understanding the track record of UN operations demands an understanding of how they have dealt with the political economy of their conflicts. The editors also spell out a clear set of questions relevant to current policy deliberations: what has been the impact of political economies on the course of UN operations? How has the UN system sought to address the resulting policy challenges? What are some of the wider lessons of the UN's experience of the past three decades in dealing with inter-state conflict?

Contributions from former UN senior mission and headquarters leadership provide an excellent set of high-level perspectives to begin the thematic section of the book. Jean-Marie Guéhenno, head of what was then the UN Department for Peacekeeping Operations from 2000 to 2008, sets the tone: the book is not a counsel of despair but rather a thoughtful consideration of the inherent constraints of international intervention in conflict. Kenny Gluck, formerly a senior official for the UN in the CAR and Yemen, argues that a critical component of missions' political work needs to be the promotion of local-level negotiation and dialogue to create a broader enabling environment for political progress. Alan Doss, former head of UN peace-keeping operations in Liberia and the DRC, highlights an important tension between the need for UN officials to consider the full texture of local politics and their ability, as outsiders, to do so.

Another set of thematic chapters offers more focused conceptual perspectives on the economic dimensions of civil war with practical impli-cations for UN operations. Charles Cater explores the impact of UN sanctions regimes and their atten-dant monitoring and reporting mechanisms, which are the Security Council's main tools for shaping the economic dimensions of a conflict. Josie Lianna Kaye shines a light on the role of private business in conflict, persuasively arguing that missions need to engage with it more systematically, business having often been seen only as an economic, and not a political, actor. Dirk Druet provides a first-class analysis of how UN operations have developed and used their tools and processes for intelligence-gathering. While constrained by the UN's politics with respect to intelligence, missions have nevertheless innovated and adapted. Judith Vorrath examines the impact of the links between the political and criminal spheres – which are not always easy to distinguish – on prospects for peace. Sanctions monitoring can provide a wealth of information on this 'grey zone' to help peace operations, but a more coherent approach would rely on clearer guidance in Security Council mandates.

UN missions have innovated and adapted

A set of well-chosen case studies follows to provide generalisable lessons for practitioners. Tatiana Carayannis and Michael J. Kavanagh assess why successive UN peacekeeping operations in the DRC (MONUC and then MONUSCO) have failed to restore central authority in the war-torn east of the country. They argue that UN operations could have better appreci-ated and addressed the political economy of the eastern DRC. Competing interests of key regional players in the conflict have also impeded UN operations. A mission's focus on building state institutions can be at odds with strong national and regional interests in not having a functional and accountable state. Examining UNMISS in South Sudan, Adam Day argues that the political logic of the country post-independence was never conducive to the UN's liberal-state-building project. A UN mandate to exploit what seemed a moment of substantial political transformation instead solidified an underlying system of patrimonial governance dominated by one ethnic group. In her chapter on UNAMA – the political mission in Afghanistan – Ashley Jackson argues that the mission had two problems: its inability to shape a broader United States-led strategy that undermined the prospects for stability and democratic governance; and the UN mission's own faulty assumptions that it could build state institutions or coordinate international donors.

Kieran Mitton's chapter on UNAMSIL in Sierra Leone stands out in highlighting an example of qualified UN success. For the mission to complete its tasks after a disastrous start required positive regional intervention and more effective deployment of the UN's own military capabilities to shape the conditions for peace. This included strangling cross-border flows of financial resources that sustained the rebel Revolutionary United Front (RUF), as well as taking a political approach that peeled away rank-and-file fighters of the group from participating in its activities. Despite the somewhat unfortunate timing of Arthur Boutellis's chapter on MINUSMA in Mali – the mission was unforeseeably terminated after publication – its analysis on how the mission tried to deal with the complex political economy of the Sahel remains relevant. MINUSMA was notable for its innovations in all-source intelligence capability and its explicit targeting of organised-crime groups.

Ken Menkhaus and Paul D. Williams cover the full spectrum of UN field missions in Somalia – from the peacekeeping missions of the early 1990s through the present Special Political Mission (UNOSOM) operating alongside a larger African Union military mission. They spell out how the international presence in Somalia has itself affected the political economy of conflict by providing ready flows of financial resources – via procurement contracts, for instance – that local actors have been keen to exploit. They also elucidate the risks of conflict that arise when local actors seek to perpetuate state-building, peacebuilding and development efforts for their own ends to the detriment of international objectives.

The concluding chapter by Berdal and Sherman synthesises the preceding contributions into a well-judged set of valuable policy recommendations to the Security Council, the UN Secretariat and the missions themselves.

Lessons for future UN operations

The book's recommendations for more context-specific approaches, tempered ambition and addressing the various politico-economic drivers of conflict and peace embody important lessons of international intervention since the end of the Cold War. They reflect the fact that dealing with civil war is plainly difficult; trade-offs abound, and outside interveners need to approach their task with humility and a readiness to get at least some of it wrong regardless. Recent scholarship on post-Cold War intervention is sobering. All intervention in conflict is political and its effects ultimately depend on underlying local configurations of power.[2] Yet too often international responses to intra-state conflict have foundered on attempts to impose technical, top-down solutions on deep-rooted economic, social and political problems.[3] Broad-brush assumptions by interveners can mask the granular motivations, incentives and power relations affecting civilians, combatants and elites that are essential to properly understanding a conflict.[4] While the UN's politics means it may be unclear how, or how consistently, specific recommendations on mandates, reform and regionally led operations can be implemented, they are all worthy of serious consideration.

Mandates: back to basics?

The recommendations on mission mandates reflect the tried-and-tested principle that peacekeeping operations should either serve an existing political settlement or at a minimum credibly create the conditions for the parties to agree on one. UN peace operations cannot substitute for the commitment of the conflict parties to a peaceful solution. Hence, the 'permissiveness' of the local and regional political economy substantially impacts the likelihood of success (p. 280). So does the peacekeeping mission's level of ambition. Berdal and Sherman expose a tricky contradiction: as peace operations have taken on politically sensitive tasks that intrude on domestic struggles for power and influence, they have called for an even deeper understanding of the fine grain of local politics (p. 7). But the central insight of a political-economy lens is that there are '*limitations* of the dominant conventional approaches favoured by the UN in dealing with intra-state conflict' (p. 11; emphasis in original). These limitations, expertly detailed in the book, raise several considerations.

Firstly, the decision to create a new UN operation must factor in the regional and international politics and economic enablers of conflict. The national interests of the key players and the extent to which they either enable or close off the space for armed groups to wage war is central to the course of conflict (p. 15). Outside players can also influence the attitude of local elites towards peace processes.[5] The attention the book pays to UN sanctions as a tool for addressing the sources of conflict is both welcome and instructive. As Cater argues, 'the most significant obstacle to the implementation of arms embargoes and natural resource sanctions is a lack of enforcement by Member States' (p. 99). In the case of the DRC, Carayannis and Kavanagh show how foreign actors sustain the ability of local armed groups to fight: 'Without them, belligerents would otherwise have neither the capital to finance a war nor the profit incentive to sustain one' (p. 175).

Secondly, the mandating and design of new missions must be realistic about the feasibility of state-building objectives such as the extension of state authority, capacity-building of state institutions and support to host-state security forces in each context. Liberal assumptions about building impartial state institutions that deliver services to the citizenry are often at odds with the aggrandising interests and motivations of local elites. But such elites and armed groups are 'unavoidable denominators in the equation of peace' (p. 65), even if they might also be part of the problem. Day makes a compelling case that UNMISS's focus on state-building between South Sudan's independence and the civil war in 2013 unwittingly empowered one set of elites. In the framework of Alex de Waal's 'political marketplace', the UN became an actor in a South Sudanese system it did not fully understand, in which political loyalty was sold to the highest bidder.[6] These arguments align with a broader pattern of scholarly scepticism about the feasibility of liberal state-building. In particular, scholars have noted that UN peacekeeping missions can buttress authoritarian regimes and undermine the UN's impartiality in a conflict.[7]

Thirdly, more context-driven approaches are needed to advance the protection of civilians under imminent threat of physical harm, which has become a common task for peacekeeping operations since 1999. Its political-economy dimensions are complex and often insufficiently understood. For all the frustration with the UN's effectiveness at protecting civilians – many go unprotected, and in some cases this has led to violent reprisals against UN operations[8] – one robust finding in the scholarly literature on peacekeeping is that missions do tend to reduce levels of violence in their areas of deployment, particularly by rebel groups.[9] Even though UNMISS failed to prevent the civil war in South Sudan, its actions to protect civilians since 2013 have no doubt saved many thousands of lives.[10] Addressing the fundamental causes of violence against civilians is more difficult, however, as it requires understanding and tackling thorny, deep-seated economic and political drivers of violence (p. 5). Protecting civilians does not, by itself, create the conditions for political success. While there are strong moral imperatives for protecting civilians, trade-offs are involved. Cedric de Coning argues that UN peacekeeping operations risk a 'stabilisation dilemma' wherein the more a mission protects civilians and helps maintain stability in the absence of a viable political process, the less incentive there is for governments to find a political solution.[11] And when host states are a source of violence, civilian protection raises tensions between missions and host states from which they require consent and cooperation. In Mali, this souring of relations was one of the factors that led to the mission's expulsion.

None of these considerations supports abandoning peace operations altogether. Even though large, multidimensional operations may be out of fashion now, there is still a demand for more focused missions. While there have been no new peacekeeping missions since 2014, Security Council-mandated observer missions have played a positive role in Colombia (UNMC and UNVMC) and Yemen (UNMHA). Although classed as Special

Political Missions, they have had the same tasks and functions as some smaller peacekeeping operations. The UN is ill-suited to conduct the kinds of counter-terrorism, war-fighting or counter-insurgency tasks for which African-led coalition operations have recently been deployed in northern Mozambique and West Africa.[12] The dearth of large-scale UN missions over the past decade may reflect the absence of suitable contexts for deploying any, which may say more about the politics of ongoing conflicts than about attitudes towards UN peacekeeping.

Security Council members should therefore approach peace operations as a spectrum of options, tailored to context.[13] What matters is whether a mission helps cement the conditions for peace. In situations with an adverse or poorly understood political economy of conflict, 'traditional' peacekeeping tasks such as ceasefire observation or separating adversary forces can still be useful. There is also a great deal of multidimensional activity that stops short of political and institutional transformation, such as disarmament, human-rights monitoring and verification of peace-agreement implementation. Even so, the ambitious multidimensional mission remains a useful tool, not least because, when the context is right for one, the UN still has the best-developed system for generating and sustaining complex multinational military, police and civilian deployments under a flag of global legitimacy.

Reform: nurture adaptation and innovation
UN reform is notoriously hard. Nevertheless, the UN can and does change. The incremental development of the structures and conduct of UN peace-keeping since 1945 is a case in point. It has occurred through a mixture of evolving mandates, self-conscious reform, on-the-ground practice and adaptation, and an accumulation of policy decisions within the Secretariat and the UN General Assembly.

There are no clever tricks to get around the inevitable political, analytical and moral complexities of engaging with the political economy of conflict itself (p. 10). Better understanding of the political economy of conflict does not provide easy solutions, and the Security Council will inevitably be faced with pressure to act before deep analysis may be feasible. But it could still improve the UN's approach in fiendishly complex environments. With this realism in mind, several of the book's recommendations stand out.

One is better mission responses to local dynamics to seize opportunities and manage risks. Gluck argues that in conflicts with weakly structured and fragmented combatants, peace operations cannot rely on the 'search for and implementation of national peace agreements' (p. 46). The inability of factionalised and incoherent groups and governments to agree or adhere to meaningful deals means missions have to negotiate successive and over-lapping agreements without clarity on whether they should be focusing on implementing weak agreements, mitigating the impact of violence on civil-ians or searching for new political frameworks (p. 50).

This argument boldly questions the UN's preference for national-level processes. On the one hand, there is a credible argument that chronically fractured, unstable peace agreements should be a reason not to deploy a UN operation. As Doss argues, there are limits on what local deals can do without cooperation from national leaders (p. 74). On the other hand, it is inevitable that UN operations are going to face this problem to varying degrees, par-ticularly given how commonly peace agreements result in 'unsettlements' that do not resolve underlying disagreements between elites.[14] UN officials may find that local deals are necessary scaffolding for a credible national-level process, to smooth its implementation or to contain local disputes – as in, for example, Sierra Leone and Mali (pp. 246, 266–7).

Credible analysis of the political and economic dimensions of a conflict is also key. Calls for better analytical capability in the UN Secretariat and missions are long-standing.[15] These have often turned on the need to under-stand the local and regional drivers of conflict. But the book, quite correctly, is clear on the need to appreciate the effect of the mission itself and, where they exist, that of parallel international interventions. One relevant factor is the direct economic impact of UN missions, which can potentially channel hundreds of millions in hard currency into the country for staff, facilities and other expenditures. Procurement contracts can be intensely political, creating financial winners and losers among local elites, as in Somalia (p. 289). Missions must also understand the trade-offs inherent in combating illicit economic actors. The chapters by Vorrath and Boutellis illuminate a vexing trade-off. Moves to tackle organised-crime networks may cut off their support to armed groups, but this may trigger violence if they fight back. And when these networks provide employment and access to goods, disrupting them may perversely reduce the ability of locals in long-neglected parts of the country to survive.

The need for better intra-mission coordination is also a persistent problem. One aspect is the bureaucratic division between the UN Secretariat's Department of Peace Operations and the Department of Political and Peacebuilding Affairs, and within missions between the political- and civil-affairs components. In UNMISS, the Civil Affairs division dealt with inter-communal matters, while the Political Affairs division handled national-level questions such as constitutional provisions on centralisation. Given the obvious overlaps between these two areas, this division of authority undermined mission coherence (p. 205).

Those seeking to remedy these problems must navigate the politics of change in the UN. A key consideration is whether the UN Secretariat can simply change existing practice or policy on its own authority, or whether change needs member-state agreement in the General Assembly or the Security Council. More broadly, the inherently centrifugal tendencies of the UN system often cut against greater operational coherence. The UN is a sprawling enterprise that lacks an overriding central authority. Its many entities are pulled in different directions by a mixture of varying legislative bases, governance arrangements, sensitivities to member-state and donor politics, and dominant personalities. Proponents of reform therefore must be realistic about the UN's general insusceptibility to institutional fixes.

Regional operations: the UN as a supporting actor

The current preference in Africa for regional, sub-regional or ad hoc coalition missions to defeat or contain rebels, insurgents and terrorists raises the question of whether or how UN peace operations should work alongside non-UN missions. UN political missions already overlap with African-led operations in Somalia, the DRC and West Africa. Present debates raise the possibility of UN operations more frequently covering political and peacebuilding tasks alongside African-led military operations.

If regional missions are to be the dominant mode of international intervention in conflict, there are valuable lessons to be drawn from Afghanistan, Somalia and Sierra Leone on how parallel interventions intertwined with the local political economy affected prospects for success. In Afghanistan and Somalia, UN political missions were at the mercy of the strategy and conduct of the non-UN interventions, whereas in Sierra Leone, outside intervention was a crucial enabler of successful implementation of the peacekeeping missions. These cases confirm the view that regional missions are both a risk and an opportunity for UN operations.[16]

Any consideration of the UN's purpose in such contexts will have to begin with an assessment of the objectives and strategies of the non-UN military operation. A UN envoy and political office cannot compensate for a military campaign that lacks political logic. Furthermore, UN political missions have far less leverage than their peacekeeping counterparts. Jackson argues that in Afghanistan, 'the incentives created by international intervention' undermined the logic of UNAMA's state-building and donor-coordination mandate, and essentially rendered it irrelevant (pp. 219–20). UNAMA could not realistically influence US strategy. In Somalia, despite Security Council action to try to diminish the jihadist group al-Shabaab's income from illicit activities, the council-mandated Monitoring Group reported that elements of AMISOM were complicit in the prohibited trade in charcoal.[17] This not only undermined AMISOM's counter-insurgency efforts, but also hindered UN monitors in determining sanctions compliance, since they relied on AMISOM for security (pp. 98–9).

On the other side of the ledger, Mitton's case study of UNAMSIL in Sierra Leone shows the positive role that 'a set of complimentary, multidimensional, and region-wide interventions', such as Guinea's and the United Kingdom's military interventions and international economic pressure against the RUF and its backers, can play (p. 238). After recovering from its severe initial crisis, UNAMSIL was able to help consolidate peace through better use of its own military component. Complementary interventions – even if not coordinated – can have a positive impact on the political economy of a conflict.

A divided Security Council

The UN Security Council's power to mandate UN peace operations and to take measures affecting individual conflicts – for example, by authorising legally binding sanctions regimes – makes the aims, capabilities and leverage of those operations highly sensitive to Security Council consensus. Council disagreement has increasingly limited the scope for effective action to shape the political economy of a conflict.[18] But it is worth remembering that peace-keeping emerged and evolved during the Cold War, when divisions within the council were profound. A divided council does not necessarily rule out effective agreement on new missions. Indeed, the revitalisation of peace-keeping could be a means of resolving second-order conflicts so that they do not escalate into riskier confrontations between global powers.

The extent to which the UN can influence the political economies of con-flicts will pivot on what forms of collective action the council can agree and the extent to which it and member states are willing to enforce them. For reform-minded practitioners, this poses a serious challenge. Mandates in the post-Cold War period have become longer, more prescriptive and more legalistic. This tendency has often advanced reform in practice. Should agreement on the content of mandates become harder to generate, innova-tion and adaptation may depend more on the UN leadership and staff's broad interpretation of more limited mandate language.

*   *   *

There is a decent case to be made that the current phase of big, multidimensional peace operations is winding down and unlikely to be repeated in the near future. The politics of the Security Council, while not deadlocked, offers relatively infertile ground for ambitious peacebuilding mandates, particularly when provisions on key matters such as human rights may be perceived as challenges to state sovereignty. Nevertheless, UN peace operations have weathered storms before and remained useful tools for states seeking to manage violent conflict. A number of long-running missions still provide pedestrian but important contributions to peace and security in, for example, Cyprus and Lebanon.

Whatever the objectives and design of future UN peace operations, they will have to grapple with the political and economic complexities of local and regional conflict. A good understanding of the political economy of conflict – and all the trade-offs it implies – is essential to the design and execution of a fruitful UN mission. *The Political Economy of Civil War and UN Peace Operations* provides an outstanding analysis of this requirement, balancing realism and a positive agenda for change.

Notes

1   See UN Security Council, 'Resolution 2666', 20 December 2022, paras 38–42, https://www.securitycouncilreport.org/atf/cf/%7B65BFCF9B-6D27-4E9C-8CD3-CF6E4FF96FF9%7D/S_RES_2666.pdf; and UN Security Council, 'Resolution 2659', 14 November 2022, para 58, https://documents-dds-ny.un.org/doc/UNDOC/GEN/N22/691/48/PDF/N2269148.pdf?OpenElement.

2   See Mats Berdal, *Building Peace After War* (Abingdon: Routledge, 2009), pp. 173–5; Christine Cheng, Jonathan Goodhand and Patrick Meehan, 'Synthesis Paper: Securing and Sustaining Elite Bargains that Reduce Violent Conflict', UK Stabilisation Unit, April 2018, p. 4, https://assets.publishing.service.gov.uk/government/uploads/system/uploads/attachment_data/file/765882/Elite_Bargains_and_Political_Deals_Project_-_Synthesis_Paper.pdf; and Elizabeth Cousens and Chetan Kumar (eds), *Peacebuilding as Politics: Cultivating Peace in Fragile Societies* (Boulder, CO: Lynne Rienner, 2001), p. 187.

3   See Severine Autesserre, *Peaceland: Conflict Resolution and the Everyday Politics of International Intervention*

(Cambridge: Cambridge University Press, 2014), p. 249.

4   See Stathis Kalyvas, *The Logic of Violence in Civil War* (Cambridge: Cambridge University Press, 2006), pp. 388–91.

5   Cheng, Goodhand and Meehan, 'Synthesis Paper: Securing and Sustaining Elite Bargains that Reduce Violent Conflict', p. 20.

6   See Alex de Waal, *The Real Politics of the Horn of Africa: Money, War and the Business of Power* (Cambridge: Polity Press, 2015).

7   See Sarah von Billerbeck and Oisin Tansey, 'Enabling Autocracy? Peacebuilding and Post-conflict Authoritarianism in the Democratic Republic of Congo', *European Journal of International Relations*, vol. 25, no. 3, 2019, pp. 698–722; and Adam Day and Charlie T. Hunt, 'A Perturbed Peace: Applying Complexity Theory to UN Peacekeeping', *International Peacekeeping*, vol. 30, no. 1, 2023.

8   See, for example, 'One Dead in Fresh Anti-UN Mission Protests in Eastern DR Congo', Al-Jazeera, 6 September 2022, https://www.aljazeera.com/news/2022/9/6/one-dead-in-fresh-anti-un-mission-protests-in-eastern-dr-congo#.

9   See Lisa Hultman, Jacob Kathman and Megan Shannon, 'Beyond Keeping Peace: United Nations Effectiveness in the Midst of Fighting', *American Political Science Review*, vol. 108, no. 4, November 2014, pp. 737–53; and Barbara F. Walter, Lise Morje Howard and V. Page Fortna, 'The Extraordinary Relationship Between Peacekeeping and Peace', *British Journal of Political Science*, vol. 51, no. 4, 2021, pp. 1,705–22.

10 See Mats Berdal and David Shearer, 'Hard Lessons from South Sudan', *Survival*, vol. 63, no. 5, October– November 2021, pp. 69–96.

11 Cedric de Coning, 'How Not to Do UN Peacekeeping: Avoid the Stabilization Dilemma with Principled and Adaptive Mandating and Leadership', *Global Governance*, vol. 29, no. 2, 2023, p. 157.

12 They include SAMIM in northern Mozambique, the ECOWAS missions in Gambia and Guinea-Bissau, and MNJTF in northern Nigeria.

13 See Ian Martin, 'All Peace Operations Are Political: A Case for Designer Missions and the Next UN Reform', in Richard Gowan (ed.), *Review of Political Missions 2010* (New York: Center on International Cooperation, 2010), pp. 8–14.

14 Christine Bell and Jan Pospisil, 'Navigating Inclusion in Transitions from Conflict: The Rise of the Political Unsettlement', *Journal of International Development*, vol. 29, no. 5, July 2017, pp. 576–93.

15 See United Nations, 'Report of the Panel on United Nations Peace Operations' (also known as the 'The Brahimi Report'), A/55/305–S/2000/809, 21 August 2000, paras 63 onwards, https:// peacekeeping.un.org/sites/default/ files/a_55_305_e_brahimi_report.pdf.

16 See Alexandra Novoselloff and Lisa Sharland, 'Partners and Competitors: Forces Operating in Parallel to UN Peace Operations', International Peace Institute, November 2019, https://www.ipinst.org/wp-content/ uploads/2019/11/IPI-Rpt-Partners-and-Competitors.pdf.

17 See United Nations, 'Report of the Monitoring Group on Somalia and Eritrea Pursuant to Security Council Resolution 2060', S/2013/413, 12 July 2013, https://documents-dds-ny. un.org/doc/UNDOC/GEN/N13/361/85/ PDF/N1336185.pdf?OpenElement.

18 See, for example, Richard Gowan, 'Major Power Rivalry and Multilateral Conflict Management', Discussion Paper Series on Managing Global Disorder No. 8, Council on Foreign Relations, December 2021, https://cdn. cfr.org/sites/default/files/report_pdf/ Gowan_MajorPowerRivalry_0.pdf.

Book Reviews

Economy
Erik Jones

States and the Masters of Capital: Sovereign Lending, Old and New
Quentin Bruneau. New York: Columbia University Press, 2022.
£30.00/$35.00. 240 pp.

On 1 August 2023, the Fitch credit-rating agency downgraded the United States' government debt from AAA to AA+, citing 'a steady deterioration in standards of governance over the last 20 years'. US Treasury Secretary Janet Yellen responded immediately to express her strong disagreement: 'Fitch's decision does not change what Americans, investors and people around the world already know', she argued. 'Treasury securities remain the world's pre-eminent safe and liquid asset.' That exchange raises important questions about how financial markets work. Why do credit-rating agencies pass judgement on government borrowers? How do they make those judgements? And what do other people 'know' that might be different?

Quentin Bruneau has written a brilliant book about the 'ways of knowing' in international finance that puts the answers to these questions in historical context. He argues that international bankers used to get to know sovereign borrowers on a personal basis. They strove to be accepted in borrowers' inner circles so that they could interact with them socially. They embraced the norms of high society and used them as a guide to trustworthiness. And they relied on reputation – both their own and others' – to communicate these judgements to the wider financial community. Those bankers who had the greatest access and prestige, like the Rothschilds, could lead the largest syndicates and so channel funds from many countries in the service of specific governments and projects.

Survival | vol. 65 no. 5 | October–November 2023 | pp. 177–184 https://doi.org/10.1080/00396338.2023.2261267

The fact that family-run banking houses like the Rothschilds' faced unlimited liability for their mistakes gave them added credibility.

At some point in the mid- to late nineteenth century, however, that way of knowing in international finance began to change. Limited-liability joint-stock corporations emerged with national rather than cosmopolitan bankers in positions of authority. These bankers may have aspired to high society, but they could never gain personal access. They therefore relied on statistics to understand prospective clients, including national governments. Bankers worried less about embracing and interpreting social norms and more about applying statistical analysis and modelling techniques. They also began to rely on specialised credit-rating agencies like Fitch to complement their own judgements. Along the way, states ceased to be a collection of individuals, becoming instead a collection of numbers.

The changeover in ways of knowing sovereign borrowers was not immediate. During the interwar period, the old and the new coexisted, with the more traditional bankers in the lead. Indeed, the most prominent members of the American financial community, such as J.P. Morgan, were eager to embrace the norms of high society in Europe and to mimic the behaviour of the top European banks. The decision to shut down international capital markets within the Bretton Woods system after the Second World War delayed things further. Once that system collapsed in the 1970s, the statistical way of knowing was fully unleashed. The result was not a re-emergence of the kind of capital markets that existed in the nineteenth and early twentieth centuries, but something entirely different, with different pathologies, as we learned during the global economic and financial crisis, and as Yellen's exchange with Fitch illustrates.

But Yellen was right to stress that Fitch's models are not the only way of knowing the creditworthiness of the US. The old ways of knowing still exist – consider the shocking access that Jeffrey Epstein had to heads of state and finance. New ways of knowing are also emerging, and Bruneau's argument about the past points to an important research agenda. Artificial intelligence could spark another paradigm shift in how creditors assess state borrowing. Anticipating who will be the key actors and what biases and volatility they might bring to international capital markets is a major challenge we must face. Bruneau's book is a great place to start.

**The Capital Order: How Economists Invented Austerity
and Paved the Way to Fascism**
Clara E. Mattei. Chicago, IL: University of Chicago Press, 2022.
$30.00. 480 pp.

The First World War was the first major industrialised war in Europe. As such, it required unprecedented contributions from members of the working class, both as fodder for slaughter on the battlefield and as the essential resource for manufacturing the armaments used for their own destruction. It is little wonder that, once societies emerged from this exhaustingly exploitative and wasteful confrontation, the working class demanded justice on all levels. This included not just participation in politics, but also the democratisation of the workplace. In making these demands, moreover, working-class representatives could demonstrate a feasible alternative to capitalism – one that was not only more just, but also more productive. The ruling class was unpersuaded. Although its members made initial concessions, they quickly sought the instruments to quell any revolution and so put the workers back in their place.

Clara Mattei sheds a cold light on how those instruments worked, focusing not on the forces of law and order but on the then-emerging domains of macroeconomic and industrial policy. In doing so, she underscores the significance of the different ways of knowing that her colleague at the New School, Quentin Bruneau, underscores in his own book (see previous review). The economists of the interwar period, Mattei argues, were quick to celebrate their achievements in building statistical models to capture the objective laws of economics. But those economists were also the products of a social class that viewed members of the working classes as lacking in virtue, wasteful and undisciplined. They even went so far as to build these characteristics implicitly into their models for interpreting macroeconomic data and labour-market performance. The result was to bake class discrimination into the value system that economists shared both across ideological divides in Italy and across the huge gulf of national experience between Italy and the United Kingdom. So long as Benito Mussolini's government followed the macroeconomic policies the economists recommended, even fascism was seen as preferable to any alternative suggested by the working classes.

Where Mattei's argument overreaches is in claiming that working-class sub-jugation was the goal of the policy mixture. She is on safer ground when she recognises the 'positivist' epistemology that underpinned belief in the law-like nature of economic mechanisms (p. 215). What economists 'knew' to be true in the early 1920s was not yet exposed to the quantum revolution in physics or Karl Popper's scientific realism. Mattei does not try to rework their reasoning. The book contains no data about outstanding government-debt levels, foreign borrowing or rollover requirements. Current-account balances, capital flows and foreign-exchange reserves are also largely absent. Without these, it is impossible to tease out how the economists of the day saw the situation in terms of their own models. If we assume that the models called for fiscal and monetary tightening to be coupled with policies to make it easier for firms to cut labour costs to restore financial stability, then it is safe to assume that was their motive. Their class bias explains why they accepted – even celebrated – that workers bore what we would regard as a disproportionate share of the adjustment costs.

This distinction is important because Mattei makes a strong argument that class bias remains embedded in these models in much the same way that racism and sexism do. Even her shift of idiom is persuasive. If we substitute 'productive investment' for 'capital accumulation' throughout the book, that changes the force of her argument in a way that reveals the power of linguistic framing. Mattei insists that we should look at the impact of policy on wages, labour shares, trade-union membership and strike action to interpret motivation; it would be better to use that information to judge whether policymakers are getting what they claim to want, particularly in the current period. If biased models are producing bad outcomes – and there is good evidence to suggest they are – then economists and policymakers should be held to account.

Why the West Is Failing: Failed Economics and the Rise of the East
John Mills. Cambridge: Polity Press, 2022. £50.00. 220 pp.

Economic growth has slowed in the West relative to other parts of the world, China in particular. That slowdown in economic growth has coincided with a slowdown in productivity growth as well. This is a problem because productivity growth is essential to raise living standards and promote innovation. Hence, Western governments should find a way to support those parts of the economy most responsible for productivity growth – and to leverage that growth and the innovation that goes along with it – to bring up real growth rates across the economy.

This prescription may sound challenging, but John Mills argues that it requires only a change in perspective. Rather than favouring finance, policymakers need to focus on the needs of the light-industrial manufacturing sector. That is where the greatest productivity growth is to be found. The key is to find ways to lower overall production costs so that entrepreneurs in this sector have the resources to invest. Subsidies may be part of the solution, but the heavy lifting needs to be done via exchange-rate policy. Governments need to target a competitive exchange rate to hold down domestic production costs relative to those in other parts of the world. The solution is really that simple, and the policy instruments already exist in the form of capital controls, sovereign-wealth funds, the withholding of taxes and central-bank mandates.

Mills makes this argument forcefully, drawing on years of experience as founder of JML, a multi-channel retailer that sells a range of consumer products including electrical appliances for everything from household cleaning to pet grooming. Mills is also widely read, and he backs his claims with a wealth of economic statistics. He is not trained as an academic economist, but he is economically literate and well intentioned. He founded an institute to devote resources 'to increase prosperity, growth and equality by putting a more successful economic future at the heart of British political discourse'.

Mills represents what John Maynard Keynes identified as a 'practical man' at the end of his *General Theory of Employment, Interest and Money*. This is meant with no disrespect either for Mills's obvious achievements or his good intentions. Rather, it is to underscore the danger of bias that lurks in the literature, as so powerfully highlighted by Clara Mattei (see previous review). Some of this bias reflects social discrimination, but some reflects methodological preferences. For example, economists like to simplify reality to make their models tractable. The challenge they face is to keep track of those simplifying assumptions. Non-economists usually do not realise the role such assumptions play.

Mills uses an argument for industrial competitiveness that assumes countries have a single exchange rate – one between the United Kingdom and the outside world, for example, or the West and the Rest (p. 144). That kind of argument makes sense in a debate about fixed versus adjustable exchange rates. In the early 1960s, Robert Mundell used the exchange rate between an imaginary Capricorn and Cancer in his analyses of competing exchange-rate regimes. But real countries have many exchange rates. That was not always obvious during the Bretton Woods system, when every country pegged to the dollar, but it is key to understanding why European countries created a 'snake in the tunnel' mechanism to coordinate bilateral currency movements within that arrangement. Multiple exchange rates also explain why Europeans formed a monetary union.

China can target its relationship with the US dollar, but which currency should the UK target? Much of the devastation visited on British manufacturing prior to the 2008 financial crisis came not from China but from the way the British pound was whipsawed between the euro and the dollar during the euro's first decade. Even a sharp drop in the labour share of value added across the economy, or a stagnation of the labour share in manufacturing, did not insulate British industry from the costs of that volatility. If economists do not promote the solutions Mills favours, they have a good reason.

Capitalism: The Story Behind the Word

Michael Sonenscher. Princeton, NJ: Princeton University Press, 2022. £22.00/$27.95. 248 pp.

Keynesian 'practical men' and academic economists are not the only ones who fall prey to assumptions embedded in theoretical models. All of us – even the most critical – are susceptible to the same mistakes. Consider the notion of 'capital'. In its modern form, the word centres on private property, wage labour and the inequitable distribution of wealth. A small few control the means of production and use that control to exploit the work of many. The only way out is to eliminate private property, nationalise the means of production and democratise the workplace.

The problem, Michael Sonenscher argues, is that this understanding of capital hides crucial elements in the functioning of the modern economy that will create problems for that solution in practice. To begin with, figuring out what should go where and when is a huge administrative challenge without the signalling embedded in market prices – particularly when there are competing priorities for the use of scarce resources. Deeper down, it is difficult for the state to reconcile the 'right to work' with the requirements for a division of labour. How can the state promote individual freedom while at the same time enforcing a rational allocation of workers to tasks?

This problem stems from an analytical fusion of 'capitalism' with Adam Smith's notion of 'commercial society' that took place in debates about the political economy long before Karl Marx and Friedrich Engels wrote *The Communist Manifesto*. Capitalism originally dealt with wealth, and in particular the kind of financial wealth that could be lent by private individuals to sovereigns. The problem of such wealth being unevenly distributed has obvious solutions in the form of progressive taxation and redistribution. In the extreme form, nationalisation – or the public expropriation of private assets – would also work. Indeed, if this capital can be used more efficiently as a means of production under public rather than private management, then there is a strong argument to go down that route.

Smith deployed the notion of 'commercial society', however, to address a different set of problems. The first problem was to create the conditions for a division of labour that would allow individuals to specialise in ways that made society as a whole more productive. The second was to extend that division of labour across national boundaries so that different societies could benefit from what David Ricardo later called 'comparative advantage'. The third was to ensure that any exchange that took place reflected notions of justice and not just the power relationships that result from structural or institutional differences across groups in society or from one country to the next.

Sonenscher disentangles the two notions tied together in the Marxist – and hence the modern – idea of capitalism to show how the problems created by Smith's notion of 'commercial society' do not lend themselves to easy solutions. We can imagine an economy without private property, but not without a division of labour. Indeed, the only way we can even begin to address those problems is to imagine a public administration capable of setting up the market as an institution, creating money and regulating credit. This administration would necessarily deal with groups as well as individuals, and would also raise taxes, borrow money, create subsidies and make its own expenditures. Sonenscher is careful to note that Ricardian comparative advantage 'had as much to do with taxation as it had to do with trade' (p. 149). He also shows how what we now call 'economic policy' is a logical extension of this line of argument.

What Sonenscher assembles from this disentangled notion of capital are the foundations for social democracy (and the mixed economy) that were laid in the late eighteenth and early to mid-nineteenth centuries. In doing so, Sonenscher effectively draws a straight line from Smith through Marx to Karl Polanyi. Sonenscher's book is essential reading for any modern progressive.

Pioneers of Capitalism: The Netherlands 1000–1800
Maarten Prak and Jan Luiten van Zanden. Ian Cressie,
trans. Princeton, NJ: Princeton University Press, 2022.
£35.00/$39.95. 280 pp.

Capitalism is a lived experience, not just a theoretical construct. That experience takes place within the context of other activities, institutions, aspirations and constraints. Of course, the emergence of capitalism can shape that context, but the reverse is also true, and those contextual factors can strongly influence how capitalism works, and therefore what capitalism is.

Maarten Prak and Jan Luiten van Zanden illustrate this notion of 'capitalism in context' by focusing on the economic history of the Netherlands over the course of eight centuries. The questions they ask are fundamental: why did capitalism emerge in this corner of northern Europe? How did the emergence of capitalism shape Dutch society? And, implicitly, how did the Dutch shape capitalism?

What they find is surprising in several respects. To begin with, capitalism in what is today the Netherlands did not emerge out of feudalism, but rather at the boundaries between the Holy Roman Empire and territories that had greater local autonomy or, perhaps better, collective 'freedoms'. The Dutch did not become capitalist because they were Protestant; they became predominantly Protestant because they were able to mobilise the financial resources necessary to win their revolt against the Habsburgs. Once they were free, they did not liberalise the market, but instead sought ways to stabilise it by nationalising foreign-exchange transactions and then monopolising trade with East Asia and the West Indies through specially chartered limited-liability joint-stock companies. They also did not oppress the working classes, but rather facilitated the proliferation of guilds as collective insurance associations, channelled resources into social-safety nets and even shifted from regressive indirect taxes to wealth and income taxes.

This telling of the story is not meant to whitewash Dutch capitalism. Prak and van Zanden are careful to highlight the many abuses – even atrocities – the Dutch committed in Indonesia and Suriname, for example. The participation of Dutch merchants in the brutalisation of indigenous peoples and the trafficking of slaves across the Indian and Atlantic oceans played an important and shameful part in the success of the Dutch economy. The authors are also careful to note that income inequality in the Netherlands increased alongside prosperity; that the urbanisation of Dutch society came at a huge public-health cost; and that political power became concentrated in an ever-smaller number of hands as the rich got richer.

These qualifications are important to recall the dangers that capitalism represents. But what is striking in Prak and van Zanden's account is how much Dutch capitalism reflects the peculiarities of Dutch society. The freedoms the Dutch sought to protect and promote were collective and not individual. The tolerance they expressed toward religious differences was instrumental – tolerating one's trading partners is good business – but it was also respectful and inclusive. The capital markets they created were designed to focus on long-term investment. The rules for participation were open, and anyone with money to invest could get involved, including as shareholders. The governance arrangements at all levels and in any form of association were deliberative.

The other striking feature is the emphasis on education, literacy and 'human capital' – meaning women as well as men. Prak and van Zanden do not pretend that Dutch society was perfectly equitable. Women were not allowed to join guilds, for example, and widows suffered disproportionately from poverty. But by the standards of the time, the Dutch were literate, well educated, professional and progressive, with equal pay for equal work. That was a key part of their success through to the end of the eighteenth century. Capitalism can always be made better, something of which the early Dutch capitalists were well aware. Prak and van Zanden do us a great service by reminding us.

Cyber Security and Emerging Technologies
Melissa K. Griffith

Underground Empire: How America Weaponized the World Economy
Henry Farrell and Abraham Newman. New York: Henry Holt and Co., 2023. $28.99. 288 pp.

Chip War: The Fight for the World's Most Critical Technology
Chris Miller. London and New York: Scribner, 2022. £20.00/$30.00. 464 pp.

A surge in international trade, foreign investments, technology exchange, communication networks and global supply chains during the last two decades has produced a world that is more interdependent than ever before. This has profound implications not just for how countries interact and cooperate in addressing shared challenges and opportunities, but also for the ways in which they compete and jostle for advantage, making interdependence simultaneously a national-security tool and a national-security problem.

Two books published in the last year – Henry Farrell and Abraham Newman's *Underground Empire* and Chris Miller's *Chip War* – expertly tackle the question of global interdependence and its consequences. In the former, Farrell, a professor at Johns Hopkins University, and Newman, a professor at Georgetown University, turn a traditional international-relations debate on its head. Rather than asking how interdependence might lead to stability and cooperation, they examine how the United States has situated itself at the heart of an international web of surveillance and control. Over the course of nearly 300 pages, they consider three questions: how this web, comprising everything from global financial systems to fibre-optic cables, emerged; why global networks have been so beneficial for American economic and security interests; and how the United States – as well as its allies and adversaries – have weaponised these networks over time.

The authors argue that, despite the early aspirations of some of the network builders, who hoped that open networks would 'undermine the old world of power politics', they 'never quite escaped the shadow of America's Cold War empire' (p. 8). Why? Inertia and path dependence meant that, 'like medieval road builders, their architects often found it easier to lay down new routes on the foundations of old ones' (p. 8). Gradually and sometimes unintentionally, the United States turned emerging and intricate global economic networks into an underground empire, one through which 'it could listen in on the world's conversations and isolate its enemies from the world economy' (p. 8). This asymmetric interdependence allowed the US to project power in new ways, if only sporadically and opportunistically at first.

As the United States has become more overt in its efforts to exert control, however, other states have taken steps to safeguard their interests by leveraging and targeting the same networks upon which US power rests. Farrell and Newman issue a sobering warning: 'If this system ever made the United States safe, it won't for much longer' (p. 16). They argue that, as tensions heat up with China, the US will need to develop a new approach to weaponising interdependence, one that preserves the possibility of action while minimising the risk of uncontrolled escalation.

Whereas one of *Underground Empire*'s strengths is its impressive breadth, Miller's *Chip War* takes the opposite approach. A professor at Tufts, the author offers readers an artfully written investigation into a single technological ecosystem: semiconductors, colloquially referred to as 'chips'.

Miller's timing could not have been better. While semiconductors' emergence as one of the world's most sought-after commodities might previously have come as a surprise to many readers, shortages in the wake of COVID-19 and an array of policy initiatives have placed chips front and centre in debates about American industrial, security and foreign policies. In 2022, the US Congress allocated $52 billion for US domestic semiconductor manufacturing and the US Commerce Department's Bureau of Industry and Security implemented a bevy of export controls to limit China's access to advanced computing. These market interventions joined a 'series of deliberate decisions by government officials and corporate executives [to create] the far-flung supply chains we rely on today' (p. xxvi), and will rely on in the future.

Chip War takes readers on a whirlwind tour of the semiconductor industry, offering insights on topics such as its origins in Silicon Valley, its centrality to the Space Race, and the growing global reliance on a single Taiwanese company. Peppered throughout are fascinating historical titbits, such as the story of how a chip-fabrication plant (or 'fab') in Russia was 'reduced in the 1990s to producing tiny chips for McDonald's Happy Meal toys' (p. 159).

Miller ultimately marshals history in support of conceptualising chips as the 'new oil'. Indeed, he suggests they may be 'even more strategic' than oil (p. 98), citing their undisputed economic, military and strategic importance. To underline this point, Miller notes that 'China now spends more money each year importing chips than it spends on oil' (p. xviii).

The argument presented in *Chip War* is an ambitious one. Miller seeks to convince readers not just that semiconductors are an important and widely used technology, but that they underpin the balance of geopolitical power between states. For Miller, 'semiconductors have defined the world we live in, determining the shape of international politics, the structure of the world economy, and the balance of military power' (p. xxvii). He goes so far as to argue that 'the rivalry between the United States and China may well be determined by computer power' (p. xviii). While this bold proposition may leave some readers unpersuaded, Miller offers one of the most comprehensive and nuanced accounts of one of the most geopolitically contentious industries today.

Proponents of globalisation have long argued that interdependence promotes global stability and cooperation. For Miller, Farrell and Newman, the very same webs of interdependence, and the technological ecosystems that shape them, have become arenas of power projection and competition. *Underground Empire* and *Chip War* are must-reads for anyone seeking a deeper understanding of how technological and economic power is harnessed, for better or worse, in the modern world.

The Ransomware Hunting Team: A Band of Misfits' Improbable Crusade to Save the World from Cybercrime
Renee Dudley and Daniel Golden. New York: Farrar, Straus and Giroux, 2022. $30.00. 368 pp.

Allan Liska opens the second edition of his book *Ransomware: Understand. Prevent. Recover*, which seeks to familiarise readers with the evolving threat posed by ransomware attacks and an array of techniques to counteract them, with a dedication to the 'thousands of people all over the world who are fighting ransomware in different ways'. In gripping fashion, Renee Dudley and Daniel Golden introduce readers to one team doing just that.

While many readers may be familiar with the technological underpinnings of this particular form of cyber crime, the story told by *The Ransomware Hunting Team* is as much about people as it is about technology. The book can trace its origins to a gathering five years ago in Golden's home of the then newly minted tech 'though not so tech' team (as Golden jokingly described it in a talk given at the 2023 Savannah Book Festival) of the independent newsroom ProPublica. What emerged from those initial discussions is a real-life technological thriller that is equal parts inspiring and alarming.

The Ransomware Hunting Team chronicles the efforts of a small group of self-taught civilians who volunteer their time to thwart ransomware operators around the world. They do so often at great personal cost and, despite saving millions of ransomware victims, they have remained largely unknown to the public. Until now.

The members of this enigmatic group – an informal, 'invitation-only' coalition of roughly a dozen malware experts – hail from across the United States and Europe. Their improbable success stories, which feature 'a technical virtuosity that's largely self-taught', are also deeply human (p. 9). Their ranks include Michael Gillespie, widely known by the handle 'demonslay335', who, with his wife, has 'eight cats, two dogs, and a rabbit'; Fabian Wosar, who enjoys displaying 'brightly colored artwork depicting scenes from video games' on his walls; and Sarah White, who bakes focaccia for her roommates and adopts the alias 'White' to 'maintain her privacy and protect herself against retaliation by ransomware gangs' (pp. 8, 67 and 73).

Filling what Dudley and Golden refer to as a 'gaping void' left by the US government, which they say was 'slow to respond to the growing ransomware threat', this unlikely band of heroes has found itself battling ransomware actors and malicious code in what feels like a never-ending game of cat and mouse (p. 10) – a game with real-world consequences. *The Ransomware Hunting Team* serves as a stark reminder of just how personal and pervasive ransomware has become, making victims both of individuals and of institutions such as schools and hospitals.

The book also serves, if unintentionally, as a tribute to the life of Vitali Kremez. The 36-year-old cyber-security researcher and ethical hacker tragically lost his life while scuba-diving near Hollywood Beach, Florida, in October 2022. While many readers will never have known him outside the pages of this book, *The Ransomware Hunting Team* memorialises Vitali's status as a cherished member of the cyber-security community.

Middle East
Ray Takeyh

Confronting Saddam Hussein: George W. Bush and the Invasion of Iraq
Melvyn P. Leffler. Oxford and New York: Oxford University Press, 2023. £21.99/$27.95. 240 pp.

It has been 20 years since America invaded Iraq. Today one is hard pressed to find anyone willing to defend the invasion, and most of its erstwhile supporters have expressed various shades of regret. George W. Bush, who issued the order to invade, has maintained his silence, neither defending his actions nor offering any form of contrition. After all the recriminations and accusations, it is time for a balanced assessment of the war. Melvyn Leffler, a distinguished professor of history at the University of Virginia, offers such an assessment – a dispassionate, judicious and even-handed diplomatic history. The Iraq War will never be redeemed by historians, but that does not mean it cannot be better understood.

The war cannot be separated from the 9/11 tragedies. Bush and his advisers were fearful of another attack and the combination of weapons of mass destruction and terrorism. It is sometimes forgotten that Saddam Hussein's Iraq was a national-security problem that had kicked out weapons inspectors and was openly gloating about the carnage wrought by al-Qaeda. The sanctions imposed on Iraq were fraying, and there was genuine concern that Saddam would escape his box and once more menace his neighbours. The official policy of the United States before 9/11 was regime change. The Iraq Liberation Act of 1998 was endorsed by the Clinton administration and enjoyed near unanimous support in Congress. All this does not justify the invasion, as there were plenty of sober voices urging caution, but the context is still important.

Leffler's even-handed approach can at times be exacting. He insists that Bush had an open mind and was hoping that his brand of coercive diplomacy would disarm Saddam and obviate the need for war. During the run-up to the war, however, Bush repeatedly insisted that he did not believe Saddam would ever come clean, leaving no alternative to invasion. The emphasis was on coercion, not diplomacy, and it is hard to see how Iraq could have persuaded America that it had cleansed itself of its weapons stock. One of the oddities of the war is that no one advised Bush not to invade. Even Colin Powell, his sceptical secretary of state, never came out forcefully against the war, only offering tepid warnings about the difficulty of the mission. It is possible that Bush would have ignored such advice, but no one in his inner circle ever attempted to talk him out of invading.

Survival | vol. 65 no. 5 | October–November 2023 | pp. 189–195 https://doi.org/10.1080/00396338.2023.2261268

Leffler is unsparing about the administration's lack of post-war planning, the so-called 'Phase IV'. Secretary of defense Donald Rumsfeld had no interest in administering a messy Iraq and was too eager to pull out after Saddam was toppled. The administration's scattershot approach contributed to a civil war that ravaged Iraq and drained American resources. Bush was a curious commander-in-chief, rarely imposing discipline on his squabbling aides and seldom insisting on timely course corrections. In the end, Leffler proves that the Iraq War was a tragedy and not a crime, as some of its more strident critics have claimed. This important book will hopefully set the standard for other authors seeking to examine one of America's costliest conflicts.

Iraq Against the World: Saddam, America, and the Post-Cold War Order
Samuel Helfont. Oxford: Oxford University Press, 2023.
£25.99/$39.95. 280 pp.

Seldom has the Middle East seen a regime as unsavoury as that of Saddam Hussein, a man who grew up admiring Josef Stalin, created his own deranged police state and abused generations of Iraqis. Saddam's crimes were not contained by Iraq's borders, as he twice invaded his neighbours. His use of chemical weapons on Iran terrorised civilians and disfigured front-line soldiers. Saddam and his Ba'ath Party also launched a semi-effective campaign to influence Western opinion in the aftermath of the Gulf War.

Iraq Against the World is part of a new crop of books that are using the archives of Saddam's regime to probe its inner workings. The book's focus is more limited than its title might suggest, but it does shed light on an important and neglected topic, making the case that even a clumsy totalitarian regime can succeed in conditioning global opinion. In the end, Iraq may turn out to be the Middle Eastern country best understood by historians. Nowhere else in the region does one have access to such a rich depository of archival records.

After Iraq's eviction from Kuwait in 1991, the triumphant allies imposed comprehensive sanctions intended to force Saddam to reveal the full scope of his weapons programme. As has become clear since the 2003 invasion, Saddam had basically disarmed, and the weapons inspectors did their job. But in the 1990s, the question of Iraq had become embedded in American domestic politics, and no administration was prepared to invite a political backlash by rehabilitating a Saddam-led Iraq. Baghdad tried to weaken Western solidarity by highlighting the suffering of Iraq's people and working with various left-wing organisations to demonstrate the human toll of the embargo. Many of those organisations had their own agenda and did not know that some of the information they were using was coming from Ba'athist operatives.

Did Iraq's public-relations campaign have any impact? To be sure, by the end of the 1990s, France, Russia and many Islamic states were complaining loudly about the cost of sanctions. Malnutrition, a lack of medicines and a shortage of basic commodities devastated Iraq's lower and middle classes. The standard American response that all this was Saddam's fault did not sit well with global opinion. In this sense, it was Iraqi suffering more than any Ba'athist campaign that weakened the sanctions regime. Belatedly, the Clinton administration tried various oil-for-food programmes that offered Iraq a means of selling its oil and using the money for targeted purchases of humanitarian goods. In a paradoxical manner, such programmes strengthened Saddam's hand, as he was the dispenser of patronage and used the money to his political advantage.

The more effective lobbying campaign during this period – one that lies beyond the author's purview – was conducted by Iraqi exiles plotting against Saddam. Ahmed Chalabi and other exiles pushed hard for Western intervention to topple Saddam, and managed to gain bipartisan support in Washington. In 1998, Bill Clinton signed a law that had passed with overwhelming support in Congress declaring America's policy to be regime change in Iraq.

Asad's Autocratic Dynasty in Syria: Civil War and the Role of Regional and Global Powers
Moshe Ma'oz. Liverpool: Liverpool University Press, 2023.
£24.95. 165 pp.

Moshe Ma'oz is one of the more esteemed scholars of the Middle East, and has paid particular attention to Syria during his long academic career. His latest book is intended to introduce the general reader to the complex maze that is Syria. Compact chapters serve up a history of great-power involvement in the country, the rise of the Assad dynasty and how it all came crashing down in 2011.

Syria has long been a conflicted land. Carved up by the mandatory powers, it became an amalgam of ethnicities and religious sects that could only be held together by force. In that sense, Syria was not that different from neighbouring Iraq or other multi-confessional states. Its post-independence politics were turbulent, with coups and counter-coups. The Ba'ath Party attempted to impose ideological discipline on this unruly land, only to become a tool of ambitious military officers looking for a veneer of legitimacy. Syria was to be governed by strongmen, not fuzzy intellectuals who sharpened their debating skills in Parisian cafes.

Ma'oz is at his best in untangling the bewildering strands of Syrian politics and the personalities bound up in them. The elder Assad, who reigned over

Syria for three decades, was one of the region's more effective dictators. He had no compunction about shedding blood, but managed to provide stability for a nation that had seen little of it. He empowered his own Alawite sect and developed an effective patronage system. He waged war against Israel, made himself indispensable to a generation of American diplomats dreaming of peace in the Middle East and took aid from the Soviet Union without becoming its client.

Bashar al-Assad was bound to have difficulty mastering the balancing act that his father perfected. He initially talked of reform in a nation whose governing compact was sustained by brute force. When the 2011 Arab Spring sent winds of change across the region, Syria was bound to falter. It seemed to shatter, becoming a venue for both great-power competition and regional rivalries. Islamists of various hues, Kurds seeking emancipation, a Sunni business class caught in the crossfire and the all-important Alawites sought their own ends in the midst of external intervention. The most successful outsiders by far were Iran and Russia. The forces mustered by Tehran, along with Russian airpower, proved decisive for Assad's survival. It was a savage conflict, with millions killed or displaced.

Ma'oz takes the Obama administration to task for drawing various red lines and not enforcing them. In this telling, the Americans became hapless bystanders, outsmarted by Russian dictator Vladimir Putin. Today, as Putin finds himself in a debilitating stalemate of his own making in Ukraine, it may be difficult to recall a time when he was celebrated as a master strategist. It is equally difficult to see how even a more committed America could have altered Syria's fate. After Iraq, both Republican and Democratic administrations have proven reluctant to intervene militarily in the Middle East, where the outcome of such interventions is inevitably uncertain.

This Flame Within: Iranian Revolutionaries in the United States
Manijeh Moradian. Durham, NC: Duke University Press, 2022.
$28.95. 352 pp.

Members of Iran's modern middle class, with their degrees from Western universities, were to be the mainstay of Shah Mohammad Reza Pahlavi's rule in Iran. By the 1960s, the shah had turned his back on the traditional classes comprising merchants, landowners and clerics, who had powered Persian dynasties for centuries. Iran's 'new man' was secular, socially liberal, politically obedient and Western-trained. The shah dispatched hundreds of thousands of young Iranians abroad for training, only to see them turn against him.

In *This Flame Within*, Manijeh Moradian concentrates on Iranian student activism in the United States. Many young Iranians perceived their struggle in the broader context of the Global South seeking emancipation from Western colonialism. It is an interesting topic too often marred by a tendentious reading of Cold War politics and incomprehensible academic jargon. There are many insightful observations here that get lost among long-winded paragraphs. The book could have used a serious scrubbing by a sharp-eyed editor.

Still, the author does grapple with the many contradictions that ultimately bedevilled the Pahlavi dynasty. For the modernising monarch of Iran, the West set the standard of development. The shah constantly compared his country to European nations and insisted that Iran would exceed their production levels within compressed timelines. He was arrogant and supercilious, often lecturing Western leaders about their lack of will and the idleness of their people. The young men sent abroad were to be the foot soldiers of the new Iran. Armed with Western development paradigms, they would refashion their backward nation and pull the benighted masses into the age of modernity. Instead, they organised protests every time the shah visited America and Europe.

By the 1970s, the situation became even more dangerous as many students joined various urban guerrilla groups that terrorised the monarchy. They attacked government offices, banks and restaurants where Western contractors and salesmen of all sorts congregated. The shah's secret police disarmed the guerrillas, but not without much struggle. The monarch, cocooned in his various palaces, could not understand why the beneficiaries of his largess were committing acts of violence that led to their own deaths.

The predicament of many of these student activists would be even worse after the revolution triumphed, as the vengeful clerics showed little compunction about casting them aside. The first post-revolutionary government did feature prominent former student activists such as Ebrahim Yazdi and Sadegh Ghotbzadeh, but they were soon excised. Under the banner of a cultural revolution, the mullahs closed the universities for several years and revamped the curriculum. Leftist student associations were soon disbanded and replaced by Islamist ones. Women who pressed for emancipation were made to cover themselves in Islamic dress, and countless young men died on the battlefields of Iraq.

Both the shah and his clerical successors misread their people in a fundamental way. Throughout the last and current centuries, the Iranian people have sought a representative and accountable government. Both young and old have grown weary of a series of despotic governments and their national compacts. The shah offered financial rewards in exchange for political passivity. The mullahs offer celestial salvation that is even less tangible to a nation that bends toward secularism after 40 years of theocratic rule.

The Regent of Allah: Ali Khamenei's Political Evolution in Iran

Mehdi Khalaji. Lanham, MD: Rowman & Littlefield, 2023.
£30.00/$35.00. 244 pp.

Ayatollah Sayyid Ali Khamenei is one of the most successful despots in the history of the modern Middle East. He is a revolutionary with a revolutionary's integrity. His ideological commitments are plain to see, and his animosities are enduring. During his more than three decades in power, he has beset his domestic rivals, outwitted a succession of American presidents and survived various internal insurrections. In *The Regent of Allah*, Mehdi Khalaji tries to come to terms with Khamenei's life and times. This is not a conventional biography, and there are curious gaps. Still, there are important nuggets sprinkled through the text.

As a young man growing up in Mashhad, Khamenei had one foot in the city's theological centres and another in its literary circles. He was a cleric whose horizons were not limited to pondering religious texts. He enjoyed Western novels and the works of Islamist revolutionaries. He seemingly befriended Ali Shariati, a philosopher who sought to infuse religion with a revolutionary spirit. Shariati would become popular with university students, but not so much with grand ayatollahs, who resented his ill-informed intrusion into their domain.

One of the shortcomings of the book is that it spends little time on the revolution that catapulted Khamenei to power. The cause of theocracy did not have many stakeholders at the top echelons of the clerical class. Most of Iran's ayatollahs were displeased with Shah Mohammad Reza Pahlavi's rule, but were inclined to work with the monarch. They were hoping to nudge him in the right direction, as opposed to changing the regime root and branch. Khamenei was part of a distinct minority of clerics who embraced Ayatollah Ruhollah Khomeini's revolutionary call from the beginning and accepted his arcane theory of the direct assumption of power by God's regent. It would have been good to know how Khamenei embarked on this journey, which sits alongside centuries of Shia thought.

The book is at its best where it covers Khamenei's tenure as Iran's Supreme Leader. It may come as a surprise to many readers that Khamenei initially had a relatively benign view of the West and was thought to be among the regime's pragmatic leaders. All this seemed to change as Khamenei embraced anti-Americanism as the best way of consolidating his power and ensuring the survival of the revolution. Khamenei was a brilliant tactician who gradually placed his own men at the regime's critical choke points. He nurtured the lethal Revolutionary Guard Corps and ensured that the force remained directly loyal to him. Today, he stands at the top of the Islamic Republic, rarely challenged by other political actors.

As a former seminarian, Khalaji is adept at explaining in digestible language the complex theological debates that rattled the shrine cities of Qom and Najaf. To understand a theocracy, one must comprehend Shia rituals and traditions. Indeed, the last section of the book tries to situate the nuclear debate within a theological context. It appears the men of God are satisfied there is sufficient justification to develop a weapon of mass destruction, particularly if its intended targets are non-Muslims.

South Asia
Teresita C. Schaffer

I Feel No Peace: Rohingya Fleeing Over Seas and Rivers
Kaamil Ahmed. London: C. Hurst & Co., 2023. £18.99. 272 pp.

The Rohingya, an ethnic minority with a large population in Myanmar, became globally known for fleeing that country after ethnic conflict and the hostility of several governments made their lives unliveable. They made their way across the border to Bangladesh, one of the most crowded countries in the world, but also one of the economic success stories of the last 50 years. Kaamil Ahmed, a UK-based journalist of Bangladeshi background, has painted an extraordinary – and depressing – picture of the Rohingya's recent history. His account, based primarily on intensive interviews with people caught up in the refugee whirlwind, makes clear that their plight is even worse than one might expect.

The title, as he explains early in the book, is a rough translation of an expression that was on the lips and in the hearts of nearly everyone he spoke to, using the evocative word *oshanti* ('un-peace'), which is shared by the Bengali and Rohingya languages. The point at which the Rohingya became a global byword for refugee misery was in 2017, when a military occupation forced them out of Myanmar and across the Naf River into Bangladesh. In fact, their involuntary odyssey had started nearly a half-century earlier, with military campaigns inside Myanmar; a governmental decision not to grant this group the automatic birthright citizenship that most of the country's ethnic mosaic enjoyed; and pogroms.

Through the eyes and words of this community, Ahmed puts the reader in the middle of their woes – people stuck without documents, terrified of anyone in a uniform, indebted from their unsuccessful attempts to resettle themselves, worn out and pressured into 'muling' drugs. He follows people to Malaysia, where most Rohingya live a bit better and Islam is the predominant religion, but where the welcome mat, such as it was, has worn out.

The Bangladeshi government has taken justifiable credit for taking in nearly a million people, but even there the authorities have long since tired of the substantial burden of this enormous and resourceless community. The ill will the Rohingya found all around them in Myanmar is absent, but there is an almost equally toxic indifference in Bangladesh.

The book ends on a more uplifting note. Momtaz, a woman who has several interviews in the book, says *shanti lage* – 'I feel peace'. It is not a complete peace, but a life with 'normal' sources of anxiety and with neighbours who are fairly neighbourly. Momtaz even dares to dream about her daughter becoming a doctor (p. 231).

Survival | vol. 65 no. 5 | October–November 2023 | pp. 196–202 https://doi.org/10.1080/00396338.2023.2261269

Ahmed doesn't provide a solution to a problem with overwhelming dimensions. The usual proposal for refugees is to either voluntarily return home or resettle elsewhere. Treating the Rohingya like citizens in distress is one bridge that even Aung San Suu Kyi, despite her earlier reputation as a human-rights icon, was not willing to cross, even before her government was displaced by a military coup. Meanwhile, the world's refugee-support institutions are far from having the resources to finance resettlement elsewhere. One book cannot solve the problem, but this one will help the reader understand it at the human level.

India Is Broken: A People Betrayed, Independence to Today
Ashoka Mody. Stanford, CA: Stanford University Press, 2023.
$35.00. 528 pp.

Ashoka Mody, born and raised in India but now a visiting professor at Princeton University, has written a searing critique of India's economic policy since its independence in 1947. Conventional wisdom faults India's governments for excessively state-centred policy. Mody, by contrast, begins and ends his account with the country's failure to produce enough jobs to employ its large population productively and to invest enough in education and health so that its citizens can achieve their potential. Jobs and agriculture were the keys to progress, he argues.

Between his introduction and conclusion, Mody stresses a more familiar parade of mistaken governmental priorities. Jawaharlal Nehru, he argues, pursued a strategy centred on 'the temples of today' (pp. 53–4): big infrastructure and state-owned industry projects such as Chandigarh, the state capital of Punjab and Haryana that was designed by Le Corbusier. He built up science instruction, but failed to make a big investment in basic education.

Nehru's successors, Mody argues, similarly missed their chance to transform India's economy. Lal Bahadur Shastri made a promising start, but his death in 1966 cut his tenure short. Indira Gandhi, the most politically powerful of the early prime ministers, was determined to maximise her political control, a process that culminated in the 'Emergency', a two-year experiment in autocracy and a bitterly contested effort at coercive family planning.

At this point, Mody's account begins to diverge from the standard one, which would highlight a degree of deregulation and a sharp rise in GDP growth. He blames Rajiv Gandhi for enabling the rise of Hindu nationalism, and the other prime ministers who preceded Narendra Modi for failing to bring job growth into the 'shining India' formula. This discussion fits most comfortably within the growing 'what led to Narendra Modi' literature. The picture Mody paints is one of unremitting corruption, both financial and political, and a continuing failure to build up human capital.

India Is Broken is a good read and brings welcome attention to the human-development issues that are still high on the list of obstacles India needs to overcome. The problem of illiteracy has been much attenuated, especially in south India. The problem of jobs has been harder to address. The author gives plenty of examples of countries that have been more successful in developing human capital and creating large numbers of jobs.

I would, however, have welcomed more discussion of how today's government could remedy these important shortcomings. Modi and the Bharatiya Janata Party have certainly given priority to economic expansion, but the main tools in their effort are familiar from earlier times, notably incentives to 'make in India'. The rise in communal violence imposes a national cost, and doubtless an economic one as well.

Migrants and Machine Politics: How India's Urban Poor Seek Representation and Responsiveness
Adam Michael Auerbach and Tariq Thachil. Princeton, NJ: Princeton University Press, 2023. £100.00/$120.00. 288 pp.

India defies important aspects of the conventional wisdom about political participation. The poor, and especially the rural poor, vote in larger percentages (and hence larger numbers) than the middle class or the rich. Locally powerful figures are believed to 'own' large vote banks in their constituencies, and these in turn are believed to be based largely on caste affinities.

Adam Michael Auerbach and Tariq Thachil are not the first scholars to plunge into the complex operation of machine politics in India. Ward Berenschot examined the working and dynamics of political machines in three neighbourhoods in Ahmedabad, the largest city in Gujarat, in his book *Riot Politics*, and Milan Vaishnav's *When Crime Pays* provides a gripping analysis of why and how so many of India's parliamentarians come to office with a criminal past.

Auerbach and Thachil take another approach. They study, in tremendous detail, how the urban machines come together, who makes them up, what kind of services they provide, what holds them together and how their responsiveness to local demands is perceived by the people in their neighbourhoods. The book is based on work in slum neighbourhoods of two mid-sized Indian cities, Bhopal in Madhya Pradesh and Jaipur in Rajasthan, in the northern 'Hindi belt'. They describe their method as looking at politics 'from the bottom up'. Many of their findings contradict the conventional wisdom. For example, they were consistently told that neighbourhood residents, including recent migrants from the countryside, participated in selecting representatives, or 'brokers', who helped the neighbourhood obtain help from official sources. They found that caste affinity was not an especially important basis for this selection, and that education was a plus. Diversity among the representatives was intensified by electoral reservations for women or downtrodden castes (the Indian equivalent of affirmative action).

Similarly unexpected findings turn up when the authors explore who are considered the most desirable followers, which services people in the neighbourhood want most and which ones brokers are most eager to supply (which tracks closely with those services the brokers can personally take credit for).

If I were planning to organise a political campaign in urban India, this book would be a terrific guide. It does very little, however, to explain the ideological side of voting, or the appeal of strong national leaders. At a time when the country's most ideological party is securely in power, and when its leader, Prime Minister Narendra Modi, is clearly more popular than his party, this account still leaves out important aspects of elections. While the cerebral approach to analysing which services a neighbourhood wants or which ones a broker is eager to help deliver is fascinating, it is not the whole story. As Berenschot wrote a decade ago, if the broker system is working, the last thing the representatives and politicians who participate in it would want is a government supply system that works on its own!

India's Military Strategy: Countering Pakistan's Challenge
S. Kalyanaraman. London: Bloomsbury, 2023. £85.00. 300 pp.

S. Kalyanaraman spent 20 years as a research fellow at the Manohar Parrikar Institute for Defence Studies and Analyses (MP-IDSA), India's best-known think tank devoted to defence and security issues. As a specialist in Indian security policy, he would have been aware that writing a book on Indian military strategy is a challenging task. At least one scholar of South Asian security, George Tanham, made a name for himself by concluding that India had no strategy and no strategic culture. If Kalyanaraman's book was intended to refute Tanham's work, it does a good job. He concludes that India has not one, but three strategies.

Kalyanaraman grounds his strategic analysis in three key factors. Firstly, India and Pakistan have incompatible concepts of their identity, with Pakistan the homeland for the subcontinent's Muslims and India a secular state. Next comes Pakistan's long-standing quest for parity with India, and finally the two countries' irreconcilable positions on Kashmir.

These three core principles have been around since the partition of the subcontinent, but the main message about India's military strategy is how it has changed. Kalyanaraman distinguishes three phases. From independence until about 1970, India followed a strategy of attrition or 'exhaustion'. It sought to wear down Pakistan's forces to the point of 'strategic success', which meant achieving all of India's major goals. Ironically, Pakistan seemed to be using the same approach, hoping to burn through enough of India's military supplies that India would give up the fight. Neither succeeded.

In 1971, circumstances handed India an opportunity to go for what Kalyanaraman calls a strategy of 'annihilation', which in this case meant breaking up Pakistan and forming Bangladesh. The strategy relied on 'multiple prongs of swift advance' in place of the previous strategy, which relied more heavily on slow but massive movement (pp. 201–5). Kalyanaraman acknowledges that the 1971 conflict took place amid a civil war, but he gives insufficient credit to the domestic factors inside East Pakistan that had a tremendous impact on the fighting: the militias – some of them strengthened by Bengali officers who had left the Pakistan army – and the overwhelming popular support for the independence movement. Looking at it strictly from the perspective of military strategy, this important victory instilled in India's military leadership a desire for better inter-services coordination and for longer-term planning.

The third phase, starting in the late 1980s and early 1990s, is what Kalyanaraman calls 'strategy in the shadow of nuclear weapons' (p. 214). He refers to the changes wrought by Pakistan's acquisition of nuclear weapons, but India's nuclear breakthrough had an equally profound impact. This basically ruled out the option of initiating a full-scale war and made it necessary to think about how to avoid escalating a limited war. He gives great weight to the diplomacy surrounding the crises that followed 1990, with active involvement by the United States and several other Western countries. India, contrary to its usual practice, played along with these diplomatic efforts – and again, ironically, Pakistan did the same. When prime minister Nawaz Sharif flew to China in 1999 in the midst of fighting around Kargil to seek support, what was meant to be a six-day visit ended after a day and a half with only a rather tepid statement to show for it. What Kalyanaraman might have said was that the same nuclear weapons that had made India and Pakistan more cautious had led outside countries to conclude that what they really cared about in India–Pakistan relations was avoiding a nuclear war.

Kalyanaraman has successfully simplified the foundations of India's strategic approach and distinguished its three main phases thus far. That should greatly assist those scholars who come after him. Unfortunately, they will also need to consider the factors that complicate the picture.

Understanding the India–China Border: The Enduring Threat of War in High Himalaya
Manoj Joshi. London: C. Hurst & Co., 2022. £30.00. 256 pp.

Writing about the India–China border is an ambitious enterprise given the extensive literature already in print. Manoj Joshi's book, reflecting his standing both as a national-security journalist and a scholar of India–China relations, situates the border in a larger context. He views its tangled history through the prism of the India–China clash at Galwan in summer 2020. He argues that the way China and India have dealt with the border reflects how both these rising powers see their own place in the world, and in particular their ties with the United States.

Joshi reviews both what one might call the multi-decade 'incident report' and the larger geopolitical picture in careful detail. He blames both sides for their failure to resolve the border dispute. He shares the prevalent opinion that Jawaharlal Nehru's naive view of the other Asian giant in the 1950s and 1960s left him vulnerable to being out-negotiated. In the run-up to the Chinese attack in 1962 that led to India's rapid defeat, Joshi acknowledges that India's 'forward policy' of moving as close as possible to its own claim lines was provocative, but notes that China was making similar moves. These competing policies of encroachment, Joshi argues, gave the 1962 war some striking similarities with those of the 2020 clash.

From 1960 onwards, India and China discussed three types of possible border deal. One that first surfaced in 1960 was essentially a territorial freeze, with India keeping Arunachal Pradesh in the east and China retaining Aksai Chin in the west. Another proposed deal in 1985 represented a harder line from China, which demanded 'substantial Indian concessions' in the east, a border area that had a significant Indian population. Finally, in 1993, the emphasis shifted toward managing rather than resolving the dispute. The two sides established institutions and protocols designed to prevent open warfare. The Border Peace and Tranquility Agreement of 1993 and the closely related agreement on confidence-building measures formalised the policy, committing the two sides to work toward a resolution but stopping well short of an actual settlement.

Why did none of these resolve the conflict? The more fundamental question is whether either country considered a border settlement its top priority. By the time the Border Peace and Tranquility Agreement was negotiated, it was increasingly clear that neither did. Both were rising powers, but China's rise started earlier, and it moved faster than India's, especially economically. Both wanted to avoid a war by miscalculation. Joshi argues that China did not want to resolve the border, preferring to keep India off balance.

This brings Joshi's narrative back to the clashes in 2020, which produced the first combat fatalities in 45 years. Peace and Tranquility had been quite successful, but the institutions it established had gradually lost some of their effectiveness as both parties started to pursue incompatible goals. China's objective had expanded to primacy not just in East Asia but in South Asia as well, with India accepting a subservient position. India's goal was still 'strategic autonomy', but this did not mean subservience. Despite China's substantial economic lead, India still saw itself as an active competitor.

Joshi concludes that the risk of Himalayan war is still considerable. Certainly, India's concept of strategic autonomy includes a desire for a meaningful and positive relationship with China. Nehru's goal of non-alignment has not disappeared. And, as the controversy over China's publication of a map in summer 2023 that shows Arunachal Pradesh inside China reminds us, neither has the border dispute.

This is a gripping, well-written book with diverse sources ranging from Indian and Chinese scholars and officials to Joshi's own experience covering some of the events he describes. One subject that is surprisingly absent is the two countries' nuclear development. Still, if the future of Asian and global security is on your mind, this book should be in your collection.

From the Archives

One Cold War Among Many?

Pierre Hassner

Editor's note

Pierre Hassner, who died in May 2018 at the age of 85, was a long-standing friend of the IISS and contributor to *Survival*. His acclaimed *Adelphi* paper, *Change and Security in Europe*, appeared in 1968. His first book review for *Survival* was published in 1965, and his first original article, 'Eurocommunism and Detente', appeared in 1977. When the journal was relaunched in 2008, he accepted our invitation to become a contributing editor, and regularly contributed book reviews and articles until poor health forced him to stop in 2016. One of those articles is reprinted below. We asked him to write it after the August 2008 Russian attack on Georgia, knowing that a Jewish witness of events in pre- and Second World War Romania, who emigrated with his family to France to escape communism, and who became one of France's most celebrated and profound philosophers on the canvas of international relations, would have something wise and important to say. He did not disappoint, and it seems especially valuable to reread this early assessment of renewed tension between Russia and the West that has now, 15 years later, metastasised into full-blown hostility.

I

Forty years ago, shortly after the Soviet invasion of Czechoslovakia, the great strategic thinker Thomas Schelling stunned the audience of the 10th ISS conference in Oxford by declaring:

> I tore up my prepared speech which was supposed to announce: 'Something wonderful has happened. I was wrong in my book *Arms and Influence*. Great powers cannot coerce small states through the use of force. Whatever damage my country may have inflicted upon Vietnam,

Pierre Hassner is Research Director Emeritus at the Centre d'Etudes et de Recherches Internationales in Paris and a contributing editor to Survival.

Survival | vol. 65 no. 5 | October–November 2023 | pp. 203–212 https://doi.org/10.1080/00396338.2023.2261273

the harm done to America's soul and self-esteem is even more serious.'
And now the Russians with this irrational action against Czechoslovakia
again commit the same disastrous mistake and I don't know what
to say.

Of course in the short run Schelling was wrong. The Soviet Union's action
was logical given the nature of its regime and its rule and, predictably, was
not a failure. Czechoslovakia's geographical and cultural conditions did not
permit a Vietnam-type resistance and the West's fear of escalation kept it
from intervening. But in the long run, Schelling was right. 1989–91 proved
that in 1968 Czechoslovakia had lost a battle, but not the war.

Could it be that, in the case of Georgia, Russia will again have shown
willingness to use brute power and the West hesitation or over-extension,
but in the long run the option of rule by military intervention will prove
sterile and untenable in the modern world? Are we, then, in for a new Cold
War before a new democratic revolution?

The parallels are too obvious to need elaboration. The two lessons drawn
by Paul Goble from the Georgian crisis (that Russia, far from being a status
quo participant in the post-Cold War international system, is a revisionist
power ready to use force to challenge the settlement of 1991 and to reconstitute
the Soviet Union in a new form, and that the United States had imprudently
encouraged some of Moscow's neighbours to stand up against this enterprise
without being prepared to protect them in their hour of need) certainly suggest
more continuity than change.[1] Yet the differences are just as important.

In a sense, the invasion of Georgia, and the recognition of South Ossetia
and Abkhazia, is more important and more ominous than the invasion of
Czechoslovakia. The latter was a rearguard action in a period of imperial
decline, and in a region which had been behind the Iron Curtain for 20 years.
The very necessity for Moscow to resort to military occupation showed the
failure of its attempt to integrate the Soviet bloc. By contrast, the invasion of
Georgia is part of a counter-offensive by a resurgent Russia profiting from a
favourable international situation ('America down, Russia up, Europe out', as
the saying goes in Moscow) to challenge the entire international order. More
generally, it does indeed confirm the accelerated decline of the two competing

visions which dominated the post-Cold War world and which can be seen as two versions of democratic triumphalism: the imperial and the institutional. The credibility of the United States as a universal promoter and protector of freedom and that of Russia as a 'responsible stakeholder' in an institutional system of world governance are badly shaken and, with them, the very idea of a world ruled by a benevolent empire and that of a world governed in security matters by rules, by multilateral institutions and international cooperation.

Of course, developments in Iraq and Afghanistan, in Darfur and Burma, in Chechnya and Tibet, the paralysis of the Security Council, and the weakness and over-extension of UN peacekeeping forces had already signalled the increasing irrelevance of both. But August 2008 will remain as the symbol of their demise for the foreseeable future.

II

What is taking their place? There are two basic visions: one 'ideological', heralding a return to the Cold War, and one 'realist', heralding a multipolar world based on regional hegemonies or spheres of influence. Both carry elements of truth but have serious flaws, as they neglect the complexity, ambiguity and fluidity of the present world.

A new cold war is indeed developing between Russia and the West (or at least the United States, Britain and some other European countries, particularly the former members or satellites of the Soviet Union) but it is one among many cold and hot wars. The historical Cold War was one of the two basic 'relationships of major tension', along with the North–South struggles of decolonisation. Of course conflicts and realignments existed within the respective camps and the idea of common interests between adversaries had emerged. But today the multiple and contradictory constellations of conflict and cooperation are such that the very idea of the Cold War as one basic conflict is hard to sustain. A few years ago, Washington hawks were divided into 'China firsters' and 'al-Qaeda firsters'. Adding a clan of 'Russia firsters' would be implausible. Alternatively, lumping all the potential or actual adversaries of the West or of liberal democracy together would be as strategically misleading as the lumping together of Saddam Hussein, Osama bin Laden, and Mahmoud Ahmadinejad.

For the West as a whole, China is, in the long run, a more formidable rival and potential opponent than Russia and, at the same time, an ambiguous partner and potential threat to the latter. One could speak of a cold war, and a potentially hot one, with Iran. Metaphorical wars abound: against terrorism, against the proliferation of weapons of mass destruction, against organised crime, against illegal migration. The competition for scarce resources, particularly energy, and between increasingly protectionist economies also can be compared to a cold war. Outside the geographical borders of the West, permanent conflicts which often have both a domestic and a regional character oppose Israel and the Palestinians or their Arab neighbours, Shi'ites and Sunnis, India, Pakistan and Afghanistan, Sudan, Chad and Libya, the countries of the Horn of Africa and of the Great Lakes region, and so on. Finally, even though the roles of states, of nationalist aspirations and enmities and of the use of force may be increasing again, they are inevitably influenced and often transformed by transnational and global challenges such as climate change, epidemics and famines.

Economic interdependence seems every bit as important as military force: it creates new conflicts, provides means of pressure and blackmail, but also tends to limit these conflicts by fear of boomerang effects and of uncontrolled escalation. The conflict over Georgia is of course primarily political, having to do with security, independence, territorial integrity, the use of force and the attempt to overthrow a democratically elected government and to punish and ruin a foreign country through military occupation. But it has a clear economic dimension as well. One important objective and consequence of Moscow's action is to throw doubt on the security of the Baku–Tbilisi–Ceyhan oil pipeline and of the projected Nabucco gas pipeline, and hence on the opportunities for Europe to reduce dependence upon Russia. It is precisely this dependence which accounts in large measure for Western Europe's and particularly Germany's reluctance to react strongly. The downside for Russia is also primarily economic: loss of foreign investments, capital flight and distrust towards its financial activities abroad.

This increasing distrust may play against Russia in a way reminiscent of Cold War times and extending beyond the West. Even its associates in the Shanghai Cooperation Organisation are ill at ease both with its imperious and adventurous behaviour and with its use of minorities. Until now such feelings had mostly been directed against the United States. The South views the United States, and to a large extent the West as a whole, as having lost most of its credibility and legitimacy. It feels there is no longer any reason for the majority of the world to accept being lectured, judged and punished by Western-dominated institutions according to Western-inspired criteria. In this sense, the United States and Europe are often more isolated than the rogue states or would-be proliferators they threaten with isolation.

Thus far this situation has spectacularly benefitted China and Russia. They often appear as the balancers, the arbiters or the beneficiaries of the West's conflict with countries such as North Korea and Iran or with states the West wants to punish for their violations of human rights, such as Burma, Zimbabwe or Uzbekistan. China and Russia share many interests with the West but they share the South's resentment against past or recent humiliations and the feeling, justified or not, that the time has come when they hold the stronger cards. Now they, especially Russia, may provoke more fear but also more distrust and resentment even in the South. Seen from the West, at any rate, China and Russia are at the same time ideological adversaries, fierce competitors and indispensable partners. It follows that Western policies, too, have to combine and balance attitudes based on the three types of relations with them. In the case of Russia, the current priority is to avoid encouraging its aggressive arrogance and its feeling of impunity by failing to react, but one should never lose sight of the two other dimensions. Those who want a definitive answer as to whether Russia is a partner or an adversary do not understand the essence of the situation.

III

Western responsibility for the Georgian crisis and reactions to it have been criticised from three perspectives, corresponding to the three visions of the post-post-Cold War world I have mentioned.

Believers in international law and organisation sharply critical of the Bush administration tend to excuse Russia's action in the name of the bad example given by the West in attacking Iraq, in recognising the independence of Kosovo and in encircling Russia through the enlargement of NATO. Followers of the Realist school tend to agree with this criticism, but on the basis of power and interest rather than of law and morality. They point out that the United States has perceived neither of the changes in the balance of power, overestimating its own clout and underestimating Russia's newly regained power. Bush administration critics from Russia, Asia, Western Europe and the United States add several more arguments. First, Georgia is less important as a partner than Russia.[2] Second, China, Iran, nuclear proliferation or Islamic terrorism are more important challenges or threats than Russia. Third, the Middle East is a more direct interest of the West than the Caucasus, whereas the Caucasus are a more direct interest of Russia.[3] And finally, the latter is entitled to its sphere of influence like any other great power, and hence NATO should not penetrate into its backyard.[4]

At the other end of the spectrum, hardliners, whether right-wing neo-conservatives or left-wing anti-totalitarians, denounce the cowardly failure of the West, particularly the West Europeans, to recognise and to fight a shameful act of conquest against a democratic nation, and to stop or roll back an imperialist Russia on the rampage.

The first school is correct that the independence of Kosovo makes it harder for the West – in spite of the glaring differences between the two cases – to be quite convincing when it proclaims the sacred character of existing borders and, like Mikheil Saakashvili's attack on South Ossetia, has provided Russia with an alibi it has used with a vengeance. But it neglects the fact that Russia did not need the Kosovo example to wage a savage war against Chechnya, that it has been pursuing a long-term strategy to rebuild its predominance in the states of the former Soviet Union, to punish those which left it, and, in particular, to prevent 'colour revolutions' from succeeding.

The Realists can legitimately claim that they had warned of the likely Russian reaction to the enlargement of NATO, which could be seen as reneging on promises made at the time of German reunification. But one can just as legitimately claim that relegating Central and Eastern Europe to the status of a buffer zone or a cordon sanitaire, and refusing the admission to Western institutions of European peoples who had been submitted first to German and then Soviet domination, would go both against European stability and against the very principles and purposes of Western policies.

More recent moves, however, like the idea of including Georgia and

Ukraine in NATO and the decision to locate anti-missile systems in Poland and the Czech Republic, were guaranteed, whatever their intentions, to look in the eyes of the Russians like the confirmation of their worst fears of encirclement. Hence the Realists are right to point out that dismissing the likelihood of Moscow's strong reaction and being caught unprepared for its consequences was both unrealistic and immoral.

Realists are unrealistic, however, when they advise the West to abandon commitments already made (such as to recognise the right of Ukraine and Georgia to join NATO in the long run) as a consequence of Russia's show of force. It is unrealistic not to recognise that giving in to pressure would encourage Russia in its feeling of impunity and in its revanchist drive, that it would dramatically weaken Western credibility everywhere, and that, in particular, it would create a Munich-like feeling of betrayal among America's last and best friends. Realists should know that there is a time to stand firm as there is a time to negotiate. Their justified criticism of America's hubris and imperial temptation under George W. Bush should not lead them to underestimate the current hubris and neo-imperial drive of the Russian leadership.

Finally, the anti-Russian Cold Warriors have, not surprisingly, the opposite strengths and weaknesses from those of the Realists. They are right to discern in Vladimir Putin's policies a passionate thirst for domination and revenge. They are right to denounce the preposterous lies directed against Saakashvili (a new Hitler, guilty of genocide), or against the Americans (accused of having provoked the crisis for electoral reasons, just as they are supposed, according to Putin's speech after the Beslan tragedy, to be responsible for Chechen criminals taking schoolchildren as hostages). They are right to proclaim that, when a leader or a movement has decided to return to the language and behaviour of the Cold War, no amount of goodwill can stop him if he does not encounter strong opposition. But they are wrong morally in their self-righteousness and Manichaeism and they are wrong politically and strategically in being blind to the fundamental geopolitical change brought in part by the failed adventures they supported.

They do not see that in a world which the West no longer controls and where its legitimacy is challenged, frontal assaults – whether military, economic, or even, sometimes, rhetorical – can be counterproductive. Indirect strategies, diplomatic flexibility and manoeuvering, are inevitable for any power or alliance which is not omnipotent yet does not give up an active foreign policy. The crucial point is not to let exceptions become the rule and necessary adjustments erase commitments and replace fundamental objectives.

The right of the former Soviet states to apply for and be seriously considered for NATO membership should not be abandoned under pressure, but avenues must be suggested and left open for better times concerning parallel structures of cooperative security for the Caucasus, as proposed by Turkey, or for a more comprehensive security pact transcending the division between NATO members and non-members, as suggested by Dmitri Medvedev before the crisis. Putin's proposal on joint work on an anti-missile system in Azerbaijan, even if technically doubtful, should also be kept open.

More importantly, the West should announce its willingness, if and when Moscow overcomes its intoxication with unilateral shows of force, to consider Russia's inclusion in a transformed NATO. Nothing less would remove the feeling of encirclement and encroachment shared by the majority of the Russian population. But before this could be realistically envisaged a real discussion about the unilateral use of force by the great powers should take place. Clearly the mechanism of the Security Council as the only legitimate source of the decision to use force is entirely blocked – but an international order where major powers would claim an unrestricted right to intervene either in the name of prevention or of protecting their nationals in foreign lands, including distant ones, or their own sphere of 'privileged interest', is a recipe for unpredictability, anarchy and escalation.[5] A discussion about the new rules of the game in a new world is extremely urgent, but one cannot expect it to take place before the present crisis and, more generally, the temptations of reckless unilateralism have been shown to be counterproductive.

In the intervening period, while the United States and NATO should actively be involved in the security of Georgia and of threatened countries like Ukraine or Moldova, probably the most visible initiatives should be taken by the European Union. Rather than sanctions against Russia, the two main tasks are to lessen European dependence on Russian energy and to pursue positive programmes in helping the threatened countries in both economic reconstruction and peacekeeping. The first task has become more difficult but also more urgent. It could perhaps even involve modifying, in the framework of a general negotiation, an unsuccessful policy of intransigence towards Iran which is restricting the possibility of alternative routes for Central Asian oil and gas.

Perhaps the most important gesture would be to open the possibility of Georgia and Ukraine starting on the long road towards possible membership of the European Union. But that will meet with strong opposition not only from Russia but from most of the European public.

The United States, while no longer able to claim world leadership, remains a global power, which can, according to circumstances, give higher priority to regions such as Asia. Europe, while increasingly sensitive to distant wars and competitors, cannot but give priority to Russia, seen by most West Europeans as an indispensable partner and by most East Europeans as an imminent threat. Balancing, combining and moderating these concerns is the key for a successful Western policy in the new era.

In the long run, if the West is firm, patient and open, the forces of economic interdependence and the constraints of global challenges should work towards reconciliation and cooperation with Russia. Meanwhile, we should brace, if not for a new cold war, at least, as Kennedy said after his Vienna meeting with a blustering Nikita Khrushchev, for a rather cold winter.

Notes

1   Paul Goble, 'Window on Eurasia: What the Georgian Events Demonstrate', http://windowo neurasia.blogspot.com/2008/08/ window-on-eurasia-what-georgian-events.html. For Putin's nostalgia for the Soviet Union and wish to revive it in a different form, see his statement in *Komsomotskaya Pravda*, 2 February 2000.

2   Fyodor Lukyanov, 'Georgian Crisis Is a Trap for US Leadership', *Moscow Times*, 21 August 2008; Kishore Mahbubani, 'The West Is Strategically Wrong in Georgia', *Financial Times*, 21 August 2008.

3   George Friedman, 'The Russia–Georgian War and the Balance of Power', *Stratfor. com*, 12 August 2008, and 'Russia and Rotating the U.S. Focus', 1 April 2008.

4   Ronald Steel, 'A Superpower Is Reborn', *New York Times*, 24 August 2008.

5   See the five points outlined by Dmitri Medvedev on 1 September 2008 as guiding Russian foreign policy, especially the fourth, about protecting its foreign nationals everywhere, and the fifth about the right to 'historically special

relations with its spheres of privileged interests'. See also Paul Reynolds, 'New Russian World Order, the Five Principles', BBC News, 1 September 2008, and the vigorous critique by Gareth Evans, 'Putin Twists U.N. Policy', *The Australian*, 2 September 2008.

6 Le Carré's Karla Trilogy consisted of *Tinker Tailor Soldier Spy* (1974); *The Honourable Schoolboy* (1977); and *Smiley's People* (1979).

7 See Karl Mannheim, 'The Problem of Generations', in Paul Kecskemeti (ed.), *Essays on the Sociology of Knowledge: Collected Works*, vol. 5 (New York: Routledge, 1952), pp. 276–322. For an astute contemporary application of these ideas to American politics and culture, see Peter Beinart, 'The End of American Exceptionalism', *Atlantic,* 3 February 2014, https://www.theatlantic.com/politics/archive/2014/02/the-end-of-american-exceptionalism/283540/.

8 John le Carré, *A Legacy of Spies* (London: Penguin Random House, 2017), pp. 350–1.

9 Raymond Aron, *Memoirs: Fifty Years of Political Reflection* (London: Holmes & Meier, 1990), p. 237, quoted in John L. Harper, 'Pierre Hassner (1933–2018): An Appreciation', *Survival*, vol. 60, no. 4, August–September 2018, p. 45.

10 Harper, 'Pierre Hassner (1933–2018)', p. 46.

11 Pierre Hassner, 'Calleo the European', in John L. Harper (ed.), *A Resolute Faith in the Power of Reasonable Ideas* (Bologna: Paul H. Nitze School of Advanced International Studies, 2012), pp. 136–41.

12 See David P. Calleo, *The Atlantic Fantasy* (Washington DC: Johns Hopkins University Press, 1970).

13 Hassner, 'Calleo the European', pp. 140–1.

14 Pierre Hassner, 'One Cold War Among Many?', *Survival*, vol. 50, no. 5, October–November 2008, pp. 247–56; reprinted in this issue of *Survival*, vol. 65, no. 5, October–November 2023, pp. 203–12.

15 Hassner, 'Calleo the European', p. 136.

16 See Thomas Row, 'Rooted in Romanticism: David Calleo's Coleridgean Sensibility', in Harper, *A Resolute Faith in the Power of Reasonable Ideas*, pp. 142–51.

17 See Lawrence Freedman, 'Remembering Michael Howard', *Foreign Affairs*, 1 January 2020, https://www.foreignaffairs.com/united-states/remembering-michael-howard.

18 Hassner, 'Calleo the European', p. 136.

19 Quoted in Ian Buruma, 'The End of the Anglo-American Order', *New York Times*, 29 November 2016, https://www.nytimes.com/2016/11/29/magazine/the-end-ofthe-anglo-american-order.html.

20 See James Dobbins, 'A Brexit Do-over?', *US News & World Report*, 2 March 2018, https://www.usnews.com/opinion/world-report/articles/2018-03-02/how-can-the-united-kingdom-remain-in-the-eu-after-brexit-vote.

21 David P. Calleo, *Rethinking Europe's Future* (Washington DC: The Century Foundation, 2003), p. 90.

22 David P. Calleo, *Follies of Power* (Cambridge: Cambridge University Press, 2009), p. 154.

23 See Robert Kagan, 'Disturber of the Peace: "Yes, We Can" Meets Conservative Europe', *Washington Post*, 2 April 2009.

24 David P. Calleo, 'The Broken West', *Survival*, vol. 46, no. 3, June–July 2004, pp. 29–38.

Closing Argument

Not Fade Away: The Children of the 1930s

Dana H. Allin

I

An unexpected sadness of getting older is to outlive the world you grew up in. I first tried and failed to put this sadness into words in December 2020, after the death of John le Carré. Probably the best spy novelist ever, le Carré was also one of the great post-war writers of any genre. A big part of his achievement was the rendering – most notably in his 'Karla Trilogy' of the 1970s, and through the owlish eyes of George Smiley, his most intriguing spy – of Britain's post-imperial reckoning.[1] The political landscape of Smiley's 'Circus' – the Cold War dread and treachery, the middle-aged paunch and office intrigue, the vaguely humiliating sub-ordination to the American 'cousins' – was both wholly imagined and easy-to-recognise reality.

These 1970s were my high-school and college years, and though at the time I had never set foot in London or any other part of Europe, I could recognise from rural Maryland and from my university campus in New England a corresponding mood of post-industrial malaise. When one is 18, however, grim newspaper headlines are mere accoutrements to the ever-refreshed novelty of youth. That decade is now distantly remembered, which might help explain why le Carré's death hurt in a surprising way. It came at a midpoint between the years my parents died, 2018 and 2022.

Dana H. Allin is an IISS Senior Fellow and Editor of *Survival*, and adjunct professor at the Johns Hopkins School of Advanced International Studies (SAIS) in Bologna, Italy. This essay is adapted in part from Dana H. Allin, 'Calleo and Transatlantica', in John L. Harper (ed.) *A Resolute Faith in the Power of Reasonable Ideas* (Bologna: Paul H. Nitze School of Advanced International Studies, 2012), pp. 111–21.

Survival | vol. 65 no. 5 | October–November 2023 | pp. 213–224 https://doi.org/10.1080/00396338.2023.2261274

They, like le Carré (a pen name adopted by David Cornwell), were born in the early 1930s, and when my mother passed away four years after my father, I was hit by the realisation that my last living link to Franklin Delano Roosevelt's administration, in which both of their fathers had worked, was now severed.

The German sociologist Karl Mannheim argued in the late 1920s that the distinct consciousness and, to a significant extent, political attitudes of different generations were shaped by the political, economic and cultural events of the years when they grow into young adulthood.[2] The children of the 1930s came of age in the first decade and a half after the Second World War, an era of general security and prosperity in the United States, where my parents grew up, and in Western Europe, where le Carré joined the British Secret Intelligence Service (that is, MI6) and then started writing fiction. It is difficult to imagine, however, that a childhood in the decade of the Great Depression, the simultaneous ascents of Adolf Hitler and Roosevelt, and the march towards the cataclysm of a Second World War did not also significantly shape their worldviews.

We can now reasonably worry that we are marching inexorably towards a world where not just the living links to, but the essential achievements of, the Roosevelt era could dissolve. Before they died, my parents feared that they were witnessing, in the rise of Donald Trump, something dark and fundamental. Le Carré, discernibly radicalised by the George W. Bush years, felt the same about Trump and, closer to home, Brexit, which inspired him at the end of his life to acquire an Irish passport. It also moved him to bring back Smiley for a brief appearance in his penultimate novel, *A Legacy of Spies*. The book is set in 2017 when Smiley, by various chronological reckonings, should have been between 102 and 111 years old. With the novelist's licence, le Carré presents him as a spry nonagenarian who, at the end of the book, receives his old protégé Peter Guillam in the Freiburg apartment to which Smiley has retreated for a scholarly retirement, then takes him for dinner to a coach inn near the cathedral. The business between Guillam and Smiley concerns their machinations in the 1963 novel, *The Spy Who Came In from the Cold*, which resulted in the death of an agent and his girlfriend, for which Guillam some six decades later is being investigated. Over wine and venison, Smiley contemplates why they did the things they did, summarily discounting the causes of 'world peace' and 'capitalism'.

> 'So was it all for *England*, then?' he resumed. 'There was a time, of course
> there was. But *whose* England? *Which* England? England all alone, a
> citizen of nowhere? I'm a European, Peter. If I had a mission – if I was
> ever aware of one beyond our business with the enemy, it was to Europe.
> If I was heartless, I was heartless for Europe. If I had an unattainable
> ideal, it was of leading Europe out of her darkness towards a new age of
> reason. I have it still.'[3]

II

This is the third consecutive issue of *Survival* in which I have devoted this space to remembering the recently departed. Readers may suspect that I have become preoccupied with mortality. I have certainly become more acutely aware of it, but the more salient reason is the death, over the course of nine weeks this spring and summer, of three men in their 80s and 90s who were important writers for *Survival*. Ronald Steel, the celebrated biographer of Walter Lippmann, who wrote for us in 2007 that the Iraq War, disaster though it was, would not fundamentally deflect the trajectory of US foreign policy, died on 7 May, age 92. James Dobbins, one of the outstanding American diplomats of his generation as well as a keen foreign-policy analyst who wrote for us frequently, was 81 when he died on 3 July. And David P. Calleo, a *Survival* contributing editor who was also my academic mentor and close friend, died on 15 June at the age of 88. (I wrote about David in the last issue and return to him at some length below.)

To this venerable list one must add the earlier deaths of Pierre Hassner (1933–2018) and Michael Howard (1922–2019). Howard, the great military historian who joined in founding the International Institute for Strategic Studies (IISS) in the late 1950s, was old enough to have fought in the Italian campaign of the Second World War, service for which he was awarded Britain's Military Cross. The younger Hassner had a different encounter with Europe's mid-century cataclysm: a Romanian-born Jew, he survived the Nazis and then fled with his parents to France to escape the communists. In Paris he became a student and then colleague of Raymond Aron, the renowned philosopher of international relations who in the 1960s was the second president of the IISS. Aron wrote of Hassner:

> [He] is at his best when he expresses himself in complete freedom, when his monologue, by itself, encompasses both his arguments and the possible objections of his listeners. His subtlety and his feeling for nuance are so superior to those of others – myself included, of course – that dialogue with him becomes difficult. He has to be left alone to conduct the conversation in his own way; each of his listeners will grasp along the way the nourishment suitable to him (or the pearls thrown out at random by an inexhaustible wealth of invention and analysis).[4]

This genius of inner dialectic was evident in Hassner's contributions to this journal and other IISS writings. His first book review for *Survival* was published in 1965, his acclaimed *Adelphi* paper *Change and Security in Europe* in 1968, and his first original *Survival* article 'Eurocommunism and Detente' in 1977. When the journal was relaunched in 2008, he accepted our invitation to become a contributing editor. The Hassner inner dialogue, expressed as monologue, delighted generations of students at the Bologna Center of the Johns Hopkins School of Advanced International Studies (SAIS), where Hassner was an adjunct professor. My friend John Harper, later a professor at SAIS and another *Survival* contributing editor, took Hassner's seminar in 1976.

> Pierre's habit, as I vividly recall it, was to circle the table for five or ten minutes, ruminating in his sing-song baritone on the day's subject (be it Daniel Bell's argument about the end of ideology, or Samuel Huntington's on post-industrial politics), then pause for breath – and questions from the brave-hearted – before launching into a new monologue. The nourishment grasped was not in the form of precise information, but of puzzling paradoxes and searching questions.[5]

SAIS became an important Cold War institution in part because its centres in Washington and Bologna facilitated a transatlantic dialogue, in which Hassner and Calleo were key protagonists. Their exchanges had an ironic twist insofar as the American Calleo, a great admirer of Charles de Gaulle, articulated the Gaullist vision, whereas the French Hassner had a more Atlanticist perspective. They respected one another immensely, as I heard from Calleo many times, and as Hassner expressed in categorising Calleo as a 'European', which he definitely meant as a compliment.[6]

Calleo was the son of a librarian and fire captain who had emigrated from Italy to upstate New York. Educated at Yale, where he also completed his PhD, Calleo spent time during the early and mid-1960s in Europe, worked briefly as a consultant to the State Department in the Lyndon B. Johnson administration, and then joined the SAIS faculty as founding director of its European Studies programme. His work is full of moral sentiment generously embracing a common transatlantic fate and a common transatlantic civilisation, but it was also directed in, notably, *The Atlantic Fantasy*, a slim masterpiece of American Gaullism, against a narrow and dogmatic Atlanticism.[7] Dogmatic, idealised Atlanticism was problematic, in the argument he laid out in many more books, because it neglected or actively denied things that were undeniable and important. It was idealistic about American power where there was a need for realism, balance and restraint against the hubris and the follies of power. And it elided or diminished nationalism when it is necessary to acknowledge the durability and, one might say, irreducible dignity of the nation-state.

Alliances are about pooling and projecting power, during the Cold War against a threatening Soviet Union. But a complex assembly of nation-states inevitably will take on various purposes relating to varying national interests. One of Calleo's great contributions was to illuminate – even at the height of the Cold War – that plurality of interests and purposes. When he called for a more balanced US–European relationship, advocating what in recent years has been called 'European autonomy', he was on one level simply joining the chorus of American policymakers from John Foster Dulles to Robert McNamara, Mike Mansfield, Robert Gates and even Donald Trump – all of whom expressed frustration that Europe did not devote more resources and greater effort to defend itself. A difference, however, was Calleo's explicit recognition that a more capable Europe would be more likely to pursue distinctly European interests, and that this pursuit would have the effect of balancing and in some senses restraining American power.

Hassner was ready in part, especially after the 2003 American invasion of Iraq, to endorse this vision, but with the caveat that 'I have always been pessimistic about things I dearly wished for, like an independent European defence'. Explaining this pessimism, Hassner invoked tensions between East and West Europeans that have been evident again in their somewhat divergent reactions to the Russian invasion of Ukraine. As Hassner put it:

> David is a West European whereas my experience is that of a Jewish East Central European who grew up under two totalitarian persecutions, luckily escaped from them, but has always known what the great Polish poet Czeslaw Milosz called the difficulty of explaining to Western friends who have always lived in the same nation and under the same regime, the essential feeling of fragility of any Central European who has more than once either had to flee his country or, even more disconcerting, seen the regime and even the name of his home country or town change several times.[8]

Hassner was writing in 2012. Four years prior, Russia had attacked Georgia, and we asked Hassner to reflect on the implications in *Survival*. His essay is republished in this issue. He suggested that it was time to acknowledge that a new cold war with Russia, among some other cold wars such as the one with China, had arrived. What is striking, however, is that the pessimism he harboured in 2008 still carried some hopes of the age, as when he suggested that 'the West should announce its willingness, if and when Moscow overcomes its intoxication with unilateral shows of force, to consider Russia's inclusion in a transformed NATO'.[9] His pessimism, in retrospect, looks mild.

III

David Calleo's summer home was on the island of Elba. It could be reached, as I first reached it 37 years ago, by ferry from the port of

Piombino. If you were a graduate student in 1986, you travelled to
Piombino by train. The connections were tedious: clanking cars stopped
at every ridiculous half station; each seemed about 80 metres from the last
one. The train shunted three times – in both directions, for some reason,
then back again – past the belching stacks of Piombino's steelworks. It was
a bleak scene. Yet, if you were a young American in Italy in the 1980s, your
heart was open to gusts of romantic exaltation, the force of which grew by
stages of atmospheric contrast: the rusted detritus of a sagging industry;
evening light on the ocean's edge; sea spray over ferry prow; and then,
suddenly, the Tuscan archipelago's astonishing rough jewel, rising 1,000
metres above the sea.

Casa Fangati, Calleo's place, was a compound of three buildings set on
the side of terraced gardens worked by generations of students, including myself and, many years later, my own children. It looked out over the
Gulf of Portoferraio and, further in the distance, a ruined Pisan castle that
stood on a tower of rock reddened by Elban iron. Beyond the castle, more
sea, and beyond the sea, the Italian mainland. More rustic than elegant,
Casa Fangati was also sublimely civilised: an old farm Calleo had purchased, reimagined and reconstructed with a certain American sensibility
that followed the tradition of Gore Vidal, Ernest Hemingway, Gertrude
Stein, Henry James and even Thomas Jefferson – pilgrim writers who
had managed to make the European landscape their own without, in any
essential way, divesting from the American landscapes and identities that
they carried with them.

Calleo 'ruled over Elba and kept an eye on Bologna for a longer time
than Napoleone Buonaparte ever did', Hassner noted.[10] This attachment
was rooted, like his scholarship and teaching, in a romantic vision, as
Thomas Row, another of his PhD students, ably documented.[11] It was at
Casa Fangati that Calleo produced most of his scholarship, putting pencil
to yellow legal pad and then – as all graduate students visiting Elba knew
well – scribbling upon, revising and re-revising the typed and then the
printed product of every generation of word processing that had ever
existed. When Philip Gordon, yet another Calleo doctoral student who
preceded me as *Survival* editor, showed me the ropes, he said that he

had adopted Calleo's notation system for editing hard copies by hand, as have I.

More significantly, Calleo influenced this journal by inspiring a romantic fusion of history, culture, politics and economics, planting the same insistence on understanding the bigger social picture that Howard had imposed on the study of military history.[12] Hassner, 'struck by [Calleo's] use of the formulation: "romantic constitutionalism"', derived from it 'a definition of David's doctrine of international affairs as "semi-romantic semi-constitutionalism"'.[13] Though hardly the most felicitous phrase to be associated with Calleo's work, it does capture his appreciation of the European Union as a *sui generis* achievement of international political organisation and, indeed, his devotion to a transatlantic relationship that would be more equally balanced and arguably more civilisationally vital than traditional Atlanticism could conceive. In a sense, Yale, SAIS–Washington, SAIS–Bologna and even the salon that was Casa Fangati were institutional embodiments of his vision of a close but balanced and autonomous relationship between his two homes: the United States and Europe. Brexit, the election of Trump and, of course, Russia's invasion of Ukraine cast a shadow on this vision. Brexit, Howard told an interviewer after the first of these events, was 'accelerating the disintegration of the Western world'.[14] Dobbins, also seeing the referendum result as a threat to his career's devotion to transatlantic relations, proposed, with an uncharacteristic lack of political realism, that Britain simply hold another referendum.[15]

Calleo was never quite so gloomy. His health had started to decline before the year of the Brexit referendum and Trump's election, but he still summered in Elba, drank wine, presided over new students and old friends, and philosophised with his usual preternatural charm. By the time Vladimir Putin launched his full-scale invasion of Ukraine in early 2022, David was quite incapacitated at his home on Capitol Hill, but he still had a twinkle in his eye and a general demeanour of cheerful confidence. Calleo had always insisted that any durable European settlement would need to take Russian interests into account. He was in no condition to articulate what this might mean during the dark winter of 2022, but there is a distinction between irreducible interests and enduring values. A nation's interests are entangled in its values, but the two are not exactly the same thing. De Gaulle had criticised Roosevelt for not recognising or admitting that the United States' proclaimed universal values were cover for specific national interests. Calleo quoted de Gaulle with approval, and criticised American excess, but he never abandoned his pride in American virtues and, particularly, in what the United States had accomplished in partnership with Europe.

In his large body of work on what I have elsewhere called 'Transatlantica', Calleo came back again and again to the magnitude of this achievement. In *Rethinking Europe's Future*, he wrote that:

> Europeans emerged from World War II with lessons and visions of their own. They were determined to escape from their vicious interwar cycle of economic stagnation, misery, social conflict, and repressive politics. They therefore sought a radical upgrading of their national economies and societies. Their ambition was not merely to 'recover' to return to the 1930s – but to transform their economies and political systems to entirely new levels of performance, security, and concord. The key to success, they believed, lay in promoting rapid growth American-style while constructing a safety net of welfare for the whole population.[16]

In *Follies of Power*, he cast Europe's entire post-war experience, culminating in the EU, in stark moral terms:

> Today's EU is the organic outgrowth of post-war Europe's own remarkable moral redemption – the unexpected good that followed the deep plunge into evil and suffering that began with Europe's Great War of 1914. The sense of community that grew up among Europe's ravaged states after World War II was the regional embodiment of what had been developing within the states themselves. The welfare state was a domestic product of Europe's renewal. It reflected what Europeans had learned from the horrors of their own recent history ... This spiritual renewal was the real post-war European miracle.[17]

That book was published in 2009, in a global financial crisis that was arguably precursor to the unravelling of order that we subsequently experienced. At about the same time, Robert Kagan wrote about the essential conservatism of European societies that above all sought shelter from the disruptions of both capitalism and geopolitics. He equated the Bush administration's bold move into Iraq with the Obama administration's bold injection of fiscal demand into a failing economy. Continental Europeans, he suggested, recoiled in their conservatism from what they regarded as both geopolitical and economic recklessness.[18]

Calleo, a progressive liberal in American political terms, had evident affinities with this small-c conservatism as well. But he recognised, like de Gaulle, that there come moments requiring revolutionary determination:

> Between the American vision – unipolar, hegemonic and unilateral – and
> the European pluralist vision – multipolar, balanced and multilateral –
> there is great potential for conflict. Both visions are radical. The American
> vision aims for a world with no balance of power – for the first time in
> modern history. The European vision, where the EU unites its whole
> continent, is attempting to reverse the results of the Second World War.[19]

Was this European vision the same as Smiley's 'unattainable ideal' of 'leading Europe out of her darkness towards a new age of reason'? It is close enough, and perhaps we can honour the children of the 1930s if we have it still.

Notes

1 Le Carré's Karla Trilogy consisted of *Tinker Tailor Soldier Spy* (1974); *The Honourable Schoolboy* (1977); and *Smiley's People* (1979).

2 See Karl Mannheim, 'The Problem of Generations', in Paul Kecskemeti (ed.), *Essays on the Sociology of Knowledge: Collected Works*, vol. 5 (New York: Routledge, 1952), pp. 276–322. For an astute contemporary application of these ideas to American politics and culture, see Peter Beinart, 'The End of American Exceptionalism', *Atlantic*, 3 February 2014, https://www.theatlantic.com/politics/archive/2014/02/the-end-of-american-exceptionalism/283540/.

3 John le Carré, *A Legacy of Spies* (London: Penguin Random House, 2017), pp. 350–1.

4   Raymond Aron, *Memoirs: Fifty Years of Political Reflection* (London: Holmes & Meier, 1990), p. 237, quoted in John L. Harper, 'Pierre Hassner (1933–2018): An Appreciation', *Survival*, vol. 60, no. 4, August–September 2018, p. 45.

5   Harper, 'Pierre Hassner (1933–2018)', p. 46.

6   Pierre Hassner, 'Calleo the European', in John L. Harper (ed.), *A Resolute Faith in the Power of Reasonable Ideas* (Bologna: Paul H. Nitze School of Advanced International Studies, 2012), pp. 136–41.

7   See David P. Calleo, *The Atlantic Fantasy* (Washington DC: Johns Hopkins University Press, 1970).

8   Hassner, 'Calleo the European', pp. 140–1.

9   Pierre Hassner, 'One Cold War Among Many?', *Survival*, vol. 50, no. 5, October–November 2008, pp. 247–56; reprinted in this issue of *Survival*, vol. 65, no. 5, October–November 2023, pp. 203–12.

10   Hassner, 'Calleo the European', p. 136.

11   See Thomas Row, 'Rooted in Romanticism: David Calleo's Coleridgean Sensibility', in Harper, *A Resolute Faith in the Power of Reasonable Ideas*, pp. 142–51.

12   See Lawrence Freedman, 'Remembering Michael Howard', *Foreign Affairs*, 1 January 2020, https://www.foreignaffairs.com/united-states/remembering-michael-howard.

13   Hassner, 'Calleo the European', p. 136.

14   Quoted in Ian Buruma, 'The End of the Anglo-American Order', *New York Times*, 29 November 2016, https://www.nytimes.com/2016/11/29/magazine/the-end-ofthe-anglo-american-order.html.

15   See James Dobbins, 'A Brexit Do-over?', *US News & World Report*, 2 March 2018, https://www.usnews.com/opinion/world-report/articles/2018-03-02/how-can-the-united-kingdom-remain-in-the-eu-after-brexit-vote.

16   David P. Calleo, *Rethinking Europe's Future* (Washington DC: The Century Foundation, 2003), p. 90.

17   David P. Calleo, *Follies of Power* (Cambridge: Cambridge University Press, 2009), p. 154.

18   See Robert Kagan, 'Disturber of the Peace: "Yes, We Can" Meets Conservative Europe', *Washington Post*, 2 April 2009.

19   David P. Calleo, 'The Broken West', *Survival*, vol. 46, no. 3, June–July 2004, pp. 29–38.